SRP 6/85   16.95   c25

MINE MILL

The History of the International Union of Mine, Mill and Smelter Workers in Canada □ Since 1895

P9-CJN-472

by Mike Solski and John Smaller

Canadian Cataloguing in Publication Data

Solski, Michael, 1918-
  Mine Mill

ISBN 0-88791-031-9 (bound). –
    ISBN 0-88791-029-7 (pbk.)

1. International Union of Mine Mill and
Smelter Workers (Canada)--History.
2. Trade-unions--Miners--Canada--History.
I. Smaller, John, 1916– II. Title.

HD8039.M62C3 1985 331.88′1222′0971 C85-090028-X

Printed and bound in Canada by Mutual Press Limited, Ottawa
Hardcover bound by Smith, Irwin & Conley Ltd., Smiths Falls, Ontario
Typeset by Slan Typesetting, Ottawa, Ontario
Cover by David Berman Graphic Design, Ottawa
Maps by Cindy Milner of Ottawa and Dublin, Ireland

ISBN 0-88791-029-7 paper
ISBN 0-88791-031-9 hardcover

Steel Rail Publishing
P.O. Box 4357, Stn. E
Ottawa Canada K1S 5B3

About the Authors

MIKE SOLSKI

Born in Coniston in 1918, Mike Solski first went to work for Inco as a yard labourer at age seventeen. Subsequently, he worked as a smelter labourer, blacksmith and plateworker at the Coniston and Copper Cliff smelters of Inco. Between 1942 and 1944, he was chairman of the Mine Mill organizing committee at the Coniston plant and was trustee of the newly formed Local 598 until he was elected vice-president in 1947, a position he filled until he became secretary-treasurer of the local in 1951. He was president of Local 598 from 1952 to 1959, and served as Eastern Canadian director (District 2) of Mine Mill during the Steel raids. He was also secretary of the first Canadian Mine Mill Council in 1953, and secretary of the constitutional committee that established Canadian autonomy in 1955. Among other civic activities, he was Mayor of Coniston from 1962 to 1972, Mayor of the newly formed Town of Nickel Centre from 1972 to 1978, and served three terms as vice-chairman of the Regional Municipality of Sudbury. He is also past president of the Nickel District Liberal Association and president of the Nickel Belt Federal Association. In 1983, he was chairman of a historical group which published *The Coniston Story*, a local history. He is now retired and lives in Coniston.

JOHN SMALLER

Born in Winnipeg in 1916, John (Jack) Smaller received his Master of Arts degree in English Literature from the University of Manitoba. From 1940 to 1942, he edited the *Northern Citizen*, the newspaper sponsored by Mine Mill members and community supporters in Kirkland Lake preceding and during the gold miners' strike of 1941-42. After serving in the Canadian army during the war, he returned to Toronto to work for the Canadian Press. From 1948 to 1958, he worked on the staff of the Mine Mill union, handling public relations, publishing a weekly union paper and producing a union radio program out of Sudbury. He is now retired and lives in Toronto.

The Mine Mill union logo was adapted from the "Three Stars" emblem originally designed at an executive meeting of the Western Federation of Miners in 1901. The three stars, E, I and O stand for "Education, Independence and Organization," the WFM motto. Originally, the three stars were W, F and M, and represented not only the WFM but also its three leaders, William D. Haywood, Edward Boyce and James Maher, who brought the "stars of heaven to the bottomless pits of the Western mines that they might shed their rays of hope" (John O'Callahan, artist). The hammer, bar (from the old hand-drill used by miners) and quill represent labour, industry and education, and were suggested for use in the WFM emblem by George Pettibone, Ed Boyce and Hon. D. C. Coates at the 1901 meeting.

Contents

Chapter IV

Kirkland Lake ▆▆▆▆▆▆▆▆▆▆▆▆▆▆▆▆▆▆▆▆ 79

Chapter V

Sudbury Local 598 ▆▆▆▆▆▆▆▆▆▆▆▆▆▆▆▆ 97

Conclusion ▆▆▆▆▆▆▆▆▆▆▆▆▆▆▆▆▆▆▆▆ 161

Acknowledgements

Much of the historical background material comes from sources too numerous for a detailed accounting of credits. The story is based upon personal interviews with many individuals from across Canada who were part of the union, some of them from its earliest days.

Records available at the Ontario Archives in Toronto, the Laurentian University Archives in Sudbury, and the Special Collection Archives of the University of British Columbia were consulted.

The papers and memorabilia in the possession of many former members of the union were made available. Of inestimable value to this study was the assistance of Sudbury labour historian Jim Tester, who made more than a score of recorded interviews available.

We acknowledge the pioneering work done on the raids in Sudbury by John Lang, a Sudbury native whose Master of Arts thesis, "A Lion in a Den of Daniels: A History of the International Union of Mine Mill and Smelter Workers in Sudbury, 1942-1962," was presented to the University of Guelph in 1970.

Dr. Wayne Roberts and the Labour Studies Programme of McMaster University permitted us to quote extensively from *Miner's Life: Bob Miner and Union Organizing in Timmins, Kirkland Lake and Sudbury.*

Special credit must go to the Canada Council and Labour Canada for grants which made it possible to interview former members of the union in several provinces and to study relevant material in Canadian archives.

And finally, to our editor, Terry Binnersley, a native of Garson, Ontario whose work to get the book into print went beyond normal editorial bounds, we are extremely grateful.

Abbreviations

ACCL	All Canadian Congress of Labour
AFL	American Federation of Labour
ALU	American Labour Union
CCF	Co-operative Commonwealth Federation
CCL	Canadian Congress of Labour
CIO	Congress of Industrial Organizations
CLC	Canadian Labour Congress
CM&S	Consolidated Mining and Smelting Company (Cominco)
IDI ACT	Industrial Disputes Investigation Act
INCO	International Nickel Company of Canada
IUMMSW	International Union of Mine, Mill and Smelter Workers (Mine Mill)
IWW	Industrial Workers of the World
MWUC	Mine Workers Union of Canada
NRA	National Recovery Act (U.S.A.)
NLRB	National Labour Relations Board (U.S.A.)
OBU	One Big Union
OLRB	Ontario Labour Relations Board
SWOC	Steelworkers' Organizing Committee
TLC	Trades and Labour Congress
UAW	United Automobile Workers
UCNW	United Copper-Nickel Workers
UMW	United Mine Workers
USWA	United Steelworkers of America
WFM	Western Federation of Miners
WLU	Western Labour Union
WUL	Workers Unity League

Preface

THE INTERNATIONAL UNION OF MINE, MILL AND Smelter Workers was a truly international union that has become legendary. Mine Mill grew out of the traditions established by its predecessor, the Western Federation of Miners. Established in 1893 to unite small unions in the western United States, the federation's aim was to counter the brutality of frontier mining conditions with a strong and unified organization of hard rock miners at a time when the industry was still in its infancy. The first WFM local in Canada was established in Rossland, British Columbia in 1895. The "pack-sack miner" at the turn of the century followed the fortunes of his trade in mining camps from the western U.S. to northern British Columbia, from Mexico to Alabama, and from Vancouver Island to northern Ontario and Quebec. Wherever he went, he took his travelling union card and the traditions of his union with him.

In the early years of the Western Federation of Miners both in the U.S. and Canada, its members were prominent among the founders of radical organizations. The Industrial Workers of the World (IWW) was founded by leaders of the WFM such as Big Bill Haywood. In the early 1900s, Canadian members of the IWW in western Canada founded the One Big Union (OBU), which played a significant role in the Winnipeg General Strike of 1919 and for a time supplanted Mine Mill in northern Ontario. Hard rock miners were accustomed to accusations that they were anarchistic and enemies of society. The metal miners of western Canada and northern Ontario in large measure have traditionally supported socialist policies and parties in order to institute change. Early on, they elected CCF members to federal and provincial parliaments. In the industrial field, Mine Mill was one of the eight founding members of the CIO, which led the way out of the American Federation of Labour and organized the increasing number of people working in the new mass-production industries. Even the CIO was accused of being communistic and part of a conspiracy to subvert an unsuspecting populace in its early days. Although it was always controversial because of the principled political positions taken by its leadership, Mine Mill maintained its role as the representative of mine and metal workers because it was a grass-roots organization effective in bettering the immediate living and working conditions of its members.

However, shortly after the end of World War II, Mine Mill came under attack from several quarters, including a fellow trade union, government and its agencies, national labour federations, the Catholic Church and the media. This assault continued for more than a decade, only to end in 1967 when Mine Mill closed its books, most of its membership absorbed into the United Steelworkers of America.

The story of why Mine Mill was the object of such sustained attack and how the union was finally overwhelmed and absorbed by an organization which could not claim equal levels of achievement richly deserves telling. When application was first made for a grant from the Canada Council to write the history of Mine Mill in Canada, the intent was to tell the story objectively and yet passionately. We have aimed at objectivity in recounting this history, but the passions generated by recalling the conflict that led to Mine Mill's demise have been accorded some room, too. The conflict became the major concern and impeded the union's positive work in the areas of labour-industry relations, community and legislative responsibilities, and general membership welfare — areas in which the union could always point to tangible achievements.

It cannot be denied that the union succeeded in achieving for its members the highest overall levels of earning and working conditions throughout Canada. Dominion government statistics for the better part of the post-war period show that Sudbury enjoyed the second highest wage levels in Canada. The first highest levels were in Trail, B.C., where Mine Mill held contracts with Consolidated Mining and Smelting Corporation, the major industry in that district. Not long after the Ontario Labour Relations Board granted Steel control over the workers employed by the International Nickel Company in 1962, Sudbury dropped to fifteenth place on the government's list of wage levels in centres across Canada.

What then was the reason for the success of the Steelworkers in the takeover of Mine Mill's membership? The costly and disruptive raids by the Steelworkers extended from as early as 1946 until the merger in 1967. The assistance of the various government agencies, overt and covert, in the destruction of Mine Mill was obvious and flagrant. The times were unsympathetic to the aims and aspirations of a militant, radical trade union; the exponents of the Cold War in the United States were determined to still all voices but their own. They succeeded by generating hysterical opposition to individuals and organizations which dared to deviate even marginally from the norm, which could be determined by them alone. In the day of the McCarthy terror, U.S. government agencies attacked militant trade unions, notably Mine Mill. In Canada, disciples of McCarthyism followed suit.

Mine Mill's relations with the U.S.-controlled Canadian metal mining industry were relatively peaceful, but it must be conceded that, by the very nature of the socio-economic system in which we live, the corporations would, to put it mildly, prefer to operate without trade union restraint on the desire to maximize profits. A reasonable assumption would be that somewhere in the conglomerate of assailants, the fine corporate hand may be found.

Then there were the leaders of the CCF (now NDP) who were embarrassed at being branded radical and fearful lest they be engulfed in the McCarthyist assault. They took up the Red-menace, Communist-conspiracy theme for Canadian dissemination. Throughout the Steel raids, CCF-NDP personalities participated in determining strategy and tactics for the raiders, meeting openly and secretly with groups posing as dissidents within Mine Mill, and providing legal advice and direction in the court battles which followed labour board actions.

Not to be overlooked is the effect of Charles H. Millard, the Canadian Director of the United Steelworkers of America (USWA) at the time. As an executive member of the Canadian Congress of Labour (CCL) and a mover and shaker in the Co-operative Commonwealth Federation (CCF), Millard was purveyor of an overflowing treasury throughout the period in which the raids took place. The late Mr. Millard was a unique figure in the Canadian labour movement and deserves a definitive biography by a truly perceptive chronicler. Defeated in a leadership bid in the United Automobile Workers (UAW) at the time that the Oshawa General Motors strike ushered the CIO into Canada in 1937, Millard was set adrift. He called on his contacts in the hierarchy of the CIO in the U.S. and had himself appointed director of the Steelworkers Organizing Committee in Canada (SWOC). He laboured quietly in his Toronto office, building a personal guard by appointing loyal followers to salaried positions and encouraging eager young rank-and-file workers in the steel industry to organize their plants until a viable union was established in the industry. SWOC then became USWA and Millard Canadian director.

During the latter years of World War II, when federal labour legislation protected workers organizing unions, there was substantial trade union growth. However, the post-war years were characterized by a tightening of the reins on unions and new organization was difficult to achieve. Millard cast covetous eyes on neighbouring established trade unions. With the McCarthyite surge at full thrust in the United States and

Mine Mill there an early target, Millard set his entire apparatus to work against Mine Mill in Canada and thereby started more than ten years of disruption and turmoil in the labour movement.

The role of the Catholic Church in the raid on Mine Mill and its effect on the final outcome was significant, especially in eastern Canada. Catholic churchmen used church publications and exhortations from pulpits to mobilize parishioners in support of the raiders. Separate school children in Sudbury were prevailed upon to carry home literature calling on their fathers to support those who would destroy Mine Mill.

Not to be left in the wings and jeopardize their role in the moulding of public opinion, high-profile journalists flooded the daily and periodical press with pseudo-researched, headline-grabbing stories in line with the Communist-conspiracy clamour. Prominent in their slander of Mine Mill were Pierre Berton in a widely publicized piece in the April 1, 1951 issue of *Maclean's Magazine*, and John Harbron, international affairs expert for the Thompson newspaper chain, in a learned spread in the December 12, 1953 issue of the *Financial Post*. David Lewis Stein, now a *Toronto Star* columnist, joined with his version of a Communist-dominated Mine Mill in the April 21, 1962 issue of *Maclean's* during the final stages of the battle for the Sudbury Inco workers. A series in the now-defunct *Toronto Telegram* in December 1959 was outrageous beyond belief. The author of the series, erstwhile reporter Frank Drea, later became public relations employee of the Steelworkers, and later still discordant cabinet member in the Ontario Tory government. Incidentally, the Drea series in the *Telegram* cost the publishers some $6,500 in an out-of-court settlement when a union member sued that paper for slander.

Some very serious problems faced the union. Although Mine Mill and its predecessor, the Western Federation of Miners, had been active in Canada since the turn of the century, its growth in the 1940s had been phenomenal. Because of its rapid expansion, growing pains were inevitable within the union. In the 1950s, Local 598 in the Sudbury district numbered from 11,000 to 18,000 members at Inco and Falconbridge mines. In Trail and Kimberley in B.C. where Consolidated Mining and Smelting Corporation employed from 8,000 to 10,000 workers, Mine Mill Local 480 and 651 became the dominant organizations in their respective areas. Visions of personal power brought many unworthy elements into prominence. When their attempts to realize ambitions were frustrated by the local membership, they unerringly established liaisons with one another and ultimately with the Steelworkers. Not only some rank-and-file members, but also some Mine Mill officers and staff members were warmly embraced by Steel leaders and given direction, assistance and, it was widely rumoured, financial support. Thus there developed a so-called dissident movement which received considerable publicity. Although they had long been viewed by loyal Mine Mill members with ample suspicion, these dissidents were paid-up members of Mine Mill and because of the union's deep-rooted democratic principles they were permitted to carry on their questionable activities. Perhaps a lesser adherence to principles in the face of apprehended dangers would have produced a more beneficial outcome for the general membership. When the final, open raids were launched, these so-called dissidents roamed through the plants and mines with fists full of Steel membership cards.

The problem most difficult to deal with at the time was the persistent charge that Mine Mill was a Communist-dominated union. It had been repeated by the media so often and by so many in official positions — police forces, government, church and lay bodies — that few involved with Mine Mill could remain immune in the prevailing political climate. Many honest union members were affected and were manipulated to absolve themselves from the accusation by changing unions.

More than 30,000 employees of the metal mining industry in Canada were dues-paying members of Mine Mill. Within the membership, some were Conservatives, others Liberals, CCFers, Communists, and still others were neither members nor adherents of any political party. The membership reflected the political spectrum of the population as a whole, with one very significant exception. Because of the nature of the industry, the men who mined and processed metals have been in the vanguard of militant and radical movements from the earliest days of mining in North America.

North American industrial history is replete with battles of miners for what they considered their rights against industrial or political repression.

The real conspiracy, of course, was to destroy Mine Mill. Charges of Communist domination and allegations of leadership involvement in an international communist conspiracy were levelled at Mine Mill. But Mine Mill leaders were far too busy fighting off the raiders to be involved in any conspiracy, let alone an international conspiracy.

Despite the totality of the forces gathered against Mine Mill, Steel won the crucial vote in Sudbury by a bare fifteen votes more than the minimum required out of a total of 14,337 ballots cast in the Inco certification vote conducted by the Ontario Labour Relations Board. These fifteen votes transferred the entire membership of Sudbury Local 598 to the Steel union. Although the union hung on at Trail and Kimberley in British Columbia, Local 598 was the flagship of Mine Mill in Canada, and the final outcome was inevitable.

The effort presented here is not intended as a definitive history. It is an attempt to tell a story that deserves to be told because of the large part the union played in the labour movement in Canada.

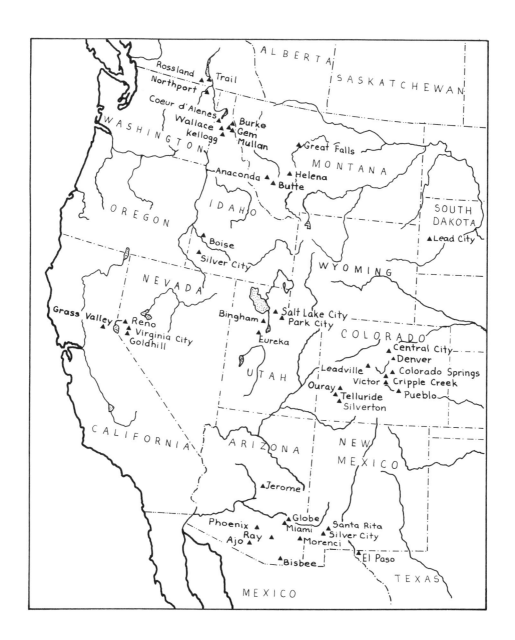

WESTERN U.S. MINING CENTRES CIRCA 1890

CHAPTER I

The Western Federation of Miners: Origins in the United States

THE INTERNATIONAL UNION OF MINE, MILL AND Smelter Workers traces its roots back to 1893, when a small group of miners' unions joined forces to form the Western Federation of Miners in the wake of brutal attacks on fledgling unions in the Coeur d'Alenes district in Idaho. Throughout the years, Mine Mill continued to honour the heritage of its militant predecessor, and kept alive the history of the fierce struggle required to obtain the most basic provision for the health and safety of the miner and his family. While this book concentrates on the history of Mine Mill in Canada, it seems only natural to include a chapter on the origins of which Mine Millers were so justly proud. Most importantly, the story of its beginnings shows that this radical, militant union, far in advance of any other union of its time, was built from the ground up by the miners themselves, out of the sheer necessity to protect themselves from brutal frontier mining conditions.

Early Beginnings

In the last half of the nineteenth century, the metal mining and processing industry was centred in mountainous, isolated territory in the western United States and Canada and the men who worked in it were accustomed to heavy labour and rough, primitive living conditions. Because of the extremely dangerous conditions of their jobs, the miners developed a reliance on each other for their very lives, creating a comradeship that carried over into their unions.

When the industry was in its infancy, mining operations were often small, short-lived enterprises. The miners were frequently on the move, exchanging information and ideas about their jobs and problems with employers. Thus, when times and conditions called for the establishment of a federation of miners' unions, the contacts had already been made. Before long, mine owners found themselves dealing with a fledgling organization rather than with individual miners, and, true to

the legendary violence of the U.S. frontier, they responded with guns and dynamite. Mine Owners' Association armed guards, deputy sheriffs, notorious Pinkerton Agency thugs and the military faced miners armed in self defence. Confinement in the infamous bull pen or deportation to the frozen wasteland or desert was the fate of many a striker pulled off the picket line. Disputes were invariably settled right on the spot; verbal agreements, without time limits, were made, and if the employer did not live up to them, negotiations were immediately reopened, with a picket line, or from behind a barricade.

One of the earliest recorded group actions was in the Comstock diggings at Virginia City, Nevada. The Comstock miners organized to protect their wage scales as early as 1863. In 1864 and again in 1867, they marched in bodies to assert their demands. The union constitution adopted in 1867 provided that all men working underground should receive four dollars for an eight-hour day. The eight-hour day became standard for all Comstock miners by 1872. They had the closed shop and the check-off, though such terms were unheard of in those days: the Virginia City Miners' Union would not permit any man to work underground if he was not a member; it deducted monthly dues of two dollars from every man's pay. The union cared for its sick and disabled, and made sure the companies chipped in too. When a miner was killed, every miner gave a day's pay to the family.

There were early beginnings in Montana, too. The Butte miners organized their union shortly after a delegation from the Virginia City Miners' Union visited them, on June 13, 1878. In Arizona, the Globe City Union was formed in 1884; in 1887 and 1888 a group of mines in the Coeur d'Alenes district in Idaho became unionized. These local unions came together to form a single district federation in 1889. Its first project was a badly needed hospital. A two-storey, $30,000 hospital was put under the administration of the Catholic Order of Providence. But unionization was viewed by mine owners as an unacceptable threat to the continued growth of their profits and soon the union-busting floodgates were opened wide with the infamous Coeur d'Alenes conflict.

Ironically, attempts by the mine owners to destroy the union resulted in the increased determination of the miners and the formation of the Western Federation of Miners.

The Coeur d'Alenes War: 1892

In 1890-91 the Coeur d'Alenes operators brought in compressed air drills and many miners were downgraded to shovellers and car-men at daily wages of three dollars instead of the $3.50 they had been getting.* A mass meeting of all union men in the district decided to demand a flat $3.50 a day for all underground workers. Although the companies initially agreed to the demand, they were determined to win back their wage differential, and before long their strategy unfolded.

They called a meeting of all mine operators in the district, and the Mine Owners' Association was formed, the first of many such associations that plagued the years to come. The mines were all shut down early in January on the pretext that the operators were trying to force the railroads to cut freight rates. The negotiations with the railroads concluded in March, but when the operators posted notices that the mines would reopen on April 1st, they announced a three-dollar daily wage for car-men and shovellers. To a man, the miners voted to reject the wage cut.

The owners' response was to bring non-union men into the district, under guard of armed detectives. The union quickly took initiatives to persuade the newcomers to leave. One night, trainmen friendly to the union intercepted a group of 80 workers brought in from Grass Valley, California to replace union men, and told them they would have to ride the rest of the way in boxcars. When the men woke up next morning, they were in Pendleton, Oregon, 250 miles away.

The next step in the strategy became a standard practice intended to block miners' unions. The mine owners got a U.S. district judge to issue an injunction forbidding the miners from "interfering" with the hiring of men. The miners had been peaceful and orderly, despite the fact they had been jobless for five months. It was the mine operators who had violated Idaho law by bringing armed men into the state. Yet the state governor issued a proclamation ordering the miners to disperse all unlawful assemblages and to cease interference with the mine owners. From then on, state governors openly sided with the mine operators in their attempts to break strikes and bust the union.

Next, the companies planted Pinkerton agents in the unions to disrupt, destabilize and sabotage union activities. This device, which became a standard tactic of mine owners throughout the years, was perfected in the Coeur d'Alenes in the 1890s. Then came the smear campaign: the cry of "anarchist" was used in 1892, just as the cry of "Red" and "Communist" was to be used in the 1950s, to discredit union members. By this time, the company properties were heav-

ily guarded by armed deputies crouched behind barricades. The battle joined.

> On July 10, an altercation and a fist fight between a guard and a striker set off a rumour that union men had been killed by company guards, and armed men poured into the town of Gem.* Difficulties were temporarily averted, but the following day a union miner was killed by the guards. The aroused miners attacked the Frisco mill and barracks, which housed the guards, but were repelled. In the midst of the fighting, the penstock, an open conduit carrying water to the mill, was left unguarded. Some of the miners sent two 50-pound boxes of dynamite down into the mill, and blew it up with one employee killed and twenty wounded.[1]

Meanwhile, guards at the Gem mine and mill had opened furious fire on the town of Gem below where the miners were congregated.

> Shortly after the engagement began at the Frisco mill, a sudden shower of bullets came into the town of Gem from the breastworks of the Gem mine. John Ward, who was standing unarmed opposite the White and Bender building, was shot in the arm. Gus Carlson was seen to fall on the walk in the rear of Daxon's saloon. Those who rushed to his assistance were driven back by another shower of bullets. Even a white flag of truce was not at first respected. Carlson was found dead . . . . No effort was made to capture the Gem mine and the firing soon stopped. Shortly thereafter, the morning train came up the canyon. The sheriff, district attorney, and deputy U.S. marshalls were on it. A truce was arranged. Finally about noon the nonunion men at the Gem mine surrendered their arms and were assembled as prisoners with those from the Frisco mill. That afternoon the union men took possession of the Bunker Hill and Sullivan concentrator, and informed (the operator) that he must discharge his nonunion men or see his mill blown up.[2]

The companies had been trying to provoke violence for many weeks. Now they could demand that the governor call in federal troops. When troops arrived, the commander, General Carlin, removed the sheriff and marshal who had been friendly to the miners and appointed a company doctor as sheriff. Some 600 union men and sympathizers were arrested and forced into "bull-pens," which were used as prisons all summer. The bull-pen became a regular strike breaking tool. It consisted of a barn-like structure in which miners were confined, often for months. There were no sanitary facilities; food was unfit for a dog. In some cases, the building was a two-storey structure, and excretions of men on the upper floor would drip through the loosely fitted floor boards on those below. Many men became sick and some died. By the time the last of the bull-pen prisoners had been released, most of their jobs had been taken by non-union men.

---

*Gem was a single street lined with houses and saloons and backed up against steep mountain slopes.

[1]Perlman and Taft, *History of Labour in the U.S.*, Vol. 4.

[2]Vernon Jensen, *Heritage of Conflict*, Greenwood Press, Publishers, New York, 1968, p. 35.

---

*The air drill, operated by a single miner, produced more ore, increasing the demand for less skilled workers (muckers) to shovel ore faster.

Troops camped at Wallace, Idaho during Coeur d'Alenes strike, June 1892. Denver Public Library Western History Department

Another pattern to emerge in the first Coeur d'Alenes war* was the harassment of the union by law enforcement agencies that blatantly acted on behalf of the mine owners and brought countless criminal charges against embattled union members. In the majority of cases, charges were dropped or the real victims were acquitted.

Thirty prisoners were held for further trial, but only seventeen were actually tried. Of these, thirteen union leaders were sentenced to jail by Judge H. H. Beatty, who found them guilty of contempt of court in violation of his own injunction. Dr. R. W. Smith, in his study, "The Idaho Antecedents of the Western Federation of Miners," remarks: "Judge Beatty, who had issued the injunctions in the first place, now heard all the testimony and arguments in the case and delivered the decision and sentences at the end of the trial. It was thus a clear-cut case of judge-made and judge-executed law."[3] Four of the seventeen were convicted of criminal conspiracy, but the convictions were reversed by the U.S. Supreme Court. Murder charges brought against forty-two strikers had to be dropped after the first in a planned series of murder trials was lost due to lack of evidence.

In spite of the strikebreakers, Pinkerton agents, injunctions and troops, the Coeur d'Alenes unions had not broken union solidarity. Gradually, as the scabs brought in by the companies began to drift out of the district, union men were rehired to replace them. The unions survived and re-established themselves. As a result of their experience in the Coeur d'Alenes, the unions saw the need to organize and unite into larger bodies, and by the next year the Western Federation of Miners was growing and stabilizing.

*For a history of the second Coeur d'Alenes battle in 1899, in which 1,200 strikers were rounded into bull-pens once again, see W. D. Haywood, *Bill Haywood's Book*, New York, International Publishers, 1929.

[3]Dr. R.W. Smith, "The Idaho Antecedents of the Western Federation of Miners," unpublished paper in the IUMMSW collection at the University of British Columbia.

The Western Federation of Miners: 1893

After the Coeur d'Alenes situation, reports of the infant United Mine Workers of America set up in 1890 by several coal miners' unions led union leaders to conclude that the next logical step would be to unite all the non-ferrous metal miners' unions of the west. In consultation with the well established Butte Miners' Union, they invited all miners' unions of the west to send delegates to a convention in Butte, Montana.

Although the delegates at the founding convention numbered only forty-two, they spoke for miners in what were then the most important non-ferrous metal producing areas in the U.S. The convention began Monday, May 15, 1893, and by Friday evening the constitution and by-laws of the new-born Western Federation of Miners (WFM) had been approved and released to the press. John Gilligan of Butte was elected the first president, and Butte was made union headquarters.

Of the original 10 points in the program, many remained high priorities for the International Union of Mine, Mill and Smelter Workers (IUMMSW). Union organizers wanted "to secure an earning fully compatible with the dangers of our employment." They demanded enactment of suitable mine safety laws "with a sufficient number of inspectors, who shall be practical miners, for the proper enforcement of such laws."

They agreed to fight for "employment of our members in preference to non-union men," in other words, the union shop. They proposed a ban on child labour. And they demanded "repeal of all conspiracy (meaning anti-labour) laws that in any way abridge the right of labor organizations."

Basic democracy, which was the pride and strength of this union for its entire existence, was laid down at that convention. The constitution required a three-fourths vote by secret ballot before a strike could be called by a local union, and it called for an annual convention of elected delegates.

Cripple Creek: 1894

The infant federation was less than a year old when a major strike was called at Cripple Creek, Colorado, where one event made the strike remarkable: Governor David Waite called in the state militia to defend the strikers. This was the first and last time a governor prevented violence by halting company gunmen.

The operators had mobilized a small army of 1,200 deputies. Members of WFM locals throughout the state assembled in defence of their brothers at a camp on Bull Hill; the company army marched to a camp nearby. In this critical situation, the governor acted quickly, ordering the sheriff to observe a truce until troops arrived. He then placed the militia between the miners and the deputies and ordered the latter to turn back immediately or the militia would fire on them. The governor had wired the militia:

> Accept surrender of the miners. Do not disarm them but protect them with all your power. Make a cordon and keep the armed deputies out. Advise the sheriff and make no arrests. Use no force to compel men to go with sheriff. Let that be voluntary. If the armed deputies resist your authority, I will call out the unorganized militia to suppress their insurrection.[4]

An agreement was reached and peace prevailed in the area for the next nine years. The governor was supported by the Populist movement, and from the outset the Populists supported the labour movement in the west, and in turn were strongly backed by the Western Federation of Miners.

The federation was at first a very loose association of unions, each fighting on its own, but the convention of 1896 launched a new era with the election of Edward Boyce as president and James Maher as secretary-treasurer. Under their leadership, the WFM became a well disciplined fighting union and its membership mounted rapidly. From its inception with fifteen locals in five states, by 1910 it had grown to 177 locals in thirteen states, Alaska, British Columbia and Ontario. From a membership of 8,000 in 1897, it jumped to 44,000 in 1907.

The Eight-Hour Day: 1896

In 1896, the WFM joined the American Federation of Labour (AFL) and moved its headquarters to Salt Lake City, Utah, where the campaign for the eight-hour day began. Employers argued the law should be applied differently, depending on occupation, because conditions in the underground mines differed from those in smelters and other reduction works. The court turned thumbs down on that argument. It said:

> Unquestionably the atmosphere and other conditions in mines and reduction works differ . . . . poisonous gases, dust and impalpable substances arise and float in the air in stamp mills, smelters and other works in which ores containing metals, combined with arsenic and other poisonous elements or agencies, are treated, reduced and refined . . . there can be no doubt that prolonged effort day after day, subject to such conditions and agencies, will produce morbid, noxious and often deadly effects in the human systems.[5]

So, said the court, if labour must be performed under such conditions, "the period of labour each day should be of reasonable length. Twelve hours per day would be less injurious than fourteen, ten less than twelve, and eight less than ten. The legislature has named eight." The Utah Supreme Court's decision upholding the state's eight-hour law was a milestone in U.S. labour's 50-year fight for the eight-hour day.

---

[4]Vernon Jensen, *Heritage of Conflict*, p. 51.

[5]Vernon Jensen, *Heritage of Conflict*, p. 98.

The eight-hour fight spread to other states and was won in many, as well as in British Columbia and Ontario. Because of the failure of the AFL to act, the WFM spearheaded the drives for almost all workers' protective legislation in the western U.S. and in Canada. This was true not only of eight-hour laws but also of workmen's compensation* and industrial safety laws.

✕

The Western Labour Union: 1898

If the WFM's affiliation with the AFL was intended to increase the western union's strength, it was soon disenchanted. The American Federation of Labour, which had developed along the lines of the old craft guilds, drew its strength from skilled tradesmen, for the most part employed in the industrialized centres of the eastern U.S. Therefore, not only did the AFL maintain a traditional bias towards the privilege due to skilled as opposed to unskilled workers, but it incorporated a regional bias as well. The AFL's lack of interest in the miners of the west became evident when striking miners in Leadville, Colorado, called upon the AFL for assistance. None was forthcoming, and their long strike ended in defeat. Delegates at the fifth WFM convention in May 1897 voted to withdraw from the AFL.

In May of 1898, the Western Federation of Miners formed its own Western Labour Union (WLU). The motivation was two-fold: first, to develop a powerful national federation of unions dedicated to genuine struggle against employers, that would be a source of real help during strikes or other crises and that would launch a major organizing campaign in the west; second, to organize all workers along the lines of the industrial unionism on which the WFM was founded. In short, the WFM was seeking to unite with allies who would match its own militancy.

Delegates at the convention from unions as widely scattered as Rossland, B.C., Texas and California, described their new organization as "an industrial, educational and political organization, uncompromising in policy."

Three years later, the WLU changed its name to the American Labour Union, and by June, 1903, claimed a membership of 100,000, of whom a good third were members of the WFM. When the ALU headquarters were moved to Chicago in 1904, it was because the leaders had determined to set the stage for another, broader organization, the Industrial Workers of the World (IWW), which was founded in 1905.

The WLU and its successor, the ALU, gave a genuine boost to the organization of low-paid and unskilled workers and to the idea of industrial unionism. Because it made the first genuine attempt at industrial unionism and because it

openly rejected and fought the rigid craft unionism of the AFL, the WLU might well be called the grandfather of the Congress of Industrial Unions (CIO).

✕

Big Bill Haywood

William D. Haywood was elected secretary-treasurer of the WFM in 1900, the year the WFM moved its headquarters from Salt Lake City to Denver. Haywood was a big man in every way: physically powerful, hard-headed, direct, and impatient of anyone or anything standing in his way, Haywood was a real son of the Rockies. He said he had risen "from the bowels of the earth" to be touched by the idealism of labour's struggle. For years, he had worked in one mine after another until he came to one that was organized by the WFM, where he rose quickly in the union from the ranks.

WFM President Ed Boyce was the first editor of the monthly *Miners' Magazine*, launched as the official organ of the WFM in 1900. Haywood took over on Boyce's frequent absences from town. "All this," said Haywood, "when I was more familiar with the stormy end of a number two shovel than I was with a pen."

The WFM constitution was written by miners, and history records that men who work underground for low wages and long hours, in miserable working conditions, have been among the most militant of all workers in every land. They were ready to campaign for legislation to improve their hours and conditions. Throughout the history of the WFM, and later the IUMMSW, the union never gave up its conviction that political action was as important as the fight on the job to obtain a better life.

Edward Boyce and Bill Haywood, the two outstanding leaders of the WFM in its early years, joined the Socialist Party of Eugene Debs in 1901. The experience of the WFM and its members during its turbulent first twelve years led straight to the decision to send federation delegates to the founding convention of the Industrial Workers of the World (IWW) in Chicago in 1905.

Boyce remained with Haywood in the union's leadership for only two years. At the 1902 convention, Boyce announced his retirement. His wife, Eleanor, a former school-teacher, had grubstaked her father and brothers in a mining claim called the Hercules in the Coeur d'Alenes. When they struck a ledge, she became a millionaire overnight. Boyce had been in poor health for several years, so the Boyces bought the Portland Hotel in Portland, Oregon, and the former president of the WFM settled down as "an inn-keeper," as Haywood playfully called him. Whenever Haywood, "Gene" Debs and others visited Portland they always had a free room at the Portland Hotel.

Charles A. Moyer took Boyce's place as WFM president, a post he held even after the union changed its name to the International Union of Mine, Mill and Smelter Workers in 1916. Moyer remained president until his resignation in 1926.

---

*In Ontario, the Workmen's Compensation Act passed as a result of a WFM campaign is still considered a model for such laws on this continent.

Gatling gun trained in front of courthouse to cover approach from depot, Cripple Creek 1903. Denver Public Library Western History Department

The Colorado Strikes: 1903-1905

The fight for the eight-hour law in Colorado, and the feudal policies of the smelter trust (including the Guggenheim's big American Smelting and Refining Company) were responsible for a series of strikes that began in 1903 and led to full scale warfare in Colorado by 1905. Despite tremendous popular support and election campaign promises, the eight-hour statute had been quashed by the legislature. Although, among the organized miners, the eight-hour day had been reluctantly conceded by the mining companies, conditions for the unorganized smelter workers were still barbaric, with wages half those of miners at $1.80 per day, for a ten- or twelve-hour day.

It wasn't long before the WFM arrived at the same destination as the ore mined in the district and sent to smelters for refining. Locals were established at the Guggenheim's Grant and Globe smelters in Denver in 1899 and again in 1902. A smelterman's local was chartered at the Portland, Telluride and Standard companies in Colorado City in August 1902, and other locals such as the one at Northport in Washington were beginning to establish themselves.

In Denver, the 1903 strike for the eight-hour day and the Guggenheim's refusal to recognize the union resulted in a stand-off. By 1905, furnaces froze at the Grant smelter, its slag congealed, and it never opened again. Its smoke stack remained standing until it was toppled as a safety measure in 1950. Called "Bill Haywood's Monument," it might better have been called a monument to the fight for an eight-hour day.

In Colorado City, to keep the union out, the smelter owners immediately hired Pinkerton agents and fired union members as soon as they were discovered. On February 14, 1903, after twenty-three men were fired, the local union called a strike demanding that the men be rehired. Portland and Telluride agreed to bargain terms, but Standard (a subsidiary of United States Reduction and Refining) refused to recognize the union. This action involved all of Cripple Creek's mining district in the dispute, as the miners were forced to lend their support to the smelter workers by cutting off Standard's supply of ore from the region. The frontier that the WFM now had to face was a frontier of a new kind as the large industries of the world-famous American monopolies began to develop in the west.

The strikes that ensued helped bring to a climax the feeling among miners, millmen and smeltermen in the WFM that more radical answers had to be found for their problems and hardened their conviction that political action at the polls was crucial: more pro-labour governors had to be elected. The methods used by mine operators and government agencies to deal with the strikers brought large numbers of western workers in to the socialist camp. The events that occurred over the next two years were to culminate in the WFM, along with eight other unions, launching the Industrial Workers of the World in 1905.

The Military and the *Victor Record*

The Colorado strikes of 1903-1905 had everything: troops, martial law, bull-pens, deportations, explosions, countless frame-ups, company vigilantes, even an attempt to suppress a newspaper. The companies and the state government threw the whole book at the workers and their families. Even sympathizers miles away from the scene of the strike did not go unscathed.

6

As the strikes wore on, more and more strikers were arrested, held for a time in the bull-pens, and then released. When the *Victor Record* protested against the continued militia outrages, the troops raided the newspaper and arrested the entire staff on a charge of criminal libel. Fortunately, they neglected Emma Langdon, a young apprentice learning to operate the typesetting machine, who happened to be at home at the time of the raid. Hearing news of it, she waited until nightfall, then stole through the darkened streets and climbed into the back of the print shop through a window. Working through the night, Emma Langdon got out an issue of the paper single-handed, writing the news stories and editorials, setting the type, and running the press by herself. The protest against this attack on the *Victor Record* was so great nation-wide that the staff was released and the charges dropped.

When merchants in the strike area announced that all business would be on a cash basis, Bill Haywood promptly organized union retail stores, owned and operated by the WFM. The stores flourished with prices twenty to thirty percent below those charged by the merchants who had hoped to starve out the strikers.

Troops protected the reopening of some mines using scab labour. Strike leaders were arrested on grounds of military necessity and thrown into bull-pens although no charges were filed. When the union instituted habeas corpus action to win the freedom of the men, Brigadier General Chase surrounded the courthouse with soldiers, drew up a Gatling gun, posted sharp-shooters on nearby roofs, and announced he would refuse to accept the judge's decision.

In June 1904, the small railroad station at Independence was blown up, killing thirteen scabs and wounding sixteen. The WFM quickly offered a reward of $5,000 for the arrest and conviction of the guilty. But now the reign of terror was started in earnest. The governor issued a proclamation suspending the right of habeas corpus. The commanding officer issued a vagrancy order calling for the deportation of all idle men in the district. At a meeting of the Mine Owners' Association, the Victor sheriff was forced to resign under the threat of lynching. An armed mob organized by the Citizens' Alliance wrecked the union stores and destroyed thousands of books in the union library. Hundreds of strikers were thrown into bull-pens, then deported to the Kansas border and New Mexico, threatened with death if they returned.

Major McClelland and Adjutant General Sherman Bell of the Colorado National Guard gave the tip-off on their arrogance and contempt for lawful methods. McClelland said: "To hell with the constitution. We are not going by the constitution; we are following the orders of Governor Peabody." And Bell declared: "Nobody knows but me and Governor Peabody and God what will be done next in this district."

One attempted frame-up grew out of a train wreck that didn't happen. Still, three union leaders were charged with attempted sabotage. During the trial, a witness for the prosecution broke down under cross-examination and admitted that detectives working for the mine owners had promised him $1,000 to wreck the train and a pardon from Governor Peabody if he were caught and convicted. The union men were found not guilty, but despite demands by the WFM, no action was taken against the real culprit or the two detectives who hired him.

Emma Langdon

Troops taking Victor Record *staff (foreground), who were in sympathy with the strikers, to the bull pen.* Courtesy of Amon Carter Museum, Fort Worth, Texas

The Contract Bonus System

The strikes spread all the way to Colorado's western slope. The Telluride mine settlement, in addition to winning the eight-hour day, ended the hated "contract" system which had made it impossible for the miners to get out of debt to the operators. Under the contract system, as Bill Haywood explained it, the Smuggler Union mine

> would give miners a contract to break ore at so much per fathom. The miners boarded at the company boarding house. They were provided with tools and powder by the company. At the termination of the contract the expenses incidental to their work — board, powder, candles, tool-sharpening and so on — were deducted from the amount owed them by the company. The price per fathom was continually reduced and the exactions of the company increased. In the beginning miners were required only to break the ore, but finally they were compelled to break it in a suitable size and shovel it down the mill-holes or chutes.

The Telluride strike settlement guaranteed the miner at least the union-set day's pay for his work and he could end the contract whenever he decided.

Fifty or more years later, Mine Mill's research department had this to say about the contract system in the 1950s:

> The principle behind all these systems (contract bonus) is essentially the same — dangle a little incentive before workers, move it back and forth as seems necessary and you can get a lot more work done at much less cost per unit. Over the years, contract systems have been used to divide workers, to prevent organization, to speed up work and to keep wage costs down.
>
> The bonus system is almost completely company controlled, with the company having sole power of decision over standards, prices, assignment of contract, etc... workers have been forced to speed up mercilessly to the point where their health and safety have been seriously affected.
>
> Company control: 1) the company alone fixes standards and price. 2) the company juggles rates as it sees fit. 3) the company may or may not pay for 'miscellaneous' items. 4) the company alone assigns contracts. 5) there is not now any effective restraint against arbitrary use of this vast control by the company.
>
> Fixing of standards and prices: Theoretically, prices for each contract are established by the mine foreman on the basis of certain general standards. In applying these standards, the foreman in turn works with mine engineers, time study men and others. The general standards used by the company supposedly spell out base prices for each type of operation (stope, raise, drift, etc.) and for breakage, mucking and timbering. Within these general classifications there are innumerable variations based on type of ground (hard, soft, medium, etc.), general conditions (hot, cold, damp), and type of equipment used. The great variation of factors that enter into the price means, in short, that the company can set whatever price it considers necessary to get the work done.

The bonus system was developed to compensate for the problem of adequately supervising men working underground. Because of the nature of the industry, small groups of two or three men could not be supervised except at an unacceptable cost. Another method that would force the men to speed up production to a level satisfactory to profit-hungry mine owners had to be devised. And so the bonus system was developed, whereby a few extra dollars could be earned by workers who accepted the self-imposed speedup and its accompanying threat to life, limb and health.

As the years go by, new generations of miners go underground, new personnel officers are employed, and cost-cutting techniques are honed to a finer edge at the expense of the workers.

Adolphus Stewart Embree:
A Biography

Typical of the early labour organizers who confronted the full power of the mining companies and government forces, Adolphus Stewart (Sam) Embree followed a career that took him from Canada to the United States, where he was involved in the Bisbee, Arizona deportations similar to the deportations that followed the Colorado labour wars of 1903-1905.

Born in Newfoundland in 1877, Sam attended Mount Allison Academy and University in New Brunswick from 1892 to 1897, graduating with a B.A. degree and a special course in chemistry and assaying. He moved to Greenwood, B.C. in 1899, where he first joined the WFM and served as secretary in the Greenwood and Phoenix locals. When the WFM affiliated with the IWW in 1905, he became a member of the IWW, and after it withdrew from the IWW, he continued membership in both organizations and was active in both. In 1908, he was sent by the WFM to Nome, Alaska, and in the succeeding years he worked continuously in the service of labour.

Sam was active in the Coeur d'Alenes and in the coal mining fields of Colorado, and he was involved in the struggle which led to the infamous Ludlow massacre. Out of work in 1916, he went to Bisbee, Arizona to work in the copper mines, where he was elected to the local IWW executive board and also acted as temporary recording secretary for Local 30 of the International Union of Mine, Mill and Smelter Workers. With copper at premium prices in 1917, safety at the Phelps Dodge company in Bisbee was sacrificed for greater production. In June 1917, resentment against the mining companies in the area came to a head. A strike 98 percent effective in the area called for the federal government to take over the mines. On July 12, 1917, Sam Embree was among 1,200 Bisbee miners rounded up by company vigilantes in the Bisbee deportations. The men were loaded onto a train and left on the desert in New Mexico. Later, they were transported by the army to a camp in Columbus, N.M. In a biography he prepared before his death in 1957, Embree recalled:

In September the camp was disbanded and we were told to leave. The day before we left the Colonel in charge called me to his office and showed me a telegram. It read: "If Embree returns to Bisbee we will give him the same kind of necktie party Frank Little got in Butte."

Five hundred of the miners had decided to go back to Bisbee. I went with them. At the Arizona line we were met by gunmen and, after many fights, the miners were taken to Bisbee, tried for vagrancy and put out on road gangs. I made my way to Douglas where I was arrested by Sheriff Wheeler. I was placed by myself in an abandoned jail at Lowell. Parties in cars came to the jail through the night but when they saw a soldier friend of mine standing in front of the jail they thought I was under federal protection.

A. S. EMBREE

Strikers deported by the army from Bisbee, Arizona were marched to the closest railroad station, apparently in Lowell, and railroaded into the middle of the desert. Photos courtesy Una Travis

After his acquittal, Sam worked on the defence committee in Chicago where Bill Haywood and 100 other members of the IWW were being held for trial on federal charges. With his health failing, Embree asked to be transferred to Butte as head of the mining department of the IWW, and in 1918 he moved there with his family, and led a strike against Anaconda Copper in April 1920. In 1921, he was arrested in Idaho on charges of criminal syndicalism, which designated almost any political opposition after World War One. He was convicted and sentenced to one to ten years in the Boise penitentiary, leaving his wife, his young daughter Una and his son without any resources but reliance upon the IWW for bare necessities. During the time he was in prison, his family travelled around and raised funds. After that, according to an interview with his daughter Una:

"He served four years and then he was in such ill health that the prison authorities thought it better to get him out of the place before he died on their hands, so we got him out of the prison and he was paroled, and we had to spend a year in Idaho, and some friends of ours from Boise found us a little place, kind of a little farmhouse . . .

"So we lived in this little house when he was paroled and we had to live there for a year. That was the parole sentence. For a living we raised chickens, my father worked in the wheat fields, my mother made bread and raised chickens . . . when my father was finally paroled, we went to a family up in B.C. and they took care of us for another year."

Sam returned to working as an active union organizer, with time spent in and out of jail, until 1929. He was inactive then, until 1937 when he withdrew from the IWW and started work once more for his original union, the IUMMSW, CIO.

The hardships suffered by the Embree family during the early years served only to strengthen the commitment of the next generation. Sam's daughter Una worked as secretary to Mine Mill president Reid Robinson; her husband Maurice Travis went on to hold executive positions in the union. In a recent interview, Maurice Travis paid tribute to the Embree family tradition:

"Throughout subsequent years her life didn't change much because instead of being deathly concerned about the welfare of her father, I was going through the same sort of thing, having been indicted under the Taft-Hartley law and subsequent indictments for alleged conspiracy under the same law, and in the course of six or seven trials by jury and appeals, Una was subjected to all this, and never lost her courage and was always a help with a positive, hopeful note on the whole situation, and never failed to attend in the court room, and helped organize support on the outside to raise funds and so forth in pursuit of these cases."

The WFM and the IWW

The outrages that broke the Colorado strikes were part of the reason that the Western Federation of Miners sent its delegates to the founding convention of the Industrial Workers of the World in 1905. The strikes had again demonstrated the need for a larger national organization, but a return to the AFL was ruled out. The Western Labour Union and their own experiences had convinced the miners, millmen and smeltermen that the industrial form of unionism was the only answer.

Bill Haywood was chairman of the Industrial Congress at which the IWW was formed. The 203 delegates who began the IWW united around three issues: the conviction that industrial unionism must replace the craft unionism of the

day; the feeling that all workers must unite for action in the political and legislative arena; and opposition to the Samuel Gompers-AFL philosophy which held that there were no basic differences in interest or aims between the workers and their employers, and that there was nothing wrong with collaborating with management. The WFM remained the "mining department" of the IWW for three turbulent years, when the factionalism that occurred in the movement was too much for the miners to stand, and they withdrew in 1908.

The IWW was active in the west as the spokesman for migrant and unskilled workers, fighting for the rights of lumber, construction, agricultural and fruit workers. In the east, it led struggles of unorganized foreign-born workers. But its effect on the WFM was to take away its most militant leaders and members. Men like Bill Haywood and Vincent St. John left the WFM to lead the IWW, and the leaders left behind, men like Moyer, became more and more conservative. Desertion of the WFM by its most militant leaders was a hard blow.

The Steunenberg Murder Case

The impetus for the rift in the WFM can be traced to the famous Steunenberg murder trial. Haywood and Moyer were still in the leadership of the WFM in February of 1906, when they and George Pettibone, a former WFM official, were kidnapped, taken secretly to Boise, and charged with murder in the assassination of the ex-Governor of Idaho.

The WFM had supported Frank Steunenberg in his successful campaign for governor in 1896. But in the second Coeur d'Alenes strike in 1899, Steunenberg threw the full weight of his office behind the Mine Owners' Association and was the man chiefly responsible for ordering the reign of terror. Steunenberg was a wealthy man when he retired in 1901, thanks to the financial aid the mine owners provided for his land speculation while he was governor.

Steunenberg was killed December 30, 1905, by a bomb attached to the gate of his Caldwell, Idaho home. The Idaho Mine Owners' Association quickly sent for James McParland, the labour spy who had destroyed the Molly Maguires (an ultra radical, secret labour organization in Pennsylvania) and who now headed the Pinkerton Agency's western division. During the week between the explosion and McParland's arrest of Harry Orchard in a Caldwell hotel, Orchard had, incredibly, remained in town with all the materials for bomb-making spread on the table in his room.

In fact, Orchard was a labour spy for the Mine Owners' Association. Before going to work for the association, he had already committed every crime possible — larceny, fraud, desertion, bigamy, arson, burglary, murder. Even though he was on the mine owners' payroll, he confessed to McParland that he had been hired by Haywood, Moyer and Pettibone to kill Steunenberg as revenge for the Coeur d'Alenes terror six years before.

Denver authorities and the Governor of Colorado then joined in a plot with Idaho officials to kidnap Moyer,

"THEIR ONLY CRIME, LOYALTY TO THE WORKING CLASS."

IDAHO

CHAS. MOYER, Denver, Colo.

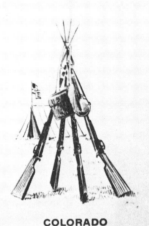

COLORADO

W. D. HAYWOOD, Denver, Colo.

SPECIAL TRAIN.

GEO. A. PETTIBONE, Denver, Colo.

KIDNAPPED BY GOVERNOR McDONALD'S COLORADO MILITIA AND GOVERNOR GOODING'S IDAHO PINKERTON THUGS

Moyer, Haywood and Pettibone were not fugitives from justice: they were dragged away from their homes and families in the dead of night---carried by special train to a foreign state.

Working Men Arouse! Protest Against This Invasion of Your Sovereign Rights.

YOU MAY BE THE NEXT.

J. C. WILLIAMS,
Acting President W. F. M.

JAMES KIRWAN,
Acting Secretary Treasurer W. F. M.
Room 3 Pioneer Bldg., Denver, Colo.

Haywood and Pettibone from their homes in Denver. They put them on a special train and rushed them to the Idaho penitentiary, where they spent the next eighteen months awaiting trial, while the state bribed, intimidated and framed witnesses, and used ministers, psychologists and a hysterical press to picture Orchard as a hardened criminal who had been converted to Christianity by McParland.

The case almost immediately became a political football. Idaho's Governor Gooding made his crusade against the accused WFM leaders the major issue in his 1906 election campaign. William Howard Taft, President Theodore Roosevelt's secretary of war, went to Idaho to urge speedy conviction. In a letter to congressmen, Roosevelt labelled Haywood and Moyer "undesirable citizens." The Idaho legislature appropriated more than $100,000 to underwrite the prosecution.

At the same time, workers all over the country demonstrated their outrage against this obvious frame-up. Not only union members, but also large numbers of unorganized workers attended hundreds of protest rallies, marched in parades, distributed literature and gave tens of thousands of dollars to the defence. The kidnappings and Gooding's boast that Haywood, Moyer and Pettibone would not leave the state alive were looked upon as a threat to the WFM and to all of labour. Conviction of the three would brand the WFM, the IWW and the Socialist Party, of which they were all members, as murder rings. Within three days of the arrest, the Illinois district convention of the United Mine workers of America voted to send $5,000 for the defence.

Clarence Darrow, heading the defence, fought for Haywood in the first trial. Fifty special correspondents from newspapers all over the country covered the case. The prosecution was led by William Borah, later U.S. Senator from Idaho, who had been in on the kidnapping plot. After a fifteen-month delay, the trial opened May 9, 1907. It took nearly two months to choose a jury; not one worker was selected. Although 160 witnesses were brought in by the prosecution, the only one who accused Haywood of a specific act was Orchard. Darrow proceeded to prove Orchard was a pathological liar and degenerate.

Darrow took eleven hours to sum up his arguments to the jury. Most quoted, perhaps, is this declaration:

> Mr. Haywood is not my greatest concern. Other men have died before him. Other men have been martyrs to a holy cause since the world began. Whenever men have looked upward and onward, forgotten their selfishness, struggled for humanity, worked for the poor and the weak, they have been sacrificed.
>
> But, gentlemen, you short-sighted people who would cure hatred with hate, you who think you can crush out the feelings and the hopes and aspirations of man by tying a noose around his neck, you who are trying to kill him, not because it is Haywood, but because he represents a class, don't be so blind, don't so so foolish as to believe you can strangle the Western Federation of Miners when you tie a rope around his neck. Don't be so blind in your madness as to believe that when you make three fresh new graves you will kill the labour movement of the world. If at the behest of this mob you should kill Bill Haywood, he is mortal, he will die, but I want to say that a million men will grab up the banner of labour at the open grave where Haywood lays it down,

CLARENCE DARROW

and in spite of prisons or scaffold or fire, in spite of prosecution or jury, or courts, these men of willing hands will carry it on to victory in the end.[6]

Haywood was acquitted. Pettibone was acquitted in the second trial, and charges against Moyer were dismissed. Orchard was imprisoned for life, and died some years later in the Idaho penitentiary.

By then, Haywood had become nationally famous, the hero of workers all over the country. When he returned to Denver, he was met at the station by a crowd of 10,000 and carried through the downtown streets in a midnight parade. Almost at once he undertook a national speaking tour, after which he left the WFM leadership to become a full-time organizer for the IWW. The long trial and the publicity generated seemed to have widened political differences and Haywood moved to the more radical IWW, leaving Moyer in a more and more conservative position.

Meanwhile, the rift that occurred within the WFM over the IWW did not prevent it from pursuing its organizing campaign. The "Directory of Local Unions and Officers" which appeared in the December 27, 1905 issue of *Miners' Magazine* listed a total of 185 locals, including 20 in British Columbia and one in Ontario. The federation had gained its first chartered local in Ontario, Cobalt Miners' Union Local 146. The union grew rapidly in Canada during the next half-dozen years, reaching a peak of 6,000 members in 1912, divided almost equally between Ontario and British Columbia.

In order to develop relations with the union representing the coal miners, the WFM rejoined the AFL on May 9, 1911. The arrangement with the United Mine Workers was especially important in British Columbia, where both the WFM and the UMW had, for several years, claimed jurisdiction over all miners. Jurisdictional disputes had become common, and in some camps, both WFM and UMW card-holders could be found. These had led to conferences among the Canadian leadership of both unions, in which they agreed to leave the coal jurisdiction to the UMW, while the WFM was to stick to metal workers. The other reason for returning to the AFL was that two industrial unions, the UMW and the Brewery Workers, were now in the AFL. This gave the miners hope that industrial unionism could be pressed from within the AFL.

---

[6]*Bill Haywood's Book*, p. 214.

The Copper Strike and Joe Hill

The biggest strike ever conducted by the federation was the Michigan copper strike of 1913, during which 15,000 miners were out for eight months. The companies used many of the same strike breaking techniques which had been introduced by western mine operators, including the vigilante mob which called itself a "Citizens Alliance" and deportation of strike leaders. These same techniques were used in Canada against Mine Mill in the 1940s and '50s during the early organizational drives and later as an aid to the Steel raids.

During the critical days of the copper strike, WFM President Charles Moyer was visited in his hotel room at the strike centre by a group of "Citizens Alliance" men who beat him unconscious and shot him in the back. Then they dragged him through the streets for a mile and a half to the railroad station, where James McNaughton, Calumet & Hecla presi-

dent, slapped him in the face and said: "We'll hang you if you come back to this district." Moyer was put on a train to Chicago. As soon as the bullet was removed from his back, he returned to Calumet.

The strike ended after eight months without a clear-cut victory. All the strike issues were conceded except the key one, recognition of the union. A depression had hit the industry, and layoffs in the west made it impossible to raise enough money to stave off starvation for the Michigan workers.

The story of Joe Hill, the workers' troubadour, has become part of the history of the union of metal mine workers for his martyrdom in the long fight of copper workers to organize. Joe Hill was a Wobbly (IWW), and the songs he

The funeral of Joe Hill. The Archives of Labor and Urban Affairs, Wayne State University

wrote are still being sung by workers in all unions. Union songs, such as "What We Want," "Scissor Bill," "Hallelujah I'm a Bum," "There is Power in a Union," "Casey Jones — the Union Scab," and "Should I Ever Be a Soldier" are a few of them.

Hill was trying to organize Bingham Canyon copper miners when he was arrested in Salt Lake City on a charge of murdering a grocery store owner. Behind the frame-up was the Utah Copper Company, later to become the Kennecott Copper Corporation, notorious for its anti-labour management. Joe Hill was arrested in January 1914. By the time he was executed by a firing squad in November 1915, his case had become world famous. U.S. President Wilson asked Utah's governor for leniency; the Swedish government protested the execution (Joel Hagglund, or Joe Hill, had emigrated from Sweden in 1902). On the eve of his execution, he wired to Bill Haywood: "Don't mourn for me — organize!" So the song, written years later by Earl Robinson and Alfred Hayes and sung at Mine Mill conventions, goes:

I dreamed I saw Joe Hill last night,
Alive as you and me.
Says I, "But Joe you're ten years dead,"
"I never died," says he,
"I never died," says he.

"In Salt Lake, Joe," says I to him,
Him standing by my bed,
"They framed you on a murder charge,"
Says Joe, "But I ain't dead,"
Says Joe, "But I ain't dead."

"The copper bosses killed you, Joe,
They shot you, Joe," says I.
"Takes more than guns to kill a man,"
Says Joe, "I didn't die,"
Says Joe, "I didn't die."

And standing there as big as life
And smiling with his eyes,
Joe says, "What they forgot to kill
Went on to organize,
Went on to organize."

"Joe Hill ain't dead," he says to me,
"Joe Hill ain't never died.
Where workingmen are out on strike
Joe Hill is at their side,
Joe Hill is at their side."

"From San Diego up to Maine,
In every mine and mill,
Where workers strike and organize,"
Says he, "You'll find Joe Hill,"
Says he, "You'll find Joe Hill."

I dreamed I saw Joe Hill last night,
Alive as you or me.
Says I, "But Joe, you're ten years dead,"
"I never died," says he,
"I never died," says he."

This same song, on a recording by Paul Robeson, was used as the pretext for banning a popular Local 598 weekly radio program in Sudbury, Ontario in the 1950s.

WFM Becomes IUMMSW: 1916

By the time of the 1916 WFM convention, the union's membership had fallen seriously. Of the 76 locals in the union, less than half (36) sent delegates. Only 7,294 votes were cast in the international election that year, in which Moyer was returned to office. The convention voted to change the name of the Western Federation of Miners to the International Union of Mine, Mill and Smelter Workers. Since the federation, as an industrial union, represented not only miners but also millmen and smeltermen, the name change was intended to recognize the full jurisdiction of the union. Moreover, the union was no longer solely a western organization.

During World War One, a combined government and industry drive against trade unions recorded considerable success, but even before the war years the union had begun to decline. Internal dissension had gradually taken its toll, aggravated by the dual unionism of the IWW in the U.S. and, during 1919, of the One Big Union movement in Canada, which had diverted much of the membership. The increased willingness of state, provincial and federal governments to join employers in breaking strikes and harassing all unions lent an additional impact.

A general breakdown of Mine Mill in the U.S. became assured as the Palmer Raids* at the end of the war heralded the onslaught of a furious anti-labour drive by American business and industry. *The Miners' Magazine* stopped publication in 1921. In 1926, Moyer resigned, and the international office was moved to Salt Lake, where its direction drifted aimlessly. The leadership became a kind of caretaker group which kept alive memories of great traditions and looked forward to a new day. Conventions were held irregularly during the 1920s. Secretary-treasurer Edward Sweeny alone worked full time for the union, able to do so only because he had a small independent income of his own. Other officers and board members were working in the mines, mills or smelters.

Mine Mill Revives: 1933

Not until the election of Franklin D. Roosevelt as President of the U.S. in 1933, did Mine Mill come to life again. One of the first acts which Congress approved at Roosevelt's urging, was the National Recovery Act (NRA). The law, which was intended to save the corporations, was still brazenly violated by employers all over the country. But tucked away in NRA was something new, Section 7A. Known as the Wagner Act, Section 7A was important because, for the first time, the U.S. government had declared support for the right of workers to organize.

By then, the international union had gone downhill to such an extent there were but six locals left. The 1,500

---

*Attorney-General Mitchell Palmer's repressive raids on labour groups took place in 1919. They were also known as the Red Scare.

members of the union in these six locals sent delegates to a special conference at Butte in June 1933. Now was the time, the delegates agreed, to get the union into motion again. Plans were laid for an organizational drive, and when the 30th convention was held in Butte two months later, the union was back in business. The convention adopted a code covering wages, hours and conditions to be submitted to the government for consideration as the industry minimum under NRA. Running through the convention was the strong theme of organizing. Thus the new era began, and during the next year the union grew rapidly.

When the 31st convention met at Salt Lake in 1934, secretary-treasurer James Robinson* reported that the year had seen the union's membership increased to 15,000 and the number of locals to 94. Robinson also announced formation of three women's auxiliaries and Mine Mill councils in three states.

At the 1935 convention in Salt Lake, Robinson reported 38 new locals for a total of 132, 27 new women's auxiliaries, three new district unions and a membership of 26,000. Mine Mill's international office was moved back to Denver where it remained except for a period in Chicago between 1945 and 1951.

---

*James Robinson was the father of Reid Robinson. Reid Robinson was elected international president in 1936.

The 1936 IUMMSW convention in Denver, at which Reid Robinson was elected president. Faces familiar to the authors include James Robinson, his son Reid, John Clark, who later became president, and their wives. William Mason later became board member of District 1, Angelo Verdu board member of District 3, and Chase Powers board member of District 7 which included California and British Columbia. Solski Collection

The CIO: 1936

The fight had already started within the American Federation of Labour for an aggressive, nationwide organizing campaign on industrial union lines in mass production industries. Mine Mill aligned itself with John L. Lewis of the United Mine Workers and other unions to press for a change in the AFL's traditional craft union policies. The debate came to a head in the 1935 AFL convention and, three weeks afterwards, leaders of eight affiliated unions announced formation of the Committee for Industrial Organization for the purpose of "encouraging and promoting the organization of the unorganized workers in mass production and other industries on an industrial basis." The next year the rebel unions were suspended and in 1938 expelled from the AFL, and the "Committee" became the Congress of Industrial Organizations (CIO).

At the 1936 Mine Mill convention, Reid Robinson of the Butte Miners' Union was chosen president, and the chief theme, "Organize," was so effective that by 1938 the union boasted 50,000 members. By 1937, arrangements had been made for a Mine Mill edition of *People's Press*, the CIO newspaper. On April 6, 1942, the first issue of *The Union*, a Mine Mill paper, was published.

In 1938, one of the main organizational areas of Mine Mill was in the southwestern United States. The union launched a vigorous campaign against the dual wage system in the mines under which Mexican-American workers were paid less than their white counterparts. The end result was a breaking down of racial barriers in the local unions and in the mining communities.

A big breakthrough was achieved for Alabama miners in 1941. Mine Mill won a long, drawn-out legal battle in the U.S. Supreme Court for collar-to-collar pay, the first such victory in the U.S. mining industry. As a result of this legal win, thousands of workers throughout the country collected millions of dollars in back pay for previously unpaid hours of work.

That same year, the sliding wage scale was virtually eliminated in the United States. Cursed by every worker in the metal mining industry, the sliding scale tied wages to metal prices: when prices went up, wages went up; when prices went down, wages went down. This put mining industry workers at the mercy of price rigging, speculation and economic instability. With the end of the sliding scale, workers were assured negotiated wage rates that would stand firm for the duration of the collective agreement.

World War Two

On December 7, 1941, the Japanese military blasted the U.S. installation at Pearl Harbour in Hawaii. This sneak attack brought the United States into World War Two on the side of the allied forces against the Axis fascist powers.

The following day, as the representative of workers in the metal mining industry, Mine Mill presented its Production for Victory Plan to President Roosevelt. It was a program for expansion of the industry to ensure increased metals output. As part of the program, proposals were made for an adequate supply of skilled workers to do the job. The union's plan dealt with the stability of wages and hours, as well as safety and health. It provided a sensible, integrated approach to the problems of the mining industry, while at the same time protecting the hard-won gains of the union. As part of the plan, Mine Mill offered a no-strike pledge for the duration of the war. Mine Mill's program and consistent record during the war received warm praise from the War Labor Board, the War Production Board, the War Department and from President Roosevelt himself.

Wage rates in the mining industry were virtually frozen during the war. However, before the wage freezes came, an expanding Mine Mill had regained the ground lost during the depression of the thirties. The last increases negotiated in 1942 brought gains of about one dollar per shift. Miners' rates in Utah were raised to about $7.50, in Butte to $7.75 and in the Coeur d'Alenes to $8.25 per day.

While Mine Mill members were turning out production for victory during the war years, the union continued to organize. Mining companies in Utah, Nevada and the southwest United States, in addition to Sudbury and Trail in Canada, were being organized into the union. In 1944, a signal victory was won at Miami, Arizona when the War Labor Board agreed with Mine Mill that the copper companies there had to stop the practice of hiring Mexican-American workers at lower rates of pay and denying them opportunities for advancement.

At the war's end, Mine Mill President Reid Robinson went to Paris with a CIO delegation to participate in the formation of the World Federation of Trade Unions (WFTU), representing 66 million workers from 56 countries. The future for labour looked bright.

Mine Mill moved to secure wage and contract gains that had been side-tracked by the war. Intensive bargaining resulted in many improvements in collective agreements. The first premium pay for shift work was established. Paid holidays and paid vacations became standard provisions in union contracts.

One of the most significant gains of the post-war period was a national settlement with the American Smelting and Refining Company. It provided a national settlement for all AS&R plants represented by Mine Mill. For the first time, a national agreement with a single U.S. corporation was made effective. This bargaining tactic became a union-wide policy, and national bargaining councils were established to bargain with Anaconda, Phelps Dodge and Kennecott, the major U.S. producers.

At the conclusion of 1946, Mine Mill held contracts with 583 companies, covering some 157,000 employees in the United States and Canada. The union had a paid-up membership of about 125,000 workers. This was the peak. Postwar layoffs and shutdowns began to cut in on the membership, and then the raids came.

The Raids

The union was faced not only with a post-war decline but with increasingly hostile employers worried about the growing effectiveness of rank-and-file organizations like Mine Mill and who felt their corporate control was being undermined. By 1947, an anti-labour campaign was initiated by industry and its friends in government and the media, in which the union movement was pictured as a giant threatening destruction of the country. This cabal was able to push the Taft-Hartley Act through the U.S. Congress, over the veto of President Truman. Then came the deluge.

The Taft-Hartley Act not only chopped away provisions of the Wagner Act, known as labour's Magna Carta, but included a new gimmick that sanctified red-baiting and made it law. It provided that any union that wanted to use the services of the National Labor Relations Board would have to sign non-Communist affidavits.

The union movement almost unanimously rejected such a purity provision at the time, arguing that the affidavit was in violation of the first and fifth amendments to the U.S. constitution. Most union leaders felt the labour movement had demonstrated its patriotism and correctly saw the Taft-Hartley Act as a legal smoke-screen behind which the unions would be purged of their militant leaders. However, some conservative union bosses saw Taft-Hartley as an opportunity to expand their union's jurisdiction and dues-paying membership. They became part of the anti-labour scenario.

At its 1947 convention, Mine Mill joined the fight against Taft-Hartley. Union officers were instructed not to sign the affidavits and to boycott the NLRD. However, it was not that simple. A serious situation developed in the 1948 strike at American Zinc when Mine Mill's non-compliance was used by the company and raiding unions to frighten striking zinc workers. Two units of this company were induced to break away from Mine Mill in the middle of the strike struggle.

The main antagonist seeking to replace Mine Mill was the United Steelworkers of America (USWA). A most violent expression of the Steelworkers' campaign occurred in April 1949, when Mine Mill's secretary-treasurer Maurice Travis was severely beaten by a gang of hoodlums led by Steel organizer Nick Zonarich. The assault took place in the studio of radio station WJLD in Bessemer, Alabama while a Mine Mill program was on the air. Travis was so brutally beaten he was confined to hospital for over a month. Both eyes were severely injured, with permanent blinding in the right eye. Strangely, no charges were ever laid against the attackers, who were well known. It was more than a coincidence that the local sheriff who should have initiated legal action was a leading member of the Ku Klux Klan and a supporter of the "white supremacy" brand of Steel unionism in Bessemer.

In mid-1949, Mine Mill along with a group of other unions decided to comply with the provisions of Taft-Hartley and sign the affidavits. This removed a serious technical roadblock in the negotiations with American Zinc, and the long and bitter strike was finally won, with a thirteen-cent wage increase, the union shop and reinstatement of all strikers.

Raids against Mine Mill continued but the union held firm in its determination to remain an independent, rank-and-file union. The Steel union sought to achieve through the intervention of the CIO leadership what it could not achieve in direct raiding. The CIO handed over Mine Mill's jurisdiction in the metal mining industry of the United States to Steel. Mine Mill refused to back down on its right to autonomy. February 15, 1950 was a sad day for labour when the CIO expelled one of its founding unions, Mine Mill.

In 1950, USWA leaders launched their first nation-wide raids against Mine Mill. They used the CIO expulsion and red-baiting as their chief weapons, but met with little success as Mine Mill won election after election against the raiders. In the following year, Mine Mill staged the first nation-wide strike in the copper industry and won substantial wage gains and the first pension plans in the industry, despite the Taft-Hartley injunction against the union.

The raiding continued but it was becoming clear that additional forces would have to be employed to defeat Mine Mill. In 1952, the notorious McCarran Committee conducted a week-long hearing against the union. The committee chairman, Senator McCarran of Nevada, had long been considered a favourite of the mining companies.

In the early fifties, a major attempt was made to crush Mine Mill through government court action. Secretary-treasurer Maurice Travis and international representative Clinton Jencks were indicted for allegedly filing false Taft-Hartley affidavits. The National Labor Relations Board attempted to have Mine Mill decertified as a bargaining agent. The union was cited by the Subversive Activities Control Board under the McCarran Act as being "Communist infiltrated." A charge of conspiracy in connection with Taft-Hartley affidavits was filed against present and past leaders of the union — a charge vigorously denied by those involved.

In 1956, the legal cases began to reach the Supreme Court. In each case, the union was upheld. Travis and Jencks were cleared, and the Jencks decision is regarded as a landmark for civil liberties legislation in the United States. The NLRB's decertification attempt was denied by a unanimous Supreme Court decision.

In August 1959, Mine Mill led a nation-wide strike against the major copper companies. The copper market was in an over-supply situation, and months of negotiations proved fruitless. It appeared that the companies were also convinced that the pending trials of union leaders in the Taft-Hartley conspiracy cases would weaken the unions' effectiveness as a bargaining agent. The companies attempted to force a cheap and humiliating settlement on the union, but they had not reckoned with the union's rank and file, who refused to surrender. The long, tough strike went on for almost six months. During that time, the conspiracy case came to trial. For seven weeks, many of the defendants were in court during the day, while they negotiated with the companies at night and on weekends.

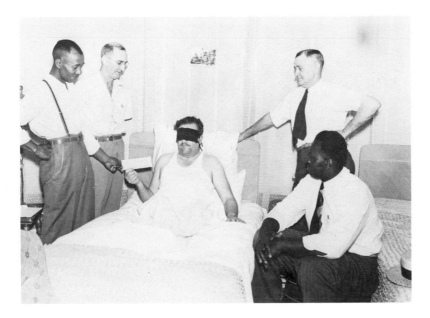

"Steelworkers' Thugs Did This: CIO Is Committing Suicide!" read a Mine Mill protest to Philip Murray, CIO president, after the brutal assault on Mine Mill financial secretary Maurice Travis by raiding Steelworkers. The attack, led by Steel organizer Nick Zonarich, took place in radio station WJLD in Bessemer, Alabama while a Mine Mill program was in progress on the eve of a bargaining election for red-iron ore miners employed by Tennessee Coal, Iron & Railroad Co., a subsidiary of U.S. Steel. Travis suffered injury to both and removal of one of his eyes. In this picture, taken in a Birmingham hospital in April 1949, leaders of Alabama locals bring messages of solidarity in the fight against white supremacist unionism. No charges were laid by the Bessemer sheriff in connection with the assault. Photo courtesy Maurice Travis

Despite the use of court injunctions, law suits, company ads, "Dear John" letters to employees, and back-to-work movements to break the strike, the strikers held firm. Close to a million dollars was raised and distributed in strike relief to the determined workers. Eventually, settlements were reached with AS&R, Kennecott, Anaconda and Phelps Dodge. The new contracts provided for substantial wage gains, pension improvements, health and welfare improvements and other important gains.

During this same tough year of 1959, the union's international vice-president Asbury Howard was beaten and jailed for six months in Bessemer, Alabama. His crime? Arranging to publish a poster urging blacks to register to vote! Howard was shackled on a chain gang as an attempt to humiliate this early activist in the civil rights struggle.

In the early sixties, the raiding continued as a time- and money-consuming stalemate. For the embattled Mine Mill, funds were running low and the battle fatigue against almost impossible odds was beginning to tell. The Steel union did not remain unscathed. It was experiencing severe internal problems, with union members restive under the anti-rank-and-file and raiding policies. In 1965, I.W. Abel defeated "Wavy Davy" McDonald for the presidency of the USWA, promising to return to basic unionism and more effective bargaining. With the McCarthy era at an end, the time was ripe for a union truce.

Discussions held by the leaderships of Mine Mill and Steel finally culminated in a merger agreement. On January 16, 1967, a convention of Mine Mill in the United States agreed with the merger terms, and Mine Mill locals became part of the USWA. In was bitter fruit for many union militants who had fought for an independent union of metal mine workers through 74 years of struggle.

Mine Mill's secretary-treasurer at the time of the merger, Irving Dichter, said in a recent interview that a number of factors had led the international board to believe the "time was opportune to merge with honour." Two factors Dichter invoked were the wearing down of Mine Mill from all the attacks against it and the defeat of McDonald by Abel, with the promise of progressive changes in Steel that would make it possible for Mine-Millers to work within it. Dichter said the Mine Mill leadership was determined "not to further weaken itself in collective bargaining, but instead to enhance the union's strength through unity in the mining industry." He argued, "We always preached unity. It is true that we never preached merger, but ultimately the only possibility of achieving unity was through merger."

Recently questioned about the merger, the last president of Mine Mill, Al Skinner, made these trenchant remarks: "During the Truman, Eisenhower and early Kennedy administrations, McCarthy hysteria almost became the number one foreign and domestic policy in the United States. Most politicians ran for cover to avoid being painted with the "red brush." No one was interested in the truth or facts. During this period the CIO and the AFL joined the witch-hunt against any union or any leader who got painted by their enemies or the companies they dealt with."

He pointed out that in the United States Mine Mill had its leaders indicted on conspiracy charges, their organization continually harassed. These officers went through twelve years of litigation, during which the cost to them and their families was beyond calculation, he added. They were finally exonerated by the U.S. Supreme Court in 1968.

It is ironic that the Mine Mill officers won their cases a year after the merger. The harassment ended. It was a small and tardy consolation.

Fourteen Indicted Mines Union Leaders Surrender to Federal Officers

Chiefs of Mines Union Staff Face Conspiracy Indictments

Thirteen of the 14 members of the International Union of Mine, Mill and Smelter Workers staff who surrendered Tuesday to face federal indictments charging them with conspiracy appear here on their arrival at the Denver office of the United States marshal. Left to right are Ray Dennis, Al Pezzati, Jim Durkin, Al Skinner, Jess Van Camp, Harold Sanderson, Jack Marcotti, Irving Dichter, Graham Dolan, Maurice Travis, Anton Lawrence, Asbury Howard and C. J. Powers. Charley Wilson, who was also indicted, does not appear in this photo. The indicted men joked, made light of their appearance, accompanied by attorneys. See story on page 2.

Denver Post, November 16, 1956

CHAPTER II

Organization in Western Canada

As American companies bought up small, independently-owned mining sites in southern B.C., miners from the U.S. moved north across the border to work, bringing with them the lessons they had learned in the bitter struggles of Idaho and Colorado. Expansion of the WFM followed the expansion of the industry as the union was carried into camp after camp.

The WFM Comes to Canada: 1895

The first recorded local of the Western Federation of Miners in Canada was the Rossland Miners' Union, WFM Local 38, chartered in 1895. District Association No. 6 covered local unions at Sandon, Ymir, Kaslo, Rossland, Trail, Nelson, Texada, Silverton, Hedley and Phoenix. During those early years the coal miners of Vancouver Island and the Crow's Nest Pass were also an integral part of the WFM. District No. 6, the Canadian district, maintained thirteen Kootenay locals, one Alberta group, an official newspaper, libraries and lecture series. From its earliest days, in the eyes of the union, all workers had equal rights and no restrictions were placed on membership except against proven enemies of the workers — police spies and the like.

The Eight-Hour Day: 1899

A further boost to the WFM came in 1899 when Attorney General Joseph M. Martin quietly oversaw the passage of the Eight-Hour-Day Act through the legislature on February 27th. Martin had been elected to represent Rossland's mining constituency by advocating eight-hour day reform. The Eight-Hour-Day Act cut two hours off the daily shift of all underground workers.

When news of this statute hit them, the B.C. Mine Managers' Association tried hard to have the act either amended or declared illegal, but public opinion was on the miners' side and the government held to the law. Twenty-three Kootenay mining companies lobbied Martin to have the eight-hour law repealed, but the WFM's petition, signed by 3,000 of the district's miners, provided support for the law.[1] Some operators accepted the law, but the Silver-Lead Mine Owners' Association, when it put the eight-hour day into practice, announced wages would be cut from $3.50 to three dollars per day for miners and shovellers, and from three dollars to $2.50 for carmen. The WFM's strike in the Kootenays against the operators in the Silver-Lead Association lasted several months. Mine operators imported strikebreakers from the Michigan iron ranges, and the *Miners' Magazine* reported that $500 was raised by the union to pay return fares to Michigan to persuade would-be scabs to refuse to act against the B.C. eight-hour law. The Silver-Lead operators appealed to the Canadian government, which commissioned Mr. R. C. Clute, Q.C., of Toronto, who travelled to the Kootenays to investigate. The federal government accepted Clute's recommendation to uphold the eight-hour day.

In 1899, The Clute *Royal Commission on Mining Conditions in B.C.* reported:

> I found reluctance on the part of some mine managers to recognize the unions as such. It is said . . . we approve of unions within proper limits, but refuse to hand over our mines to the control of the union or to permit any interference with our policy or management. We will listen to complaints from the men, but will not submit to dictation by the union — least of all a union affiliated with the WFM.
>
> In a new mining district the owners of capital there invested usually reside elsewhere, and the chief benefit to the locality, and often to the country, at all events in the early stages of a mining camp, is

---

[1]Merle Wells, "The Western Federation of Miners in the Coeur d'Alene and Kootenay Region, 1899–1902," unpublished paper delivered at the Pacific Northwest Labour History Conference, Seattle, Wa, 1976.

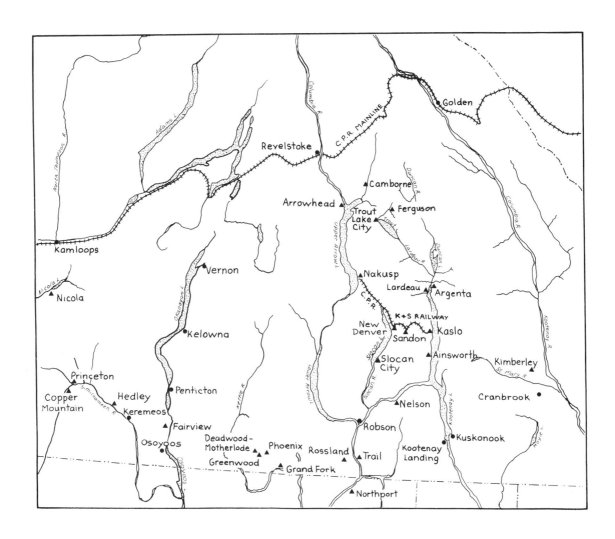

MINING CENTRES IN SOUTHERN B.C. CIRCA 1900

Western Federation of Miners meeting in Ferguson, B.C. 1900. Vancouver Public Library Photo 100

derived from the cost of production, wages, plant, etc., and not from the expenditure of dividends which are usually received and spent elsewhere.

Wage earners throughout the civilized world believe in the necessity of organization . . . to protect themselves from competition and starvation wages and the hardships which, in most cases, ensue where there is no union to support just demands or right grievances. . . . If an establishment employing a large number of men antagonized them at the start by refusing to recognize in any way their organizations, must not this tend to irritate, annoy and finally create a breach?

Large aggregations of capital organize and speak through one man; why should not labour do the same? . . . I desire to bring to your notice an instance where the utmost accord and results perfectly satisfactory to the management have been attained by full recognition of the union. The Vancouver Coal Company of Nanaimo, with a capital of 265,000 pounds sterling, has been in existence since 1862, and employs 1200 men . . . the union is fully recognized and all disputes are settled through its committee.

The *Miners' Magazine* commented that there was more protection for the worker in Canada than in the U.S., where the courts were always ready to grant injunctions and rule out progressive legislation.

The following letter describes the eight-hour day strike at Sandon, B.C. Much to the regret of the organizers of the Eighth Annual Convention of Mine Mill, held in Sudbury the last week of February 1956, it wasn't until after the convention ended that this letter to the *Sudbury Daily Star* revealed another WFM leader from B.C. before the turn of the century. Senator Thomas Farquhar, then living in northern Ontario, would have been a guest of honour had the union been aware of his existence.

The Editor   March 3, 1956
The Sudbury Daily Star

I read with much interest in Monday's Star, the early history of the International Union of Mine, Mill and Smelter Workers of Canada, and of its origin in the Western Federation of Miners, chartered at Rossland, B.C. in 1895.

I arrived in Sandon, B.C. in 1896, where I joined the Sandon branch of the Western Federation of Miners and was working in the Slocan Star Mine when the Eight-Hour Day Act was passed by the B.C. Legislature. Until this Act came into effect we worked 10 hours underground.

To offset this, the mine owners asked us to accept a reduced wage from $3.50, which had been the daily rate, to $3. Our refusal to accept this led to a bitter strike of nine months duration.

In those days when miners went on strike, the mine owners at once began to devise every possible scheme whereby the strike might be broken. They even brought in men from Nova Scotia, telling them to bring firearms, representing that these would be needed to fend off the attacks of fierce grizzly and silver-tip bears. These men, on arrival, were landed at the Pain mine without reaching the town of Sandon, and, to prevent them from making any contact with the striking miners, were taken directly from the train and loaded into the buckets in which the ore was brought from the mine, and were taken this way into the mine.

That evening a meeting of the enraged miners was called, and many were determined to go into the mine and bring out the new men by force. However, a cool-headed Scotsman, Bill Davidson, who later became a member of the B.C. Legislature, gained the floor and by his good advice persuaded them from this course. He told them that he had been through strikes in Montana and Idaho, and advised working against the owners instead of with them, and it was his belief that the Nova Scotians were ignorant of the fact that there was a strike on, and that a small committee of the miners should be appointed to talk with the newcomers and explain the situation.

This was done, and when the actions and intentions of the owners became clear to the Nova Scotians, they came out at once. The unions assisted them in raffling off their guns, and they left town.

When the owners realized that their plan to cause a riot had failed, they asked the B.C. Legislature, then in session, to send in the militia, claiming that lives were endangered. A Mr. Green, who represented the riding, asked the Legislature to postpone action until he could investigate. The result was proof that everything had been conducted peaceably, and that the request of the mine owners was quite unwarranted. The troops were not despatched.

Later, the mine owners made a slight concession and the strike was settled. I was later, in 1903, elected president of the Sandon branch of the W.F. of M.

A coincidence is that I now occupy the office in the Canadian Senate formerly occupied by the late Senator Green, who was a member of the legislature at the time of the long-ago strike, and who prevented the militia from going to Sandon to break up our miners' union.

Thos. Farquhar
Senator
Little Current, Ontario

"I attended a large meeting of miners assembled in the Hall of the Miners Union and saw 21 witnesses," R. C. Clute, Q.C. wrote of Sandon in his 1899 report which favoured the eight-hour day. The Sandon local of the WFM was active, with 530 members. It not only built the Miners Union Block shown above, but its membership also supported a hospital, opera house, gymnasium and library. Nevertheless, the union was not recognized by silver-lead mine owners. (Sandon Miners Block exterior view, Provincial Archives of British Columbia Cat. no. 40671; interior view (above) Provincial Archives of British Columbia Cat. no. 53247.

Tom Farquhar (right), president of the Sandon local of the WFM in 1903, later became Senator Farquhar. Photo courtesy Ruth Ashely

The Rossland Strike: 1901

A major strike that shook all of Rossland area's mines was provoked in 1901, as mine owners began an intensive onslaught on the union. The local union had been trying to obtain at Rossland, as was in place in other mines in the Kootenay district, the same daily wage for carmen and shovellers who were making $2.50 a day as for machine men at $3.00 a day. Operators of the Le Roi mines, assisted by the manager of The War Eagle and The Centre Star mines, owned by the Gooderham syndicate of Toronto, hired "spotters" posing as union men and instituted a regime of firing and blacklisting union men and replacing them with non-union men. The WFM had further cause to believe the companies were trying to break the union. The Le Roi Mining Company,* which had several mines operating in the district, had shut down its smelter at Northport, just across the U.S. border, in order to rid itself of the union which was trying to establish itself there. For the Rossland miners to continue feeding ore to Northport with the smelter closed meant strengthening the hand of the company by allowing it to stockpile ore, giving it the opportunity to close down the mines in the future.[2]

At a membership meeting on July 3, 1901, the following resolution was passed unanimously and recorded for posterity:

> Whereas: It has come to the notice of organized labour and the general public that the managers of the principal mines within the jurisdiction of the Rossland Union for the past fifteen months have been using every means in their power to force the labouring elements in their employ into industrial slavery.
>
> Time and again those same managers have asserted that they have no grievance against organized labour, yet we find them all through the past year discriminating against active members of organized labour, and at present we see the M.&S. Union of Northport, Wash. locked out for no other reason than that they dared to organize to protect their rights.
>
> Whereas: We the members of Rossland Miners Union, No. 38, W.F. of M. have reason to believe that this blow at the Northport Union is also aimed at the Union in Rossland and if they succeed in crushing the Union in Northport, we may expect to see a cut in wages within our camp in the near future.
>
> Therefore be it resolved: That we the members of Rossland Miners Union No. 38 W.F. of M. in regular meeting assembled, extend to our Bros. in Northport our hearty co-operation and assistance. And be it further resolved: That we the members of a Union who believe that an injury to one is the concern of all believe that the time has arrived when we should act in concert with our Brothers at Northport. And be it further resolved: That it be the sense of this meeting that all members of our union who are not at present employed be requested to refrain from seeking employment from any of the mines within the jurisdiction of this Union and that those who are at present employed be requested to quit work until such time as the difficulties at Northport are adjusted and the carmen and shovellers within our jurisdiction receive three dollars per day and the managers of all mines within our jurisdiction agree that no discrimination be practised against Union men.

Publicity aimed at keeping the district fully informed was quickly launched in a printed leaflet addressed to the citizens and businessmen of Rossland and vicinity and the general public from the executive board of Local 38, dated July 11, 1901:

> Since the agreement between the big corporations of Rossland and Rossland Miners Union in April, 1900, this city has apparently enjoyed industrial peace; yet all who are conversant with the industrial affairs of Rossland for the past 15 months know there has been a secret warfare waged against this miners' union which has been nearly as destructive to the business interests of the community as an open struggle between the two industrial forces, and worse in that there is no apparent end to be seen.
>
> The foundation of the trouble rests on the fact that nearly one half of the employees in the mines of this community receive about 20 per cent less wages than the same class of employees in surrounding camps. We believe it is to continue to enforce this unjust scale of wages that so many annoying practices have been introduced to undermine the prestige of this Miners Union of Rossland.
>
> 1) An annoying system of espionage and blacklisting.
>
> 2) By connecting with bogus employment agencies seeking to flood the overcrowded labour market with cheap foreign labour.
>
> 3) By the largest corporation in this vicinity openly seeking to crush a sister Local in Northport, Wash.
>
> We believe these efforts are mainly to enforce this unjust scale of wages and to prevent all efforts towards an increase. Therefore, we have fully resolved that there can be no industrial peace in Rossland until this wage question is finally and satisfactorily settled. Then this fair city will enjoy the prosperity for which nature has evidently intended it.

An interesting comment on conditions prevailing at the time is a letter from the Denver, Colorado headquarters, dated October 16, 1901, from Bill Haywood, secretary-treasurer of the WFM, to F. E. Woodside, secretary of Rossland Miners' Union Local 38, cautioning against open use of the telegraph: "You know that under the present circumstances that a message from you addressed to this office would not be cold before the manager of the company knew of its contents."*

---

*The Le Roi Mining Co., owned at this time by the British America Corporation of London, was part of an early multinational company controlled by Whittaker Wright. The financial manipulations of worthless securities, combined with the outbreak of the Boer War which caused a drop in the London stock market, plunged the company into bankruptcy by October of 1901. In a celebrated fraud case, a London court found Wright guilty and in the court room he "took a lick of cyanide concealed in his cigar and died in his tracks" (in the words of Frank Woodside). The effect on the Rossland mines of the removal of millions of dollars of profits to cover Wright's failing empire was crucial to the workings of the mines. Mechanical breakdowns, dangerous short-cuts and low wages were used to make up drained-off capital.

[2]"The Rossland Situation," *The Labour Gazette*, December 1901, p. 363.

---

*This is comparable to a situation some forty years later in Sudbury, when Bob Miner, transacting personal business via long distance telephone with his bank in Timmins, found his boss at Inco telling him about this telephone conversation the very next morning.

Group of miners at the Le Roi Mine, Rossland 1900. First organized in 1895, Rossland WFM Local 38 had a membership of 1,300 by 1899. Provincial Archives of British Columbia Cat. no. 41872

Nine hundred to a thousand miners went on strike on July 11, 1901. Frank Woodside, on behalf of the executive of the Rossland union described the first strike day:

> . . . pickets armed with the strike order were posted on all the trails and roads leading to the mine. . . .
>
> The officers of the mine came out on the steps of the offices. They made no attempt to interfere with the picket. [Mine manager] McDonald stood on the porch of the general office watching the men as they slowly came up the hill.
>
> Had McDonald, as he claimed, made a non-union mine of the Le Roi or not? The question would soon be answered.
>
> The first man was a new employee, not a member of any union. The picket handed him a copy of the order. He took the notice, read it carefully, then turned and walked down the hill. McDonald was answered. The victory was won. Not a man, union or non-union, underground or on the surface, Italian, Austrian, Swede, American or Canadian at any of Bernard McDonald properties reported for work except those specially exempted in the notice.

Strikebreakers from Northport were immediately brought in. While the miners tried to obtain an injunction against importation of labour under the Alien Labour Act of Canada, the company retaliated with a $25,000 damage suit for financial losses due to the strike action.

By October, McDonald was bringing in strikebreakers from Winnipeg; the union set up a picket at the CPR depot. The companies obtained a comprehensive court order preventing "a union man from taking a full breath within a radius of twenty miles of a company office." This severe restriction on the union and the continued supply of labour essentially broke the strike, although it was not called off.

By November, although assessments on all locals had been authorized by the Denver office to help the strikers financially, the help was too late. The federation had provided legal assistance and approximately $20,000 from its strike fund, now depleted from the heavy costs of struggles in the Coeur d'Alenes.

Mackenzie King and Labour

On October 31, 1901, the union appealed to the federal government "to act under Conciliation Act, 1900, to investigate and adjust strike here at the mines." Responsibility for labour problems was then assigned to the Postmaster General, and in 1900, he had employed a Canadian student who had completed all but his thesis for a doctorate in economics at Harvard University, to assume publication of the *Labour Gazette* and to handle conciliation problems as Deputy Minister of Labour. William Lyon Mackenzie King had gained a little experience in mediation under the National Conciliation Act of 1900 when he arrived at Rossland on November 9th.

King went to Rossland to mediate the situation but his open friendship with the anti-union mayor and his total acceptance of the mine owners' view of the WFM as a radical union controlled by Denver and not representative of moderate Canadian members did not reassure the union. King told the miners that he could arbitrate for them only if they agreed to accept his conclusions, but since there was nothing in place which would make employers agree to a conclusion in the union's favour, the union could not hope to win. After a week in Rossland, King left for Ottawa convinced that he had done his duty, although in fact his position of flat opposition to labour unions had been evident to the rank and file, who declined King's request to address them in the union hall. His report in the *Labour Gazette* failed to mention the violations of the Alien Labour Act, and accepted the companies' position, that the non-union men now working the mines were satisfied with the hours and wages and "that it is useless to discuss a past condition of affairs which no longer concern us."[3]

---

[3] "The Rossland Situation," *Labour Gazette*, December 1901, p. 364.

By January 18, 1902, the Rossland miners were forced to negotiate a settlement and wound up with a compromise. Terms, by mutual agreement, remained secret. Although the union did not get the muckers' wage increase it had been asking for, the strike resulted in important new legislation being introduced in B.C.

The Rossland Strike and Taff Vale

The damage suits brought against the WFM by the Rossland companies were modelled on the celebrated Taff Vale case of 1900, wherein the British House of Lords had upheld recovery of damages assessed against the Amalgamated Society of Railway Servants to compensate for financial losses during a strike. In Rossland, damages claimed against the union for financial losses during the strike were especially punitive and included a legal wrangle for the union assets, including the union hall. The union's fight against these claims resulted in passage of the Trade Union Protection Act on June 20, 1902, which protected unions in B.C. from being held liable for employers' losses in a strike situation, and a dangerous precedent was quashed before it became entrenched. In effect, the Taff Vale decision no longer would endanger labour unions in British Columbia. The Rossland strike thus helped to prevent the Taff Vale decision from having a substantial future impact on the WFM and other unions in B.C. This was the first legislation of its kind in North America.

William Lyon Mackenzie King (centre) with John D. Rockefeller (right) posing as the working man's friend with Archie Dennison in Colorado in 1915. King's anti-labour stance, evident to early labour leaders in B.C., became glaring after the defeat of the Laurier government in 1911. For a time King went to work as a labour expert for John D. Rockefeller in the wake of the bad publicity generated by the Ludlow Massacre of 1914. The situation in Ludlow, Colorado began when some 9,000 miners with the United Mine Workers went on strike against the Rockefellers' Colorado Fuel and Iron Co. and were forced to move out of the town's company-owned housing and spend the winter with their families in tent colonies. In April 1914, with the strikers still unmoved from their demands, militia men and company police fired on and burned the tents, killing women and children. King attained a quiet notoriety for his solution: his "Rockefeller Plan" was nothing more than company unionism which ignored the right of the miners to choose their own union to represent them. The UMW was expelled from the region in time-honoured fashion by arrests of union leaders on charges of murder and of 191 miners on other charges. King's advice to the Rockefellers did not change company tactics, but it did create a new public image such as this one. Public Archives of Canada C-29350

Rossland Miners Hall on Columbia Avenue built in 1895. Miners' band assembles for a parade about 1900. British Columbia Provincial Archives Photo no. 37078

ROSSLAND UNION HALL

In the time-honoured tradition of the Western Federation of Miners, a membership meeting on March 16, 1898 empowered the Rossland Miners' Union Local 38 executive board to purchase lots and build a hall. On January 25, 1899, the board reported the following:

Lots purchased, $658. Architect E. J. Weston hired; Foundation cost, $938. Superstructure bid accepted, $3,560; Borrowed $3,000 from Mr. O'Brien Redding, cost of loan including three months interest in advance, $146.75; Borrowed $700 from five individuals, now repaid; Three hundred chairs for upper hall, $293.75; Including architect's fee, total cost of building, $6,537.75.

Everybody took the day off to celebrate the opening, with drilling contests, sports in the local ball grounds, and a dance

in the new hall. The parade, led by Local 38 President Robert Adams, was over one-third of a mile in length.

In the early 1920s the mines of Rossland closed down and the miners left town. The hall, abandoned and forlorn, was sold for taxes and purchased by the Knights of Pythias. During the depression in the 1930s, the first public organization meeting for the area CCF was held in the hall. Leo Nimsick, the chairman at that meeting, was later elected member of the B.C. legislature for the Co-operative Commonwealth Federation.

Not until May 7, 1952, did a meeting in the hall mark the return of Mine Mill to the centre first unionized by its predecessor, the Western Federation of Miners, over half a century earlier. Present at that occasion was George Casey, Prince Rupert, B.C., alderman, who had been secretary of Rossland Local 38 in its heyday.

"It was just 52 years ago that I was initiated into the Western Federation of Miners in this same hall," Casey told the meeting. "It was in this hall that the first Eight-Hour Day Act for underground workers was drafted in 1898, and in this hall in 1902 the first Workmen's Compensation Act was drafted."

Casey recalled the many famous labour leaders he had heard speak in the hall: James W. "Jim" Hawthornthwaite, outstanding B.C. Socialist Party leader and M.L.A. in the early years of the century, Eugene Debs, Ed Boyce, Charles Moyer, Big Bill Haywood and Elizabeth Gurley Flynn.

Mine Mill International President John Clark complimented the union for recovering the old miners' union hall and added, "as one who fought to organize this union in the early days and who married and spent my honeymoon in the Kootenays, I feel as though I am reliving past experiences in being once again present at a miners' union meeting in Rossland."

John Clark, born in Sheffield, England, joined the Phoenix local in 1906 as a young miner. Phoenix Local No. 8 was one of the early WFM locals of B.C. metal miners, organized by the light of coal oil lanterns in the bush outside the camp on a night in August 1899.

From his retirement in Tucson, Arizona, on February 1, 1967, one year before his death, Clark sent a cheque to the Phoenix local "to cover paid up membership. I don't think I need initiation or transfer as I am a paid up member in Great Falls Local 16. I think the Local will give me the honour of again being a member in my — shall I say my alma mater — Local 8 of the Western Federation of Miners."

George Casey, secretary of WFM Local 38 in its heyday (left) with WFM colleagues at a meeting in Rossland, May 7, 1952. Solski Collection

Members who joined Rossland Miners Local 38 IUMMSW in 1917, some of whom began with the WFM (undated photo, taken at a later date). Front row sitting: W. McKay, Frank Naccaratto (WFM 1912), Bill Murphy, Joe Mauro (WFM 1912). Standing: John Lepash, John Evans (WFM 1912), W. J. "Scotty" Jamieson (in door) (WFM Centre Star Mine 1906), Frank Fadra, D. F. McIntyre (membership transfer from Kimberley), Jim Nichols (WFM 1913), Jack Lloyd, Nick Michaley. Photo courtesy Leo Nimsick

COAL MINERS AND THE WFM

By 1902, the WFM had organized enough coal miners' locals in eastern B.C. and at Nanaimo, Ladysmith and Cumberland on Vancouver Island to form District No. 7, with 2,000 members. Employers began discharging workers wholesale for going to union meetings. The collieries were managed by a Mr. James Dunsmuir, ex-premier of B.C.,* who flatly refused to recognize the union, arguing that the locals were under the control of foreign leadership. When the coal miners struck in the Crow's Nest Pass and the Vancouver Island mines, the Royal Commission on Industrial Disputes in the Province of British Columbia (1903) under Mackenzie King charged the union with putting Canada's sovereignty in peril.

The WFM had organized the B.C. coal miners because they needed to be organized; they were miners, and the United Mine Workers of America had not yet been ready to send in organizers. Within a year after District No. 7 was set up, it was turned over to the United Mine Workers.

In 1911, the WFM joined the American Federation of Labour, partly because of the desire to develop relations with the UMW. This was especially important in British Columbia, where the WFM and the UMW had for several years claimed jurisdiction over all miners and jurisdictional disputes had become common. Conferences between the Canadian leadership of the two unions agreed to leave the coal fields to the UMW and the metal mining industry to the WFM.

---

*The Dunsmuir family empire, consolidated in the 1880s and 1890s in B.C., included mines, railways and steamers. James Dunsmuir was noted as the most ruthless union-smasher in the west.

GREENWOOD MINERS' STRIKE: 1909-1910

The strike at Greenwood, which lasted from March 1909 to May of 1910, underlined the ineffectiveness of Mackenzie King's new labour legislation in dealing with the problems faced by the country's work force. His Industrial Disputes Investigation (IDI) Act of 1907 was, however, extremely effective in making it difficult for unions to go on strike.

Under the guise of government conciliation, the act restricted labour while giving management an opportunity to continue union-breaking activities. Both parties in a dispute were prohibited from taking direct action, either as lockouts or as picketing, pending a hearing and issuance of a report from a tripartite board representing the union, the company and a "neutral" chairman. This "cooling off" period deprived unions of their main bargaining tool, while the company could continue to discriminate against union members and hire non-union labour. Meanwhile, boards weighted in favour of management often attempted to arrange an agreement with a so-called employees' committee rather than the elected union representative.

As the following series of letters illustrate, the Greenwood strike was initially precipitated by an attempt by the B.C. Copper Company to enforce a wage cut in its mines around Greenwood, the principal mine being the Motherlode at Deadwood Camp, four miles from Greenwood, and in its smelter at Greenwood. But, above all, the union, with 90

British Columbia Copper Co. smelter at Greenwood 1913. Cheap coal from the Fernie mines was used to fire smelters in the Boundary area. Provincial Archives of British Columbia Cat. no. 9994

percent of the workers as members, was fighting for the principle of union recognition, a principle which was not supported by the IDI Act, as the letters testify.

On March 31, 1909, Charles Birce, president, and George Heatherington, secretary, of the Greenwood Miners' Local No. 22 of the WFM declared in an affidavit in the matter of the Industrial Disputes Investigation Act, 1907: "That failing an adjustment between the British Columbia Copper Company, Limited, and the Greenwood Miners Union, or a reference of such dispute to a Board of Conciliation and Investigation under the above Act, a strike will, to the best of our knowledge and belief, be declared, and the necessary authority to declare such a strike has been obtained."

Negotiations had been proceeding for some time with little progress, and tension mounted as the community braced itself for the probability of an industry shut-down. First to move publicly against the union was the Greenwood Board of Trade with a resolution passed on May 7, 1909, declaring:

Whereas it has come to our attention through recent developments that we have in our midst those who seek to create dissension between employer and employee; It is hereby resolved that we the undersigned members of the Greenwood Board of Trade and citizens of Greenwood, which being in hearty sympathy with properly directed organized labour, wish to place ourselves on record as opposed to any further attempt to create such strained relations and we strongly oppose all effort of the labour agitator and trouble maker tending towards industrial unrest and furthermore will do our utmost not to harbour such characters in our community.

Negotiations and exchange of letters between the parties continued without concessions on either side. The conciliation board report favoured the company, but was written in a form that apparently displeased the company on the matter of firings and discrimination.

A letter dated June 24, 1909, from the local management to the New York head office of the company states that if a strike is called "we shall decide whether to attempt to operate. The attempt to reduce wages in the month of March strengthened the hands of the agitating elements to such an extent that they were able to completely upset our labour situation, and I do not think that it is at all possible to operate until we again have control of our labour."

From George Heatherington, secretary, Greenwood Miners Union, Local 22, to J. E. McAllister, manager, British Columbia Copper Co., June 24th:

I note what you say about a spirit of fairness, and that the chairman of the Board states that we did not substantiate our charges of discrimination, but the members are not overlooking the fact that Judge Wilson left Greenwood on the same train as your representative. And when we consider that Mr. Cronyn (company representative on the Conciliation Board) was your guest while in Greenwood, and the opinions expressed in his report must naturally be your opinion, we fail to see any spirit of fairness as far as this organization is concerned.

We are willing to acknowledge that you are the representative of the British Columbia Copper Co., but we also expect that you shall recognize Greenwood Miners' Union as representing your employees, and until such time as you recognize this organization as representing your employees I fail to see any possibility of our arriving at a settlement.

I wish to repeat to you what I have told you before that the Greenwood Miners' Union is not looking for trouble, and I will delay taking any action until 7 p.m., June 25, and I will expect that by that time you will let me know if you are willing to submit a wage schedule for your employees and also if you are willing to meet a committee from the union to adjust our grievances.

From McAllister, manager at Greenwood, to company representative Edward Cronyn, July 10th, complaining about Judge Wilson's attitude:

It was too bad that Judge Wilson gave you the slip at Calgary as a joint report from both of you would probably have been of more service ultimately than the two reports. However, no one can say otherwise than that you did everything that you possibly could and I know that it was due to your strenuous efforts that he was held down as he was. He must have made some exceedingly wild statements during his various drinking bouts with the agitators.

July 14th, a communication from Local 22 to E. G. Warren, local mine manager, following an attempt by the company to discuss the situation personally with the union secretary:

For your information, I will state that anything you may have to say to a member of this union who has not been authorized by the union to deal with you will carry no weight. But if you meet a committee from this union it is not in the nature of a verbal discussion as the committee must present a written report to the union and that report can be acted upon in the same manner as a communication from your company.

Mine galleries at the Glory Hole, Phoenix 1906. Public Archives of Canada PA 122107

July 17th, to McAllister from E. G. Warren:

I enclose a synopsis of what took place at the meeting with the committee of the union yesterday. In case they come back here with any more propositions, I will turn them down flatly.

Regarding the eight hours in the Glory Hole [Phoenix] work, the Granby mine works their men nine hours, so this point is only a myth. My only idea in trying to get this affair fixed up is to get to work and then attend to these fellows afterwards, the same as Granby does.

Since starting this letter I have had a telephone communication from Wm. Embree (secretary-treasurer of Local 22) in which he tells me that everything was agreed to by the union as regards the wage scale, the only points remaining in dispute being the free choice of doctor and the demand of the union for a written agreement. To this, of course, we cannot accede, unless you think it better to do so, although I fail to see any good that would come of making a written agreement with the union. I guess it is your desire as soon as we possibly can to get work started at the Mother Lode, and we are using every effort to get these fellows to call off their strike.

July 20th, McAllister to Norman Erb, New York, president of the British Columbia Copper Co.:

Dear Sir: I telegraphed you yesterday, as per enclosed instructions, and we have been today officially notified by the union that they have declared the strike off.

August 9th, special meeting of Greenwood Local 22:

Regularly moved and seconded that unless the British Columbia Copper Co. gives us a written agreement to re-employ every man who is in the camp who was working for the company at the last shut down we will call the men out again at twelve o'clock tomorrow. Carried unanimously.

December 20th, Norman Erb, New York President of the B.C. Copper Co., to McAllister:

The conditions appear to be that the Miners' Union is particularly strong in our Company, controlling nearly 90 per cent of the employees of the Mother Lode mine and with a large representation scattered in other departments. If they have singled us out in making the demand for the closed shop, I judge it is because they feel they have a better chance of success and are more strongly entrenched with us than they are with other companies in your territory.

I would consider it extremely unfortunate for the Company to be involved in a strike at this time. The price of copper is advancing and the prospects of successful operation appear to be exceptionally good and I have in mind your letter just prior to your last discontinuing operations, dwelling upon the difficulties of securing a satisfactory force after your men had once disbanded.

We are confronted with a condition and I feel certain that this condition points to a strike because a demand such as contained in the notice once made would make it impossible for the miners' union to retract without weakening their position in British Columbia for a long time to come.

The best course seems to me to be to resort to the Industrial Disputes Act because it is clear that the ministry appointing the third arbitrator will be sure to select one who will not involve the government in such a serious embarrassment as to commit it to a recognition of the request of unions to insist upon a closed shop and that we will seek to

December 23rd, from Erb ordering McAllister to seek a Board of Conciliation:

Of course it is quite possible that the Federation may disregard the findings of the Board and order a strike notwithstanding, but that is a contingency that I would rather face with the findings of the Board against them, than to have a strike precipitated now, without having made an effort to avoid it. At all events they cannot strike during the arbitration without subjecting themselves to the penalties of the Disputes Act, and you may well be able meanwhile to increase the number of your non-union men in the mine. I assume you will have to reduce your mining force through weather conditions in any event.

January 7th, 1910, from A. Flumerfelt, Victoria, B.C., to McAllister:

I have seen Mr. Mara who has consented to represent you on conciliation. He was one of the originators of Columbia Shipping Lines who subsequently sold to the C.P.R. A member of the Dominion House for a number of years, and thoroughly conversant with procedure, [he] is a man entirely in sympathy with the capital side of labour disputes.

January 12th, McAllister to Erb:

. . . up till the time we attempted to pay a lower wage than any other property in America where the WFM is represented we had our labour situation well in hand, but the average union man will fight a wage reduction to the last where he will think more than once before striking for a closed shop.

By our action last spring, we effectually strengthened the hands of the agitating element, and this condition will probably continue and their demands become more unreasonable until there is a change in the personnel of those who direct the union's affairs.

I note in your letter your suggestion that this company is involved more than other mining operations in labour disputes, but I would remind you, and the stockholders should also remember, that this company has a record second to none for operating efficiency and its work has been performed more cheaply than that of any other similar concern.

. . . the union has appointed John McInnes to the Conciliation Board, who was defeated on the Socialist ticket for the B.C. legislature at the recent elections.*

---

*John McInnes had run in Grand Forks for the Socialist Party of Canada, which in 1909 was at its peak with 22 percent of the provincial vote.

The Greenwood strike was called April 19th, 1910 after a referendum vote: the tie-up was complete. The strike was called off May 12th.

Trail-Rossland Activity: 1916-1917

The British Columbia Smelting & Refining Co. smelter at Trail Creek 1898. Trail City Archives, Trail, B.C. Cat. no. 154A

Stanley H. Scott, professor at Notre Dame University, Nelson, B.C., has described the conditions under which smelter workers were employed by Consolidated Mining and Smelting, a CPR subsidiary, in the Trail-Rossland area during and after the Rossland strike of 1901:

> Many men were hired after slipping a foreman $20. To hire one, of course, meant another man was fired. No one was ever sure of continued employment. Few jobs were far removed from the blistering heat of 160 degrees of the lead furnaces. Huge 12-ton pots had to be tapped by hand — numerous workers literally caught fire while performing these tasks.*
>
> If someone got hurt his friends took care of him because the company didn't have anything to do with that. Lead poisoning began to affect workmen as early as 1900. No first aid existed on the Hill. If someone broke an arm or a leg, both common injuries, then a big, strong friend would load him on his back and take him to the hospital. Naturally the healthy friend lost wages, if not his job, for the trip to the hospital was on company time.[4]

---

*Tapping: A clay plug made into a cone was put onto the end of a long rod and was pushed into the hole by a tapper and a helper to stop the flow of molten ore.

[4]Stanley H. Scott, "Profusion of Issues," unpublished paper delivered at the Pacific Northwest Labour History Conference, Seattle, Wa., May 1976.

Toxin in the zinc plant sickened the entire district. No dogs or cats were to be seen in burnt-over Trail; all had been killed by the smoke.

> Down-wind from the smoke stacks the ethnic communities at the foot of the hill suffered dreadfully, while management, safely guarded by town and mill security, retired each evening to Tadnac, a village constructed by immigrant labour but by 1916 forbidden to them.

The smelter companies had been quick to take advantage of the large scale immigration undertaken in Canada from 1896 to 1914, and had hired largely from this pool of new immigrant labourers. The influx of people from Europe, the U.S., Latin America and Asia created a large surplus labour pool and drastically affected union attempts to organize. Not only were the newly-arrived immigrants reluctant to involve themselves in union activity for fear of reprisals or deportation for anything that could be interpreted as political activity, but others were faced with the prospect of being fired or black-listed for joining a union at a time when many were anxious for jobs.

Smeltermen worked 365 days of the year. Actual hours varied, even though British Columbia had adopted the eight-hour day in 1899 for the metal mining industry. "Each day

Italian smelter workers pouring moulten zinc into moulds with hand ladle, Trail 1918. The man in the foreground with a skimmer in each hand is Joe DiGiorolomo. Public Archives of Canada C-80552

when we came to work we didn't know whether we would work eight, ten, eleven or twelve hours,'' recalled an aged pensioner. Overtime was unknown since pay was for the day, not by the hour. Rates only rose from $2.50 in 1907 to $2.75 per day in 1911, regardless of the hours worked.

Edmund S. Kirby, manager of the War Eagle Mine in Rossland, in his letter to T. C. Blackstock, provides an example of the tactic of fostering divisions along ethnic lines to promote labour disunity:

> In all the lower grades of labour, especially in smelter labour, it is necessary to have a mixture of races which includes a number of illiterates who are first class workmen. They are the strength of an employer and the weakness of the union. How to head off a strike of muckers or labourers for higher wages without the aid of Italian labour I do not know.[5]

[5]Letter of Edmund S. Kirby to T. C. Blackstock, Jan. 31, 1901, *Laurier Papers* (Public Archives of Canada).

Several decades later, when Steel turned its guns on Trail Local 480, Remo Morandini, whose father had been in the 1917 Trail strike, rallied to the support of the union his father had fought for in his day. A native of Trail, Remo had worked in the smelter in 1938 when Mine Mill was again organizing, and joined the union before serving in the armed forces.

In 1952, Remo was elected financial secretary of the local, which post he held for eighteen years. "I wouldn't trade off those years . . . they were the better part of my life," he said in an interview.

In 1955 during the McCarthy era, Morandini had been stopped at the U.S. border and barred from all future entry into that country. He recalls that, after the merger with Steel, he had been elected a delegate to a convention in Chicago: "I said to the Steel representative, 'you fixed it to stop me in 1955, now fix it to get me through.' I was cleared by the U.S. immigration in time to attend the convention."

In the early 1970s, Morandini resigned from his job with Cominco and his place as an officer in the union to join the B.C. Workmen's Compensation Board to work on rehabilita-

Smelter workers tapping floor of lead blast furnaces, Consolidated Mining & Smelting Co., Trail circa 1913. Trail City Archives, Trail, B.C. Cat. no. 148

tion problems of injured workmen, where he spent some ten years, "still working on behalf of the working man."

The fateful Rossland miners' strike of 1901 and the ensuing dismissals and blacklisting were legendary at the big smelter in Trail. Since more than 600 of the 1,000 smelter workers in Trail were Italian, unionization of the plant was slow to develop, but by 1915 the idea of a union in the smelter was becoming more and more attractive. When Albert "Ginger" Goodwin, a WFM organizer, arrived early in 1915, he began making substantial progress. Goodwin had formerly been vice-president of the B.C. Federation of Labour, and had run for the Trail Socialist Party nomination during the 1916 provincial elections.

The Maple Leaf Union, a company-dominated group, provided some opposition at first, but soon it, too, was recruiting for the WFM, much to the dismay of management. By winter 1916, the majority of the workers voted to become Local 105 of the International Union of Mine, Mill and Smelter Workers. Helping celebrate the victory, Charles Moyer, president of the international union, addressed the

newly expanded District 6 annual convention in March 1916.

Negotiations started in May with demands for an increase of 50 cents daily. With the intervention of the Department of Labour, a compromise agreement was reached: wages would be a minimum of three dollars per day for all employees but a sliding scale* was enforced based on the price of metals.

Consolidated Mining and Smelting called for "a firm government policy under which production would be assured through the operators being ordered to operate the mines with such men as are willing to work, with adequate military protection being provided. Union advance must be checked or the country will go to the dogs." C.M.&S. refused to consider the check-off system; apparently, it was more important to restrict the financial well-being of the union than to fight the wage increases.

---

*The concept of the sliding scale was first adopted by Comstock mine owners in the U.S., based on the notion that miners should share in the ups and downs of the market. Their wages were pegged to the world price of metals, but no provision was made for the effect of inflation.

The next year Mine Mill was adamant in its demand to get the eight-hour day enforced: on November 15, 1917, 1,200 men struck the company. Immediately the local police were reinforced by additional constables who began night and day patrols at the smelter. Premier H. C. Brewster vehemently attacked the strikers, whom he termed "the employees of the smelter who are mostly foreigners."

On December 21, 1917, the strike was called to an end, with no victory for the men. C.M.&S. did not recall more than 500 workers and shortly afterwards the IUMMSW local disintegrated. During this time, the international union was undergoing a general decline in membership that would ultimately lead to its virtual collapse. The Hill was without a viable union until 1938 when reorganization started in earnest.

During the war years, jobs were more plentiful as war industries flourished. However, few gains were passed on to the miners as the cost of living soared. In the west, labour complained of scandalous war profits by businesses and opposed conscription. During the Trail strike in 1917, Ginger Goodwin, who had been classified as physically unfit for military duty, was suddenly declared fit and conscripted. When Goodwin was shot to death by a special federal policeman for resisting conscription, the western labour movement was outraged. In Vancouver, a one-day general strike on August 2, 1918 protested Goodwin's murder. Mine Mill had lost a valuable organizer.

The following year, the Borden government responded to the Winnipeg General Strike by passing the notorious Section 98 of the Criminal Code, under which any organizations deemed to be revolutionary in intent were declared unlawful associations. A person attending a meeting of or distributing literature for such an organization was liable to serve twenty years in jail. Moreover, Section 133 of the code, which declared that it was not sedition to point out the mistakes of the government in good faith, was repealed.

The One Big Union

The decade from 1920 to 1930 was one of slow erosion of the trade union movement throughout Canada, and British Columbia was no exception. Much of the trade union support went to the One Big Union (OBU), which was motivated more by political beliefs than by trade union concerns.

The OBU was launched at a western labour conference in Calgary, Alberta, in March 1919. Several Mine Mill locals in British Columbia held a meeting at Nelson and went over to the OBU in a body to form District 1, Metalliferous Miners of the OBU. By 1920, the OBU had 20,000 members in B.C.

The OBU had its main strength in western Canada, just as the IWW was strongest in the western U.S., and was strikingly similar to the IWW in other ways. It championed the cause of industrial, as opposed to craft, unionism, and the organization of the unorganized. It relied on "direct action" and refused to lobby for progressive labour legislation. Its effect was to pull the militants out of the old unions — dual unionism. But, while the IWW organized on a loose industrial basis, the OBU set up its units on a geographical, or area, basis as well as on industrial lines. The idea was that this kind of structure would make it possible to call a complete general strike on any city or area, and thereby win demands more quickly.

The OBU petered out by 1922, partly because of government persecution of its leaders, partly because of a vigorous attack by the international and national unions of Canada whose existence was threatened.

Miners' union meeting, Hedley, B.C. circa 1920. Photo copyright Pat Wright Collection, Interior Photo Bank, Kelowna Centennial Museum, Penticton Museum no. 4310

GINGER GOODWIN.
Provincial Archives of British Columbia Photo no. 67650

As well, factionalism had disrupted the OBU and resulted in a severe disorganization of the trade unions in the province. The unions were so demoralized and weak that in 1920 the B.C. Federation of Labour disbanded. The companies got stronger and bolder: the B.C. legislature passed the Industrial Conciliation and Arbitration Act which restricted bargaining powers to employee committees, not real unions. This encouraged the spread of company unions like the one at C.M.&S.

The Company Union

Les Walker, secretary of Mine Mill B.C. District Union, in a recorded interview in 1964, recalled conditions prevailing during the twenties.

"Following the breakup of the OBU and the IUMMSW, Blaylock [S. G. Blaylock, president and general manager of C.M.&S] picked up Mackenzie King's idea that he had brought back with him from Chicago and organized this Workmen's Committee.* Blaylock's idea was that each of the smeltermen would come to own part of the company; therefore he wouldn't have any labour problems because the men would all be shareholders. And every year he would issue one share of stock to each employee. But he discovered that the men were selling the stock faster than he could issue it to them, so he finally gave up that dream.

"But he organized the Workmen's Committee and that was a committee composed of one man elected from each department on the Hill . . . men appointed to the committee promptly quit work; that is, they came to work each day and punched in the clock but they never put their working clothes on . . . they managed to get themselves on various subcommittees, such as fuel, gardening, fertilizer and all that sort of thing. At that time you could order your winter's coal through the Company. In fact, on the back of the cheque there were 99 different items that could be deducted from your pay cheque; consequently, when the man got his pay cheque there wasn't very much left.

". . . these conditions existed pretty well until 1944 when the Mine Mill Union became certified in Trail. In other words, you could get garden lots up at Warfield to grow your vegetables on, you could get free fertilizer, you could order your coal through the Company, you could pay your Legion dues through the Company, you could pay your insurance through the Company, you could have anything you wanted deducted off your pay cheque; in other words, you could get anything but money or wages. When the company found out that with a union to deal with the men were going to receive wages instead of bologna, then all of the fuel and fringe benefits and garden lots and the privilege of growing your own vegetables all of a sudden disappeared."

*Mackenzie King published *Industry and Humanity* in 1918 and thus became the theoretician of company unionism and the so-called "profit-sharing" system.

ART EVANS

Art Evans and Mine Mill: 1938

The first serious Mine Mill membership drive in the 1930s was in Trail, and by 1938 some success had been achieved in the struggle to get certified. With the company no longer supporting the Workmen's Committee, the Independent Smelterworkers' Union was set up. The members of that organization wore the Maple Leaf as their emblem and were known in the smelter as the "maple leaves."

"Opposed to them," Walker recalled, "of course was Mine Mill. The company gave every facility to the company union. In fact when they were stumping the plants looking for members, the foreman would order you to leave the job and go and listen to them, but the same courtesy wasn't extended to Mine Mill organizers. They were run out of town.

"Arthur Evans [international union staff]* was escorted out of town by Chief Campbell. He came back again. He had

*Arthur "Slim" Evans, appointed as an organizer for Mine Mill in 1938, was a well-known figure at this time. Born into poverty in 1890 in Toronto, he had left school at thirteen to help support his family, and had worked in many western mining towns in his youth, as a carpenter. He had been shot at Ludlow, Colorado, in the massacre of 1914, and joined the IWW before returning to Canada to work for the OBU. He had organized for the Workers' Unity League in the dirty thirties and had led the spectacular On-to-Ottawa Trek which set out from Vancouver June 3, 1935, to call attention to the numbers of young unemployed men forced to work in government relief camps in isolated areas for next to no pay, just to have a place to live. The Relief Camp Workers' Union wanted to bring their message, "Work and Wages," to R. B. Bennett in Ottawa, but the RCMP stopped the trekkers in what is dubbed the Regina Riot, July 1, 1935. Trek leaders were arrested, but only months later, the Bennett government was defeated. In 1936, Mackenzie King kept his election promises to close the camps and repeal Section 98 of the Criminal Code.

Evans speaking from car during Trail organizing campaign in 1938 (left). Company goons burned Evans' car October 5, 1938 (right).
Evans photos courtesy Trade Union Research Bureau, Vancouver

a black panelled delivery truck and used it for general office business, and had his records and equipment in there. The truck was taken one night from in front of the B.C. Cafe on Bay Avenue, was hauled up the smelter hill right past the two gates where there were guards on the gates so that there was no doubt but that it was seen, but it was hauled out to Stoney Creek and pushed into a ravine and burned — and yet nobody very conveniently saw anything at all.

"However, after Arthur Evans, John Peak came in as international representative around '42, and then Harvey Murphy in 1943, and after Harvey was made Regional Director for the union with an office in Vancouver, Don Guys came to Trail, and Don was the international representative when we were finally certified in 1944. Kimberley had been certified the year before.

"The first agreement was signed in 1945, but it was not signed by S. G. Blaylock. He negotiated the agreement; that is, he sat in on the meetings, and he would listen and discuss this, that and the other thing, but when they reached an item he didn't like or had no intention of talking about, he'd just swing his swivel chair around, turn his back on the meeting, look out the window and say 'when you boys are through talking about that we'll discuss something else.' That was the bargaining. But he never did sign an agreement; the agreement was signed by R. W. Diamond, who at that time was General Manager, whereas Blaylock was the Managing Director."

Organization in the 1940s

In the early 1940s, organization throughout British Columbia mushroomed in the wake of progressive labour legislation that for the first time guaranteed the right to collective bargaining. This legislation resulted from the political pressure on the King government following the Kirkland Lake gold miners' strike of 1941-42, a strike led by Mine Mill in northern Ontario.

The first issue of Mine Mill's *B.C. District News*, edited by B.C. District regional director, Harvey Murphy, appeared

June 10, 1944. The headline read: "Trail is Certified! 27-Year Struggle Results in Victory." On June 2nd, the Minister of Labour had certified Trail and District Mine Workers' Union Local 480 as the bargaining agent for the Consolidated Mining and Smelting Company (Kimberley Local 651 had been certified the previous year.)

In the June 28th, 1944 issue of Mine Mill's *B.C. District News*, George Anderson, veteran Mine Mill organizer, noted: "For the first time we have completely organized B.C. in the hard rock mining field. Copper Mountain Miners Union Local 649 was the first to sign an agreement."

Local 649 was the first local to have maintenance of membership in an agreement which stated: "All future regular employees, together with all present employees who are now or may later become members of the union shall remain members in good standing during the life of this agreement as one of the conditions of employment with the company."

In the July 10, 1944 issue of the *News*, the directory lists the following locals: Kimberley Local 651, Hedley Local 655, Gypsum Workers' Union 578, Copper Mountain Local 649, Britannia Local 663, Silverton Local 662, Wells Local 685, Pinchi Local 661, Retallack Local 698, Premier Local 694, Pioneer Local 693, Hedley Nickel Plate Local 656. Later listings include more locals, as well as several ladies auxiliary groups which were organized wherever mine properties included family residences.

The first signed agreement ever consummated between the C.M.&S. company and a legitimate union was concluded on January 16th, 1945. The bargaining committee for Trail Local 480 included president F. W. Henne, vice-president Rene Morin, Alex Grey, Leo Nimsick, H. H. Odell and international representative Harvey Murphy. By the end of 1944, there were 39 Mine Mill locals in Canada from Quebec to British Columbia, representing more than 15,000 members.

Opposite page: *Local 649 union office in Copper Mountain after a bargaining session. (L-R): Lorne Salmon, Andy Stewart, Arnie Bennett, ———, ———, Bill White, ———, Harvey Murphy, Dave Koch, Max Patrick, George "Scotty" Anderson.* UBC Collection

Signing the first agreement with Consolidated Mining & Smelting Co., Trail, January 16, 1945. Standing (L-R): M. Mason, company attorney; W. Gillaume, Peter McIntyre, E. W. Campbell, industrial relations officers; Fred Henne, Local 480 president; Rene Morin, Local 480 vice-president; Leo Nimsick, and H. H. Odell, Local 480 bargaining committee. Seated (L-R): W. S. Kirkpatrick, assistant general manager; R. W. Diamond, general manager; Harvey Murphy, International union representative.
UBC Collection

The 1946 Strikes

Following World War One, the mining companies in Canada had been successful in smashing all the Canadian locals of Mine Mill. One reason for the defeat was lack of unity and a common program; such factionalism was no match for well-organized companies bent on destruction of the union. Following World War Two, a lesson had been learned. The new generation of Mine Mill leaders realized that the union would have to fully unite behind a program to achieve much needed gains for workers in the mining and smelting industries of Canada.

Consequently, a forward looking bargaining program was hammered out at a District 8 (eastern Canada) convention held in Kirkland Lake on November 17 and 18, 1945. The eight-point program was unanimously endorsed by the District 7 (western Canada) convention held in Vancouver on December 7, 1945. That program became the basis for collective bargaining by all Canadian Mine Mill locals in 1946.

The eight objectives were: the 40-hour week; $1.10 an hour minimum rate for miners; time-and-a-half pay after 40 hours, six paid holidays with double-time if worked; shift differential pay of 5, 7½ and 10 cents an hour depending on the shift; one week vacation pay for two years or less of service, two weeks for two years or more; sick leave pay of up to two weeks per year; severance pay equal to one month's wage for each year worked; and guaranteed annual work or wage equivalent.

This program may seem modest by today's standards, but in 1946 it was plowing new ground for industrial union bargaining. Many critics contended it was a "pie-in-the-sky" approach. However, it was a realizable, unifying program for action, it appealed to the hearts and minds of mining industry workers, and union membership support was solid.

Meetings with the Consolidated Mining and Smelting Company began early in February 1946. By May, a joint bargaining committee of Trail Local 480 and Kimberley Local 651 was ready to report to the union membership and to present a tentative collective agreement. The Local 480 bargaining committee members were F. W. Henne, R. Morin, R. Fletcher, Dan Dosen and Disc Gopp. The Local 651 committee members were J. R. McFarlane, J. A. Byrne, J. Rollheiser, Dave McGhee and George Thompson. Chief negotiation spokesman was regional director Harvey Murphy, assisted by international representative Claire Billingsley.

On May 7th, a packed meeting of Trail smelter workers unanimously recommended adoption of the new contract, and Kimberley miners enthusiastically approved it at their meeting two days later. There were a number of outstanding gains. For the first time, a set wage-scale was put in place of the variable bonus, providing rates from 77 cents per hour for surface labour to $1.10 for trades. Shift differentials of three cents and five cents were established. The work week was reduced from 48 to 44 hours, to be further reduced to 42, then 40 hours in future contracts. Paid vacations of one week for employees

with up to five years service and two weeks after five years were established. The pension plan was to be completely revised and improved. A wage increase of 15½ cents per hour plus five cents per hour for adjustments in classification resulted, and a guaranteed miner's rate of eight dollars per shift was won. These gains put the Trail and Kimberley workers in the lead of all industrial workers in Canada. It was a historic, precedent-setting pattern.

The C.M.&S. contracts with the Trail and Kimberley locals covered more than half of the mining and smelting union membership in B.C. The other half was in twelve locals scattered throughout the province. Each of these locals approached its respective company management and presented the union's eight-point program as a basis for bargaining.

On May 26, 1946, the Policy Committee of the Mine Mill B.C. District Union issued a statement to the union membership which declared:

> In view of the fact that the mine operators in B.C. have to date been unwilling to meet in good faith with the bargaining committees of the local unions, and in view of their refusal to establish with us a proper wage which would provide the basic security necessary for a decent standard of living, and because of the failure to arrive at a proper agreement through the means of collective bargaining and negotiations in all properties outside of the operations of the Consolidated Mining and Smelting Company, the District Policy Committee, representing all local unions in the metal mining industry in B.C., recommends that every local union finalize negotiations at once, and failing agreement on the 8-point program within 10 days, shall proceed to take a strike vote . . . the International office in Vancouver to press simultaneously for recognition, negotiations and settlement through the mining operators association on a provincial-wide basis . . . in order to establish uniform wages, hours and conditions within the industry.

The June 24, 1946 issue of the *B.C. District News* reported that the negotiating committee had met twice with the mine operators' association and that "the employers confirmed their previous position in refusing to grant any increases above 6½ cents an hour." The District Policy Committee issued a call on June 22nd for a strike in all Mine Mill locals in B.C., except for Trail and Kimberley where collective agreements had been signed.

On July 3, 1946, 2,500 workers in twelve local unions of Mine Mill struck twelve mining operators in B.C. These were at Britannia, Cariboo Gold Quartz, Granby Consolidated, Hedley Mascot, Island Mountain, Kenville Gold, Base Metals (two operations), Hedley Nickel Plate, Pioneer Gold, Sheep Creek and Silbak Premier. The strike was solid.

On the same day, acting on the request of the B.C. Minister of Labour, the federal Minister of Labour appointed the Hon. Mr. Justice G. M. Sloan, Chief Justice of British Columbia, to act as Industrial Disputes Commissioner. Luckily for the union, Justice Sloan was not only a wise jurist, but had a keen sense of fair play. After ten days of talks, it became clear to the commissioner that the "mining companies had no intention of entering into a master contract with the union on an industry-wide basis." In reporting to the federal department of labour, he offered to resign but was persuaded to continue to mediate the dispute.

For nearly four months, Commissioner Sloan met with the union and the companies. The union refused to budge from its position based on the Trail and Kimberley settlements, while the companies were bitter and divided on settlement terms. Britannia and Copper Mountain reluctantly agreed to Sloan's recommended settlement for the copper producers, and on October 16th, members of the two locals voted overwhelmingly to accept. On November 4th, Local 655 at the Hedley Mascot gold mine accepted a negotiated agreement which provided a pattern of settlement for all other gold mines in B.C.

Because of different market conditions for the metals being mined, there were some slight differences in the various terms of settlement, but the basic terms were the same as those set at the C.M.&S. operations. The miners of B.C. emerged from their determined struggle as the highest paid in North America. For the first time in the history of B.C. mining, the workers had won through on a district-wide scale. With their new collective agreements, they set the pace for all other Canadian industrial unions.

The Steel Raids: 1950

On February 9, 1950, the United Steelworkers of America launched its raids on Mine Mill in western Canada, augmenting its takeover attempts in Port Colborne and Sudbury in Ontario.* On that day, the *B.C. District News* reported:

> . . . a raiding party of Steel "organizers" moved in on Local 480, Trail and District Smelterworkers Union, Mine Mill, along with their camp followers of the CCL and CIO, and commenced the signing of the workers up in Steel, immediately prior to the opening of the Wage, Contract and Policy Conference in that city to which delegates from all Canada and officials of the International had been called to discuss negotiations with the industry.
>
> The raid was aided and abetted by traitors in the Local 480 executive, and among the shop stewards, who had for two months previously been holding meetings with William Mahoney, a Steel functionary, and with Herbert Gargrave, former CCF MLA for MacKenzie riding, who was put on the CCL payroll as an organizer following his dismissal as a legislator by the workers of Powell River and other plants last year.
>
> First intimation to the International was given by Claire Billingsley, president of the Local who turned over the keys to International Representative John Gordon on the morning of the ninth, announcing that he had resigned and the executive with him.
>
> The first the workers knew of the desertion was when a full page advertisement in the Trail Times that evening announced the treachery and invited the members into Steel. Layout of the ad, except for the names of the stewards who signed it, had been supplied to the paper some days before . . .

---

*The background on the impetus for the Steel raids is provided in the chapters on the U.S. and Sudbury.

J. A. MacDONALD
FIN. SEC.

A. KING
PRES.

E. L. WALKER
VICE. PRES.

C. B. McMARTIN
REC. SEC.

D. DOSEN
CONDUCTOR

J. E. GORDON
ADMINISTRATOR INTER. REP.

G. CARTER
WARDEN

M. WALSH
TRUSTEE

H. N. SMITH
TRUSTEE

F. A. PEARSON
TRUSTEE

F. E. DeVITO
INTER. REP.

"BLITZ" EXECUTIVE
TRAIL & DISTRICT SMELTERWORKERS UNION
LOCAL 480 — I.U.M.M. & S.W.
— 1950-51 —

Photo courtesy
Nels Thibault

The International union appointed John Gordon as administrator of Local 480, and on February 10th members elected a "Blitz Executive" on a temporary basis. They elected Al King president, E. L. Walker vice-president, Cliff B. McMartin recording secretary, J. A. MacDonald financial secretary, and Dan Dosen, M. Walsh, G. Carter, F. Pearson and H. N. Smith to the executive board after the sudden desertion of the Local 480 executive to Steel.

That same year, the union acquired the services of a young veteran of considerable standing in the Trail community as an international union representative to assist in the campaign against the Steelworkers. His name was Francis E. (Buddy) DeVito. An officer in the Canadian Legion, later to become the Mayor of Trail, DeVito was attracted to the cause of the Mine Mill union through his friend Al King. He remained on the union staff until the raiders were decisively defeated,

and then returned to his own business. In reviewing some of the events of the raid, DeVito recalled how the union had difficulty in finding a place to meet and even getting office space:

"Nobody would rent us a hall to operate from; that's how tight a control the company and the reactionaries had over that town. This one day, King, Murphy and I were meeting in my house and talking concerning what we are going to do about providing a hall. I said, 'There is this huge empty house now owned by Andrew Walldie, one of the original blacklisted workers of the 1917 Trail strike, a Scots or English chap, honest, straight as a die, and one of the old breed who had a real estate and insurance business, a very trusted man in the community. Let's go and see; maybe he will sell us the house.' 'But we have no money,' it was said. 'Never mind, let's see what we can do.' I remember it was about three o'clock in the morning and here were these rugged characters peering through the windows of this huge old house. Had the police seen us, we would all have been arrested.

"The next day I went to see Walldie with a few guys and he said, 'Sure, I will sell you the house; why not, it's my business what I do with my property.' I remember it was $7,200. So a number of us went to the bank to ask for a loan ending up with about fifty of us signing a note; and that's how we bought the property. We had rooms for meetings and offices, and a large open square outside to handle large meetings. We beat Steel in Trail and I left the union."

In 1961, Buddy DeVito left his assistant town clerk job at Grand Forks, B.C., and once again joined the Mine Mill staff, this time in Sudbury where he handled publicity during the Steel raid.

The raids on Mine Mill quickly spread to other locals throughout the district with Steel staffers attempting to disrupt established locals and hound Mine Mill organizers wherever they worked. At the same time, however, support for Mine Mill's struggle to ward off the raiders came from many Mine Mill locals. The *News* reported that "Britannia Local had donated $1,000 to help fight the raiders in Trail . . . this follows Taku's lead of a $1,000 donation. Good friends also are the Nanaimo coal miners who have voted an assessment on each member to fight the raiders, and the West Coast Seamen's Union, ready with a generous donation." From Tulsequah Local 858 came word that $1,000 had been voted unanimously by a membership meeting to aid in the fight against the raiders.

On April 14th, members of the American Federation of Labour and the Canadian Congress of Labour unions, attending a labour unity conference in the Vancouver Pender auditorium, condemned Steelworkers' officials and voted by unanimous resolution their full support for Mine Mill. A message from Jack Stevenson, president of the Vancouver and District Trades and Labour Council, referred to the Steel raiders as "pseudo-unionists who, through despicable raiding methods seek to destroy an established and militant union." Fred Horton, secretary of Steel Local 3302, replied: "It is not the members of the United Steel Workers of America who are raiding in Trail. . . . It is their top leaders." Other supporters included John Cameron, president of the Cumberland local of United Mine Workers; Fred Jackson, president of the District Council, International Longshoremen and Warehousemen's Union, CCL-CIO; and Jack Ross, international representative of the International Brotherhood of Electrical Workers, AFL. Tom Uphill, Labour member of the B.C. Legislature, commented: "I heartily commend your committee in taking action to prevent raiding and splitting in the unions as threatened in Trail at the present time. I cannot express myself as much as I would like as I consider if this continues it will sap the strength of the whole labour movement."

Following its usual course, the Steelworkers applied for certification of Steel as bargaining agent for the Trail workers. Mine Mill finally defeated the Steel raiders in a certification vote in May 1952, but the battle and further raiding continued right up until the merger in 1967.

When Murray Cotterill, Steel's Canadian public relations director, announced following the vote that all Steel supporters were to join Mine Mill, C. H. Millard, Steel's Canadian

director, repudiated Cotterill and ordered an immediate resumption of the raids.

W. L. White, president of the Marine and Boilermakers Union, told delegates to the annual convention of the B.C. District Union of an attempt at subornation on the part of Charles Millard. On the advice of Pat Conroy, secretary of the CCL, White had approached Millard, among others, for funds to help bring the celebrated Kuzych case to the Privy Council.* Millard had told him that, if the Boilermakers would reverse their stand on raiding at Trail and go along with him, Steel could quickly find the funds needed.

Mine Mill Organizers Persist

While the raids were being fought, organization at new properties and servicing of established locals had to go on, although in more difficult circumstances. Often, Steel staffers followed Mine Mill organizers to disrupt their work and if possible take over their territory.

During the 1940s, as new mining properties were opened, Mine Mill organizers were kept busy bringing the union to the isolated, small properties where from a few score to rarely more than 300 men were employed. The miners' living conditions were primitive and the operators had little concern for safety. The operations were short-lived, so the major concern of the operators was to bring out the ore as speedily and cheaply as possible.

The Mine Mill organizer was welcomed in the camps and, in many instances, organization was completed in a single visit. These remote and isolated locals were serviced and assisted on a regular basis.

Local 289 veteran Tom McEwen reported from the Yukon, in the November 27, 1944, issue of the *News:* "Within the period of the last three months, two events have occurred in the Yukon Territory which have given a tremendous morale push to labour in the North. One was the signing of the first collective agreement in the Yukon between the Dawson Miners' Local of the I.U.M.M.&S.W. and the Yukon Consolidated Gold Corporation; the other was the presentation of a brief to the Western Labour Board by the Whitehorse and District Workers Union Local 815, also an affiliate of the I.U.M.M.&S.W."

---

*Myron Kuzych, a Vancouver welder and member of the Boilermakers and Iron Shipbuilders Union of Canada as it was then called, had been expelled in 1945 for persistent anti-union activities, including appearing as a witness for the employer and denouncing the union. Financed through undisclosed sources, Kuzych had conducted a costly media campaign against the union from a suddenly acquired office. In the first court action, he won his case and Boilermakers president William L. White and secretary William Stewart served short jail sentences for refusing to reinstate Kuzych. The seven-year legal battle finally upheld the right of the union to expel anyone found guilty of anti-union activities, but only after the Privy Council of England overturned the B.C. Appeal Court in 1951. A cause celebre in Canadian labour history, the court battles were funded with thousands of union dollars (Mine Mill Local 598 in one year contributed $500). The Kuzych case established an important precedent in safeguarding unions against enemies within their ranks.

Local 802 union office in the Yukon.
Photo courtesy Nels Thibault

Mine Mill proved itself a different kind of union, most visibly in the work of its organizers who, unlike their counterparts in other large and established unions, did not go from one local to the other by streetcar or a short urban walk. Mine Mill organizers arrived at their destinations by bush plane, crossed turbulent waters by canoe or inflatable boats and walked miles through underbrush in sweltering heat or on snowshoes in 50-below-zero weather. Monthly reports from men in the field reveal the persistence with which these organizers brought the union into small, isolated camps and towns.

BARNEY McGUIRE

In 1949, Barney McGuire reported from locations as far apart as Yellowknife, the Northwest Territories and the Yukon in the west, and Timmins, Toronto, Marmora and Kirkland Lake in Ontario. In February and March he reported from Ontario, on April 15th he was in Vancouver, and on April 30th he was in Wells, Bralorne and Hazleton in B.C.

On January 15, 1952, McGuire was in Prince Rupert, B.C., in contact with the workers in the Alcan tunnel project who were in the midst of a work stoppage. He spoke at a public meeting supporting the demands of the tunnel workers (in another union). For his pains, the RCMP shipped him out on the 19th, aboard the S.S. Costala.

His June 15th report recorded a trip "into the Emerald Glacier Mine, situated about 110 miles out of Burns Lake."

On May 1, 1953, McGuire arrived in Port Radium to start organizing. He reported that he came out on the last plane before break-up and advised that someone be sent in as soon as possible after break-up, around the last week in June. By car he went from Edmonton to Keno City, stopping over at Whitehorse to contact truck drivers of the United Keno Mines. From Keno City, Yukon, he reported on June 30th: "Have purchased a log cabin which needs some fixing up to be a suitable living quarters. This will serve as a suitable living quarters and office out of which to operate."

His July 15th report read: "Organization progressing favourably. Money is being collected to send to the striking Torbit Local." Then, on a demanding note: "The supplies I have ordered have not been received. They are needed badly. Such needless laxity results in anything but good to the union and the time is long past due when steps should be taken to rectify this matter. To my knowledge this laxity has existed ever since I have returned to the West from Eastern Canada, and much more than sufficient time has elapsed to have this rectified. Also, along this line, on June 12th last I ordered a 300 bundle of 'the Union' and to date no bundle has arrived."

Three Mine Mill organizers who were kept busy bringing the union to isolated camps (L-R): Don Guys, George "Scotty" Anderson, Barney McGuire. Photo courtesy Barney McGuire

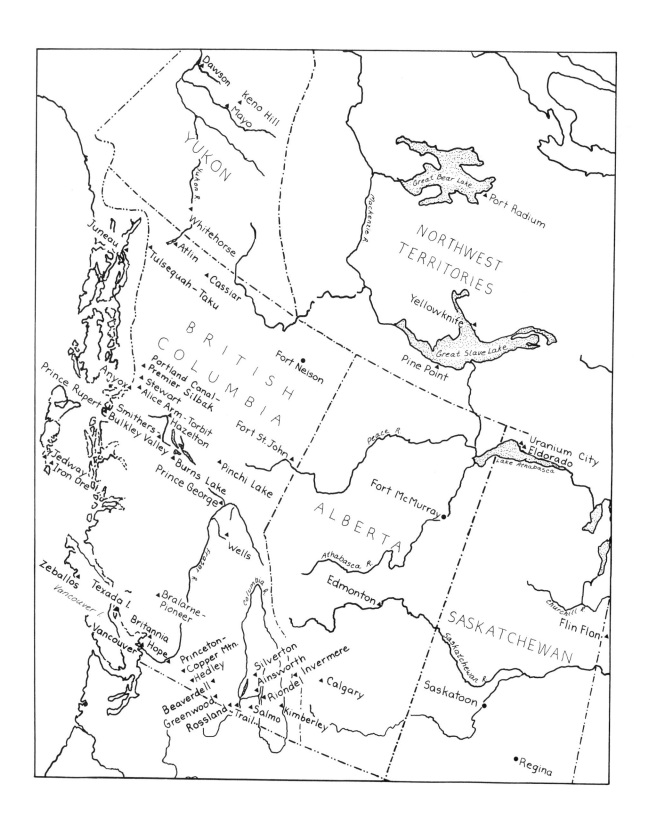

WESTERN CANADA MINING CENTRES 1940S

Having registered his complaints, he noted "good progress among convoy truck drivers hauling ore to the concentrators. This Local has sent a donation of $89 to the Torbit Local on strike at Alice Arm [B.C.]. Have solicited a few more ads for the B.C. District News."

On December 1, 1953: "When in Whitehorse I made a trip into the Cassiar Asbestos property at Cassiar, B.C. Have sent in an application for a charter to cover these workers . . . winter has started here (October 31) with the usual snow and temperatures as low as 20 below zero."

Of interest is a hand bill signed by McGuire and issued by the Mayo District Mine, Mill and Smelter Workers, Local 924, December 9, 1953:

WE ARE HERE TO STAY!

Certification has been received from the Canada Labour Relations Board covering all workers (exclusive of staff) at the Elsa Mill, Calumet Mine, and Whitehorse Garage and Transportation.

Contract demands have been approved by the workers. Contract negotiations are expected to be under way in a matter of days.

Certification has also been received covering the workers at the Mackeno Mine and Mill. Negotiations will start soon with this company.

LABOUR PRODUCES ALL WEALTH

Labour deserves the first consideration in the distribution of the wealth it creates!

Barney McGuire worked in the mine at Port Radium in 1943 and came back to organize it in 1953. (L-R): Gus Schorell, — Fraser, Barney McGuire, Red McKinnon. Photo courtesy Barney McGuire

MARTIN WALSH

Organizer Martin Walsh, in his report of July 15, 1952, noted that "one of the big problems of organizing and maintaining a union in the remote northern areas is the continuous turnover of workers, all good union men who would join Mine Mill immediately on being hired, but there has to be an ongoing organizing job."

On November 30th, Walsh reported a work stoppage over food at the Giant Mascot Mines, located some 140 miles north of Kimberley.

On February 15, 1953: "From Regina I went to Prince Albert via Saskatoon and from Prince Albert directly to Stoney Rapids where we were forced down by bad weather and had to spend the night with the Indians. The next day we flew to Stoney Rapids right into Uranium City, but don't let the word 'city' fool you. My first problem was in getting a place to stay as the hotel talked about so much in the press just isn't there yet. Furthermore, I had no sleeping bag or parka, and let me tell you — a person who goes into that country without being properly clothed is a damned fool. I bought a pair of moccasins, pair of leather mitts, pair of woolen mitts, three pairs of woolen socks, and one of the pilots gave me the loan of an extra parka he had. I was ready to face the elements." He added: "There is a large turnover — there are actually three crews, one going, one coming and one working."

Torbit/Alice Arm Local 906 strike committee. From top down (R-L): *Pratch, Cook, Monahan, Gillis, Ditto, McIntosh, Le Duke, Morrison, Jamieson, McGuire, McGillivary, McLean, Smith, Kelly.* Photo courtesy Barney McGuire

Organization progressed despite difficulties settling down. On July 31, he reported: ". . . had a very good membership meeting; the issue was another brother getting killed. This is our third death accident in less than a year. Eldorado agrees to a payroll deduction for a death benefit. We are also pressing for safety representation."

On August 31, 1953, the uranium miners voted 241 to 62 for Mine Mill, as opposed to no union, and Walsh wrote: "As for myself, I certainly don't wish to stay here forever and I must give full consideration to Maria, my wife, because she played a very important role in this campaign and all our household goods and furniture are sitting in Trail, and we have concern over these things."

By September 15th, problems at the Rix Mines occurred when the company refused to bargain to an acceptable agreement; conciliation proceedings were begun. Rix was a union stronghold, with 100 per cent check-off. Walsh wrote, "As for my shack, I suppose I will have to winterize it because by the look of things bargaining will be quite a drawn out affair. And winter is already upon us even though only in the middle of September."

Walsh noted that wherever Mine Mill started organizing, Steel followed in to disrupt on the pretext of also organizing. "I am sure that Steel and the Company have some connection because I saw the letter that Mitchell — Steel staff — sent "Red" Ryan — supposed to be organizing for Steel — and the letter advised him to see Mr. Gilchrist, assistant manager at Eldorado, about employment, and Ryan was hired right away."

On November 15th, Walsh wrote: "Am returning to my home station, Trail, and my wife and I are taking our first vacation since I have been on the International staff. . . . At a meeting with the local union people I stressed that they must take over the leadership without an International staff member there all the time."

Local 913 organizing team in front of tent accommodation at Eldorado Mining and Smelting Co. property, Uranium City, Saskatchewan 1953. (L-R): Barney McGuire, Martin Walsh, William Longridge, Mike Ellis. Photo courtesy Josephine Longridge

MIKE ELLIS

Taking his turn at organizing and servicing Mine Mill locals in the north, Mike Ellis reported on April 1, 1953, that certification had been achieved for Local 913's Nesbit LaBine and Beaverlodge mines. On June 15th, he noted that a building for living quarters and a union office was being erected with local workers helping with funds and work, because tents were impractical. On July 15th, Ellis stated that while several small mines were under organization with good results, companies were not bargaining in good faith and that the Nesbit LaBine company refused to put the check-off into effect, contrary to the provincial trade union act. However, he reported on July 30th that bargaining rights were won at four other mines.

On February 15, 1954, Nesbit LaBine moved to decertify the union. With the property under the control of the Atomic Energy Commission, Mike was not allowed on the grounds without permission. Needless to say, permission was not granted. Despite the fact that Eldorado barred Mike from its property March 15th, the union was able to sign an agreement

Tent office replaced by donations of funds and work from Local 913 members. Photo courtesy Nels Thibault

with Eldorado on July 31st, the first ever agreement for Mine Mill in uranium. On September 7th, an agreement was signed with Rix Athabasca.

On February 28, 1955, Ellis found it a problem to maintain union strength with a big turnover of men. He noted that with the booming uranium stock market, miners were buying stocks in the companies in hopes of becoming millionaires.

ANDY CAVIL

Andy Cavil then moved into the field with a report on December 15, 1954, from Local 898 in Cassiar, B.C., announcing contracts with Red Rose and Silver Standard mines. On January 15, 1955, he reported from the Yukon that Local 924 had signed up United Keno Mines, and on March 15th, that an agreement had been reached with Yale Lead and Zinc in Ainsworth, and that Local 902 had made an agreement with Salmo Mines.

On June 30th, he attempted a flight into Kitchikan, Alaska, by charter plane (Canadian) to the Granduc property, but "could not go in because of too much trouble with Canadian customs, also need a plane with skis but none to be had. The only plane with skis is the company plane."

DAVE McGHEE

Organizer Dave McGhee reported on June 30, 1954, from Keno City, Yukon: "Cassiar Asbestos Company Local 927 is in negotiations. A meeting with the Yukon Council re Holiday Act and various other acts, including mine safety, hours of work, fair wage ordinances, to be amended at Yukon Council sessions and want Mine Mill to make representation." Dave did his travelling on truck convoys.

On July 15th, "Just received my kit from the International — may have come by dog sled . . . huge distances between the different mines, with travel by plane . . . Vancouver to White-horse, 1680 miles, Whitehorse to Cassiar, 350 miles, to Calumet, 300, to Dawson, 350 miles."

On August 15th: ". . . heard Hudson Bay mining develop-ing new nickel mine and bringing men from East . . . couldn't find road into property . . . when snow comes and until freeze-up surface operations shutting down."

On November 15th: Uranium City . . . "Eldorado mines under Atomic Energy Control Commission . . . security, policy, plain clothes cops, etc., and when worker is fired the company uses security reasons." November 30th: ". . . can't get clearance from A.E.C.B. to enter property . . . finger print-ing and screening." January 15, 1955: ". . . my expenses will be higher because of travelling; this is because half the camps do not have two-way bush radios and have no way of getting the cabs back to camp . . . as soon as freeze-up is complete and am able to travel across the lake by car will begin to organize Ridge and Lorado uranium mines."

On March 31st: "Break-up is coming here soon and will want to get all of the outlying camps certified before then, and will then get the camps near town." On April 30th: ". . . have at length been cleared by A.E.C. so am now purified and I can go on the property of Eldorado . . . the weather has turned cold again so was able to go over the ice again . . . went back to Black Bay Uranium and was ordered off the property as a trespasser. Told the manager I was like MacArthur — I would be back."

On May 31st: "The ice has broken on the lake now so will be able to go to Meta and Lorado by boat." On June 30th: ". . . have started campaign to get cost of living subsidy for married personnel who have families here."

NEIL McLEOD

Three decades later, in a recorded interview in 1981, Neil McLeod recalled that "every place I went to in the North, 90 per cent was by bush plane . . . the most remote was Jedway Iron Ore, located on the very southernmost point of Queen Charlotte Island . . . you fly in with weather permitting. . . . One runway, if the wind was blowing in the proper direction you could land, if not, you just couldn't. . . . Crosswinds of more than 90 miles an hour were common and many times you'd land but couldn't get out. The guys at Jedway would phone by radio saying the weather was good and we'd come in . . . they'd get their mail and there would be someone waiting to fly out. . . ."

DOUG GOLD

Doug Gold, Kimberley Local 651's long-time business agent and board member of the B.C. District Union, related a few of his experiences, also in a 1981 recorded interview. He recalled one instance when he was sent to Tulsequah to help negotiate a contract and flew into the camp sitting on a box of asparagus. In the same plane, equally uncomfortable, were company executives. "The plane landed on a river; the bridge having been washed out, we had to cross by rubber boat, an inflatable, probably a U.S. army surplus deal."

Frank Jurick, present during the Gold interview, reminded his compatriot that it was he who navigated that rubber boat across the river "scaring the hell" out of Gold. Frank had spent ten years in the northern camps as on-the-spot union organizer. Conditions were deplorable "both on the job and in the camps. Men were being killed and injured constantly. Bunkhouses were heated by firing oil drums, while outside 40-mile-an-hour winds fanned 30-below temperatures through poorly fitted doors and windows." He recalled that at the time "the fight for butter, ketchup and meat fit to eat was just as important as wage increases." Frank, then in his fortieth year working for C.M.&S. in Trail, stressed that the union changed all those conditions with militant job action and tough bargaining.

The three mines in the Tulsequah mining camp, situated up the Taku Inlet northeast of Juneau, Alaska were organized under Local 858 Taku and District Mine and Mill Workers. The Polaris Taku Mine was organized by Barney McGuire in 1946 with the help of Frank Jurick, who also played a part in organizing the Chief Mine in 1948 and the Big Bull Mine in 1949.

Big Bull Mine and dry or change house in 1950. Photo courtesy Frank Jurick

Bush or float plane was the only means of transportation in and out in 1953. Photo courtesy Frank Jurick

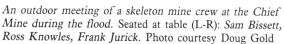

An outdoor meeting of a skeleton mine crew at the Chief Mine during the flood. Seated at table (L-R): Sam Bissett, Ross Knowles, Frank Jurick. Photo courtesy Doug Gold

The union committee used a rubber dinghy to go from mine to mine after flooding carried out the bridges on the Tulsequah River each summer (L-R): Ross Knowles, Local 858 financial secretary; Doug Gold, District office; Frank Jurick, Local 858 president. Photo courtesy Doug Gold

CLEM THOMPSON

In 1981, at 87 years of age, Clem Thompson, a former president of Kimberley Local 651, recalled his experiences. Born in the Northwest Territories, Clem had started with C.M.&S. in Kimberley in 1927, when two men firing four boilers by wheelbarrow hauled 65 tons of coal per shift: "There was no mechanical stuff to work with."

He had worked for the CPR in Saskatchewan in 1919 and had joined the OBU, which even then opponents were calling communist and subversive. He remembered hearing the legendary Art "Slim" Evans speaking for unionism on the high school grounds in Kimberley when refused use of the auditorium.

"We went into the little camps to organize," Clem recalled, "one on top of a mountain, in the middle of winter, 7,000 feet altitude, where the men worked in the mine till midnight." He remembered an especially aggressive manager of a Nelson mine who would go around tearing down meeting notices. "When the men threatened to go on strike over cookhouse conditions, he took a bulldozer and bulldozed the cookhouse into the creek and said: 'Okay, go ahead.' "

"SEAHORSE" JOHNSON

"Seahorse" Johnson, also 87 in 1981, had his first contact with the labour movement when he joined the IWW in Copper Mountain. "I packed a card for several years — secretly." In the early 1920s he worked in Anyox where there was no organization. Then, for several decades, he was in almost every mining camp in North America, a "hobo driller" he called himself, but carrying the union story with him wherever he went. In South America in the 1920s he drilled in a Peruvian copper mine at 18,000 feet altitude, but lasted only three weeks before he started to bleed. In Idaho, he drilled in a quicksilver mine where every time they blasted it threw up a cloud of quicksilver, "so I didn't stay there very long. But they sure had a nice graveyard."

From 1927 to 1929, he drilled in Noranda, then known as the Horne Mine. He worked in Flin Flon in the 1930s and in Kirkland Lake, where he "saw men pulled out dead nearly every day . . . worst mine ever worked for safety."

"I was an honest member of Mine Mill," he said, "and I hated like hell to see someone come in and try to bump us off. We had a meeting in the K.P. hall and, Mahoney [Steel staffer] speaking, said we were communists and all those kinds of things, and I got mad as hell and stood up and said 'What in hell are you saying? Do you take us for a bunch of school kids that we don't know that we have communists here? There isn't an organization in the country that hasn't a communist.' Mahoney stopped talking and left."

James Patterson, former business agent of Kimberley Local 651, participating in the interview, added: "It was largely as a result of discussion with Clem Thompson and Seahorse Johnson that the union developed the Medical Society in Kimberley and many other social projects . . . to show you that from the 'communist' union and all those other things they were calling us, Clem was mayor of Kimberley, Seahorse was an alderman, and I am the chairman of the Community College . . . so we couldn't have been all that bad."

One of the many achievements of Kimberley miners was the establishment of a new approach to the contentious contract bonus mining system in universal effect in the mining industry. As Jim Patterson described the system in the Kimberley mines, two experienced contract miners were selected by the miners themselves to work full time with company officials in setting contract bonus prices and they were on constant surveillance duty on behalf of the contract miners. A levy of two per cent of bonus earnings was deducted by the company to cover the salary of the union representatives.

JACK KELLY

Jack Kelly came to Canada from the U.K. in 1928 at the age of 17. After a few years in the east, he arrived in Trail in 1934 and was one of the lucky ones to get a job almost immediately with C.M.&S. Shortly after his arrival he was elected to the Workmen's Committee (the company union) where he tried to do all he could on behalf of the workers. He said at that time it seemed to him that all the bosses at the Trail smelter were Scottish and all the labourers Italian. Also, he recalls, organizers for Mine Mill came in about 1937.

"After war started, the government made outfits like the Workmen's Committee illegal, and to abide by the new law the Committee formed itself into the Maple Leaf union which did not last very long, but the company did not give up the effort to keep a legitimate union out." He remembers that Art Evans came in and did a lot of educational work and organizing and that later Harvey Murphy came from the coal mines in the Crow's Nest.

"The company had people prominent in the Maple Leaf union to run for office in the Mine Mill Local 480 and a slate of officers who were former Maple Leafers took over. These people promptly negotiated some kind of understanding with the Steelworkers, and that's when I became active, and we had a devil of a fight for some time."

Kelly became a shop steward, then chief steward, and vice-president of Local 480 at the time of the merger with the Steelworkers in 1967. "Mine Mill was a human union," he reflected, "interested in helping people on a man-to-man basis, not as an automated, council-oriented affair of labour relations such as we have today."

Recalling some of the highlights during his days in Mine Mill, Kelly told of Art Evans' incarceration in Rossland jail early in the organizational stage. "Art Evans was a powerful and aggressive character. When Evans got to Rossland for a special meeting, he was arrested and put into jail for the weekend. Since Evans was to be the main speaker at the

meeting, local unionists asked police how they could get him out of jail. They were told that the only way was to get a magistrate to sign a release order. The magistrate wasn't at his home, but it was known that he had a girlfriend, so a group of women went to the house of the girlfriend and pounded on the door, and after a while the lights came on. In the meantime, two of the ladies went to the rear door and a dishevelled magistrate appeared at the back door and into the arms of the women. In a short time the order to release Evans was signed and Art got to the meeting, which was very well attended."

Union members active in Kimberley Local 651, 1955. Back row (L-R): *H. Baker, Clem Thompson, Bill Booth, Doug Gold.* Front row (L-R): *J. Jenkins, F. Malone, D. Cook, K. Farron, Ed Clemmer, Alex Fergus, James Patterson, J. A. Glennie, R. Labrash.* UBC Collection

AL KING AND LOCAL 480

Al King was elected president of Trail Local 480 in 1950, following the defection of the entire previous executive board to Steel. He remained in that office for the next ten years and aided by new and loyal Mine Mill board members, led the fight against the Steelworkers' raid. In a recorded interview conducted in 1977 by Sudbury labour historian James Tester, King reflected on his years in the industry and his role in the union.

King worked in the district mines and then in the Trail smelter in 1936 and 1937, when the company-controlled Workmen's Committee was the only union in the C.M.&S. properties, a situation which prevailed until the outbreak of war in 1940. S. G. Blaylock, general manager and president of the company, was chairman of the committee. When wartime labour legislation outlawed obvious company unions, the committee transformed itself into the Independent Smelter Workers' union and because its emblem, worn by members, was the maple leaf, it was popularly known as the Maple Leaf Union.

However, King recalled, the workers were successful at times in using the committee to their advantage. For example, during the Pioneer Mine and Kirkland Lake strikes in 1941,

the men forced the committee to put through an assessment to aid the strikers in both areas. Blaylock, of course, would have none of it and the money collected was sent to the church, over the objections of the men.

In reviewing developments at the time, he noted that Art Evans had come to Trail in the late 1930s and was organizing into Mine Mill Local 289 which had been chartered with the intent to have one local for the entire province. This proved impractical and Local 480 replaced it: "It was Art Evans who really started the union." Although not a charter member of the union, King was number 65 on the membership lists. Having served in the armed forces until the end of the war, King returned to Trail and participated actively in the union, which was then certified as Mine Mill Local 480 and working under a collective agreement with C.M.&S.

Commenting on the early days of the union, he referred to men who were "the backbone of the union . . . who did the groundwork and were later persecuted and victimized, lost their jobs and had to leave to seek employment elsewhere." Later, for about two years, he said, "we had this kind of opportunistic leadership who tore the guts out of the union. . . . They were the ones who tried to get us into the Steelworkers without taking a vote or having a meeting . . . and they got turfed out by the members . . . and that's when I became president. . . ."

Al King (centre) poses with a group of predominantly Trail delegates at the 10th Annual B.C. District Convention in January 1953. Seated (L-R): Olive Anderson, Gladys LaForte, Marie Walsh, Marg Bystrom. Standing (L-R): Jack Billingsley, Frank Barnes, George LaForte, Bill Longridge, Remo Morandini, Harold Stadford, Les Walker, Al King, Al Warrington, Dan Dosen, Martin Walsh, Rene Morin, Pete Jensen, Marty Graham, Bill Muir, Arnold Laarz. UBC Collection

One result of the Steel raid in 1950, said King, "was the elimination of the company union elements which earlier had been in the leadership of the Independent Smelter Workers union and had formed the nucleus of the Steel raid." Another result, of course, was the rallying of the rank and file in support of Local 480.

King recalled the incident of the first meeting between Blaylock and a Mine Mill union committee (under wartime order P.C. 1003 which obliged industry to recognize unions) when the C.M.&S. president, seated in a swivel chair at the window, said: "The law requires that I have to recognize the union — Hello union. Good day!" He turned back in his chair and that was the end of the meeting. Blaylock, he continued, was a "ruthless man, a dictator . . . he vowed he would never sign a collective agreement with the union." And he didn't; he had other executives perform that formality.

Looking back to the 1930s, King said, "there was only one enemy and that was the boss, and the challenge to the workers was to organize but then afterwards came the raiders and dividers doing the boss's work."

LEO NIMSICK, MLA

Leo Nimsick, one of the longest serving MLAs, was elected nine times for a total of twenty-six years in the B.C. legislature. He first came to work for C.M.&S. in 1928. "Conditions in Trail were bad," he recalled in a 1981 interview, "they gave you a pint of milk a day to offset the lead and for the arsenic, a mask — a sack with all kinds of holes around it."

He remembered the first union meetings when Art Evans came to Trail in the late 1930s, the granting of a charter by the international union in 1938 on which he was number six, the organizing that carried on until after certification in 1943, and the first bargaining committee on which he was a member.

It was at this first bargaining session that Blaylock, "very upset, said: 'How about us getting the conciliation officer draw up something that both Henne [F. W. Henne, Local 480 president] and I could agree on. If Nimsick draws it up I'll be looking for something with horns, hooves and teeth on it.'"

Nimsick had been elected CCF MLA in 1949, around the time of the Steel raids on Local 480. Despite the provincial CCF leadership support for the raiding Steelworkers, Nimsick expressed strong opposition and unremitting support for Mine Mill during the entire period of the Steel raids on the union throughout Canada. In later years, when he was B.C. Minister of Mines in the NDP government, his ministry introduced 120 new safety regulations.

Commenting on the final outcome of the raids — the merger of Mine Mill with Steel in 1967 — Nimsick said: "I was really sorry when Mine Mill went over to Steel. I think it was the end of an era."

KEN SMITH, PRESIDENT

One of the leaders of Mine Mill in Canada from the early 1940s, K. A. (Ken) Smith, hard rock miner with Britannia Copper Mines, was successively vice-president of Britannia Local 663, financial-secretary in 1946, president of the B.C. District Union, and president of the Canadian Mine Mill Council in 1954. After the Canadian section of Mine Mill achieved autonomy in 1955, its first president Nels Thibault resigned in 1960 to contest the presidency of Sudbury Local 598, then in the control of the Steel-backed Gillis administration. Ken Smith was then elected president of the International Union of Mine, Mill and Smelter Workers (Canada), which post he held until the merger with Steel in 1967.

In 1934, at the age of 21, Smith experienced his first intimation of the discriminatory racial practices the mining industry used to keep its working force divided. A friend who had worked at Britannia advised him to apply by mail, first using his own name; if there was no reply from the company,

to apply again using a Scandinavian name; if still no reply, to use a Central European name. His own name won him employment, for he had applied during the Anglo-Saxon quota period.

In a 1981 interview, Smith recalled that his first job was mucking sixteen tons per shift by hand, and that when he first went to work, safety conditions were a low priority, with the mine killing about three men a month. His first awareness of job conflict was the 1933 strike at the Anyox mines where, in the "Battle of Kelly's Cut," the B.C. provincial police fired on demonstrating strikers.* That was his first exposure to Harvey Murphy, later B.C. Regional Director of Mine Mill, who had been sent to Anyox by the old Workers Unity League to help the strikers.

As a leading Mine Mill officer in the local, provincial and national fields, Smith represented his members at union conventions and in contract negotiations, and he led delegations to all levels of government. As president of Mine Mill in Canada, he was chief administrator of the union and finally negotiator in the merger with the Steelworkers.

In retirement in the mountains of B.C., Smith is fond of recalling some of the less serious incidents in his career in the union. He enjoyed relating his experience in getting to inter-

---

*Approximately 400 miners belonging to the Mine Workers Union of Canada went on strike February 1, 1933 against the Granby Copper mine and smelter. Wage cuts had been made for the third time in just over a year: the men were working twenty to twenty-two shifts per month for $2.25 to $2.40 per day, out of which they paid $1.10 per day every day of the month at company-owned boarding houses. Provincial police fired on the strikers as they attempted to march to company offices on the other side of town. Afterwards, more than 100 extra police recruited from the ranks of the unemployed were flown into Anyox to arrest the men and order them out of town in what became known as the "Anyox deportations." Clashes with police occurred again at the docks at Prince Rupert and Vancouver as the strikers attempted to prevent scabs boarding sea-planes or boats to work at Anyox.

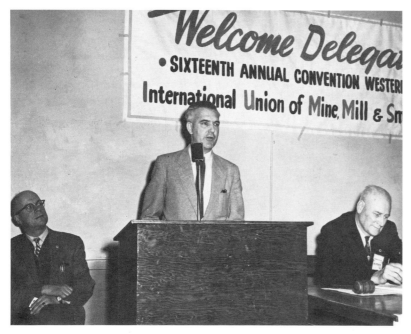

Leo Nimsick MLA, Cedric Cox MLA, Clem Thompson, Kimberley Local 651 president, at 16th Annual Western District Convention.
UBC Collection

national union gatherings in the United States during the time that Mine Mill members were being turned back at the border. As a Canadian delegate to the 1948 Mine Mill convention in San Francisco, he knew that he would most likely be stopped at the U.S. border if he undertook the normal crossing. Accompanied by his wife Kay, he flew to Victoria, B.C., where the American Bar Association was holding a convention. When the ferry carrying the conventioners left for Seattle, "we got on with them and when we arrived at Seattle the loud speakers on the wharf were announcing that the Bar Association people would disembark first, and I said to Kay 'that's us, let's go.' We got to San Francisco and our own convention."

On another occasion, Smith was asked to aid the Tulsequah Mine Mill local negotiate a new agreement. The most direct route was to fly to Seattle, go north by Pan American Airlines to Juneau, Alaska, and then over the Mendenhall Glacier by plane. However, on reaching Seattle, he was apprehended by U.S. immigration officials, refused entry, and jailed until his return to Canada was arranged. In jail he was told that since he had been refused entry into the U.S., he had never really been in the U.S. and therefore was not eligible for any of the privileges customarily allowed prisoners. "Although I had some $300 in my pockets, I was not permitted to buy anything while waiting to be returned to Canada. Apparently, immigration regulations were such that the plane that brought me in was obliged to take me out. The following morning, I was escorted to the airport to await the United Airlines plane that brought me in. I was not permitted to buy my breakfast but my guard, a decent fellow, said 'the law says I can't let you spend any money but there's nothing in the law that says I can't buy you a breakfast,' and he did, a very good one. Well,

Canadian president Ken Smith (right) in a serious discussion with International president Al Skinner at National Convention in Trail in 1966. Solski Collection

I got back to Canada and I found another method of getting to Tulsequah."

In a more serious vein, Smith stressed that "if we never got one cent increase for the worker, we did something when we gave him dignity. We made it possible for people to lift their heads."

Some B.C. members at the 49th International Mine Mill Convention, Hotel de Soto, St. Louis, Missouri, September 14-19, 1953. (L-R): George "Scotty" Anderson, Copper Mountain Local 649; Doug Gold, Kimberley Local 651; Virginia Jencks, New Mexico; Percy Berry, Trail Local 480; Arnie Bennett, Britannia Beach Local 663; Al King, Trail; Clint Jencks, New Mexico; Bill Booth, Kimberley Local 651; Remo Morandini, Trail Local 480. Solski Collection

First conference of Alberta Mine Mill unions, April 24, 1949. Front (L-R): *Frank Rogers, W. Ure, William Longridge, B. Scott, Robert Michel.* Photo courtesy Josephine Longridge

Alberta Organization

Alberta in the early 1940s could hardly be described as an industrial province and, apart from traditional organization in the coal mining industry and partial success in unionizing meat-packing plants, relatively little union organization was evident. William Longridge was an early Mine Mill organizer in that province, and his own history serves as a record of Mine Mill organization in Alberta.

Coming from the farm in 1940 to work for the Alberta Nitrogen Company in Calgary, Longridge first tried to organize his plant into the Trades and Labour Congress (TLC) but failed because of craft differences in that organization. When Consolidated Mining and Smelting took over Alberta Nitrogen, and with Mine Mill organizing C.M.&S. operations in British Columbia, Longridge undertook the task of bringing the plant into Mine Mill Local 690. He later organized the Calgary Dominion Bridge plants into Local 800 and became business agent for both locals. From 1943 to 1950, Mine Mill had organized some 1,700 workers with seventeen certifications and was the third largest industrial union in Alberta.

In 1954, Longridge left Alberta to take up office as executive-secretary of the Mine Mill Council and later as secretary of Mine Mill in Canada at its headquarters in Toronto. In addition, Longridge assisted in the fight against Steel in the raid at Trail and in organizational work in Saskatchewan.

When the Steel raids on Mine Mill intensified in the late 1950s, Alberta Mine Mill locals were immediate targets, not only for Steel raiders but for other CLC unions as well. However, Mine Mill maintained a presence in Alberta, servicing and organizing locals in the Northwest Territories and northern Saskatchewan from the office in Edmonton. Bill Berezoski was the last of the staff to remain at that post before Mine Mill merged with Steel in 1967.

Pottery and clay workers organized at Medalta Potteries, Medicine Hat, Alta. (L-R): Christine Steigel, Laura Rife, Bill Longridge, Olga Bierbach, Josephine Longridge, Irene Entzminger, Barney McGuire. Photo courtesy Josephine Longridge

CHAPTER III

Organization in North Eastern Canada

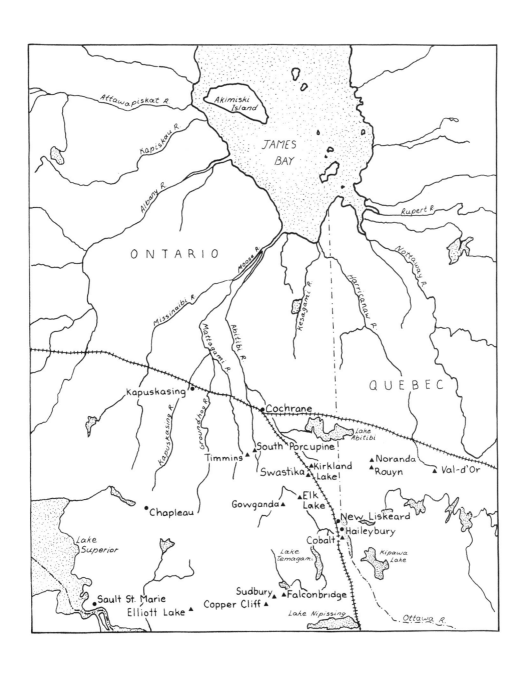

HARD ROCK MINING BEGAN IN ONTARIO FOLLOWING a government survey in 1900. The discovery that several thousands of square miles of land were suitable for mixed farming opened up the northern part of the province. Townships were mapped out and settlers moved into the area in such numbers that, by 1904, construction of the Temiskaming and Northern Ontario Railroad (now the Ontario Northland Railroad) was begun.

Legend relates that during the building of the railroad, a blacksmith named LaRose first discovered silver in Cobalt in 1905. Apparently, he had seen a fox on a rock a few yards from his shop, and had thrown his hammer at it, but missed and hit the rock. Upon retrieving his hammer, he noticed that the spot it had hit glowed. Claims were staked by LaRose, by his foreman McMartin, and among others, by contractors Noah S. Timmins who, on the foundation laid in Cobalt silver mining, developed the Hollinger Gold Mine and had the city of Timmins named after him. He continued in mine development to become one of Canada's wealthiest men.

When news of the find spread, Cobalt was transformed into an active mining centre with several operating mines and a population of thousands of miners and prospectors.

Just as the discovery of silver and cobalt attracted mining magnates, it also attracted miners from all over the continent, from Montana, Idaho, Colorado, Mexico, British Columbia and the Klondike. They came fresh from the blacklists of Colorado and the bull-pens of the Coeur d'Alenes. Most were from the northwestern U.S. and were either active or former members of the Western Federation of Miners.

The main property of LaRose Consolidated Mines Ltd., where railway blacksmith Fred LaRose first found silver during construction of the T. & N.O. Railway. The LaRose company also controlled the Lawson, University, Princess, Fischer-Eplett and Violet properties. Total production of LaRose properties to the end of 1915 was 22,891,037 ounces, valued at $11,514,043.79. Dividends paid to January 20, 1916, including profits to original owners amounted to $6,907,409.56. Photo courtesy Mike Farrell

Miners in cross-cut, Mining Corporation of Canada Ltd. property, Cobalt 1914. Mike Farrell

Cobalt WFM Local 146: 1906

Early in the winter of 1906, a group of miners decided they should have a union. Union records show that the meeting elected Paddy Fleming acting president and William Walsh acting secretary. Application was made to the Western Federation of Miners on March 24, 1906, and Cobalt Miners Union Local 146 was established soon after.

The mine operators' first reaction was to set up the Mine Managers' Association. In May of 1907, the mine managers posted a schedule of wages and working conditions to go into effect at all the mines. Under this schedule, the machine men were to receive $3.25 a shift, and helpers and muckers $2.75, while board and room cost 75 cents a day. Hours of work were from 8 a.m. to 10 p.m. or midnight.

The union immediately posted its own schedule: $3.50 for machine runners, $3.00 for helpers and muckers, 60 cents for bed and board, and the eight-hour day. A meeting of miners unanimously approved the union demands and on July 8, 1907, the first strike in Cobalt was on.

The strike was relatively short-lived, because several of the mines agreed to most of the union's demands within the first two weeks, others after some six weeks, while a few never did give in. Most of the miners returned to work an eight-hour day and the balance on nine hours, without loss in pay. Bunk and boarding house conditions and mine safety and sanitation rules were improved considerably. In most instances, however, the mine owners refused to recognize the union, but no one was discriminated against because of membership.

Police guarding scab labour during WFM strike at Cobalt 1907. Jim Tester

Cobalt Mine Mill Local 146 union members' badge. Solski Collection

The Union Grows

Meanwhile, federal and provincial governments continued to survey the north, and more reports came in of rich gold, silver, copper and other mineral discoveries. Spur lines and roads were built into mining camps at Silver Centre, Boston Creek, Elk Lake, Gowganda, Swastika, Kirkland Lake, South Porcupine and Timmins. Union locals were established and union halls built in each camp.

The second WFM local in the area was the Elk Lake Miners Union Local 140, established in the early spring of 1909. The third local, also established in 1909, was the Gowganda Miners Union Local 154. This local succeeded in obtaining the highest wages of any mining camp in the area and some of the best working conditions.

The second president of the Gowganda local was Jack McGee, a colourful WFM character in northern Ontario. In August of 1953, Mine Mill representative, William Kennedy, found Jack McGee living in a shack in the bush seven miles southwest of South Porcupine. Jack was living on some patented claims which were considered quite valuable, he having refused many offers from mining companies. He said he was quite happy to be living the life of a hermit, going into town only when he really had to.

"Jack was then 74 years old and his mind was as clear as a bell. He remembered quite distinctly most of the things that took place then, recalling the fight for the eight-hour day when both the miners and the mine owners were in Toronto in full force to lobby for and against the eight-hour day. With the union was a delegate by the name of Tom Mills. Tom was dressed up more in style with the mine

Finnish miners in the Porcupine mines (Timmins). Mike Farrell

Union members in Porcupine or Timmins 1913, wearing their badges from Cobalt. George Prusila

operators than as a union delegate and, before the interview with Premier Whitney began, Tom went over to the mine owners' section of the lobby. Being unknown to many of them, as soon as the interview started, Tom spoke up in favour of the eight-hour day. This caused considerable confusion on the mine owners' side of the assembly and was responsible to a great degree in Premier Whitney ordering the vote among the miners in the province, which resulted in the eight-hour day.

"Then there was the 'Gospel of Discontent' which happened about 1910 or 1911. A young minister by the name of Reverend A.J. North was sent from England to Canada to do missionary work. When he arrived in Toronto he was told that his assignment was Gowganda and that his job would be a very tough one as he was going among heathens and wild men.

"Coming to Gowganda by stage coach he found that the only possible place to hold divine service was the WFM union hall. He approached Jack McGee, president of the local, to see if he could have the hall on Sunday nights to preach divine service. Jack told him that he would have the matter on the agenda for the membership meeting the following Sunday afternoon.

"At the meeting, one of the members made the motion that Reverend North could have the hall on Sunday nights provided he preached the gospel of discontent. The motion was passed unanimously and McGee relayed the decision to Reverend North. The minister said he would like to have some material to study in order to learn something about

the gospel of discontent. McGee gave him copies of the *Miners Magazine* and other literature. After a few days, the reverend accepted the proposal of preaching the gospel of discontent.

"Naturally, most of the congregation at these services were members of the union and as the gospel of discontent got better so did the collections and very often, after expenses were met, there would be enough left over to send to Elk Lake for a keg of beer and, although the reverend did not join in the boisterousness, he did enjoy a glass of ale with the boys.

"This arrangement continued for some time; then the union officers got a job for Reverend North at the Blackburn Mine; thereby he was able to have an income and still preach the gospel of discontent. He joined the union members in all their activities and on one occasion, when word came to town that a couple had been frozen in the bush about ten miles from Gowganda, the boys got two dog teams and set out to find the bodies. The reverend went with them in weather of 50 below zero. Shortly afterwards he made up his mind to leave Gowganda and return to England.

"At a party in his honour, he told the miners that when he was sent to Gowganda he was told that he would meet nothing but wild men and heathens. Instead, he found a group of people who had more Christian principles than those who condemned them. He told his union brothers that if any of them ever met him in England, they would find him on a street corner preaching the gospel of discontent."

59

Porcupine Miners' Strike: 1912

The Porcupine Miners Union Local 145 of the WFM was founded April 23, 1910, and had the largest membership in the area until it went out of existence in 1919. In the autumn of 1912, a strike lasting several months closed down most of the mines in that area. Demands were for improved bunk and boarding house conditions, health and safety rules,* 50 cents a day wage increase, and the eight-hour day.

The companies' response was to import, for the first time in Canada, the notorious Pinkerton Agency; professional scabs and strike breakers were brought in as well. The union countered with its own tactics: sister locals were asked to send in reliable miners to work as scabs at the struck mines to perform "confidential duties."

The story is told of one such miner, an old WFM member from the U.S., hired on at the Hollinger Mine as an "experienced but willing miner," whose helper was an alleged farmer. They were given a machine in a drift some 40 to 50 feet from the shaft station and put to work. When

*Health and hospital provisions were a main concern throughout northern Ontario mining camps. The Mathers Commission hearings in Cobalt in 1919 recorded health and safety as frequent causes for concern by miners.

Local 145, Western Federation of Miners hall in South Porcupine, shortly after it was completed in 1912. Designed by Tom Ryan and Charles McGuire, brother of "Big Jim" McGuire, it was built by the miners themselves. Identified in the group are Tom Ryan, Local 145 secretary William Thompson, — Kerr, and Charles McGuire (fourth from right). Bob Miner lived in the same building, after it had been converted into an apartment building, from 1944 to 1977.
Photos courtesy Mike Farrell

May 1st, 1918 Labour Day parade in South Porcupine. George Prusila

it came to blast, they not only loaded the holes to the collar, but placed several cases of powder on the other side of the station and set the two blasts off simultaneously. No one worked on that level for some time.

Another dedicated WFM member, also hired on as a scab, was given a machine with instructions to finish off a round that was all drilled off but one last hole. He was told that the shift boss would help him load and blast when he was finished drilling and had "torn down the machine and bar." He blasted the whole set-up.

When asked by the shift boss why he had used this means to tear down the machine and bar, he explained: "I tried every way in the world to get that s.o.b. of a machine off the g.d. arm and finally had to use the hammer . . . . I tried everything I could think of, the hammer, the chuck wrench and everything else to get the g.d. bar down, and finally had to blast it . . . the s.o.b. who set that machine and bar up is a hell of a lot better than either me or my partner."

The Pinkerton agents were finally driven out, the strike breakers and scabs beaten back, and the struggle ended in a partial victory, with some of the union demands won.

According to a report in the *International Socialist Review,* February, 1913, the miners

held a mass meeting and resolved to demand the union scale of wages and the adoption of an 8-hour work day and decided to strike. Not

only did the boys affected walk out, but every miner in the whole camp joined them and made the tie-up complete.

Immediately the mine owners wired for detective agents, and these thugs began to appear with guns and clubs . . . . Fortunately they soon overplayed their hands and the general public refused to stomach the rowdies who were on trouble bent. Also the Ontario police held aloof . . . . So the plug-uglies abandoned the field and the police took to scab-herding, and are saving the mine companies a lot of money thereby and placing the burden upon the taxpayers who have no interest in the struggle between the bosses and the men . . . .

All of the forces of the government, except the military, are now lined up against us. It is easy to distinguish friend and foe. The Porcupine boys, who speak in a dozen different tongues, are standing together as one man. After five weeks of strike, their ranks still remain unbroken . . . .

This strike was eventually defeated, and three leaders were sentenced to three months at hard labour in the Sudbury jail. Ironically, they had to be transferred to North Bay. According to a later report in the *ISR:*

Sudbury is a mining camp, the home of the Canada Copper Co., whose proud boast has been that no organizer for the Western Federation of Miners could remain in the camp. Apparently they were afraid to even have one locked in the district jail on account of the demoralizing effect it might have on the wage slaves.

Labour meeting at Pottsville (Porcupine) circa 1913. George Prusila

Further Growth

The fifth local in the district was established at Silver Centre in 1910. A leading force in this local was Harry Jones, who had been an active WFM member in British Columbia. Harry had originally been a member of the United Mine Workers, but had transferred to the WFM in 1893. When interviewed in 1951 he was in his middle 80s. Harry's membership in Mine Mill expired with the end of the Gowganda Miners Local 154 in the autumn of 1919, at which time he was secretary of that local.

Under the leadership of Harry Jones, the first dispute between the Silver Centre local and some of the mines took place early in the winter of 1911. Up until that time, miners in Cobalt had set the wage pattern for the district, earning from 25 to 50 cents a day more than miners elsewhere, but when Silver Centre began operation, the operators started out by paying 25 cents a day more than in Cobalt in order to attract such efficient miners as Harry Jones.

However, when the operators had secured sufficient miners, they reduced wages to the Cobalt level, a cut of 25 cents a day. The miners succeeded in preventing this cut, after a strike that lasted for several weeks and was finally settled through government conciliation. The Silver Centre local also played an important role on the political front in the fight for the eight-hour day, workmen's compensation, old age pensions, mothers' allowance, and improvement in the mining laws of the province.

The Boston Creek local, established in 1910, was short-lived like the gold mining town itself. It seems to have come and gone, leaving no record of its achievements. Boston Creek is just one of the many ghost towns in northern Ontario.

Swastika Miners Union was established in 1910, but after a few years its activities were transferred to Kirkland Lake.

To consolidate the expansion of the union, a district union was set up in 1910, encompassing approximately 7,000 members. The achievement of the Eight-Hour Day Act, old age pensions, mothers' allowance, and minimum wage legislation in Ontario could be considered results of the work of District 8, WFM.

The earliest record found of Kirkland Lake Local 149 involved a strike for union recognition and wages in the summer of 1919. The local had tried to upgrade wages to Cobalt levels, where miners earned from 25 to 75 cents a day more. After three months, the miners were forced to return to work without having their union recognized or wages adjusted.

⬌

"BIG JIM" McGUIRE

"Big Jim" McGuire was not only big in stature, he made a huge contribution to the growth and importance of the Western Federation of Miners in northern Ontario. He lived to a ripe old age in retirement in Sturgeon Falls, still in his beloved north. Before his death he left his version of the story of the hard rock miners' union.

In his address to delegates at the 1959 convention of the Canadian Mine Mill in Toronto, Big Jim was an honorary guest, where he had this to say: "Today I see you young fellows going here and about with shining new brief cases under your arm. Sometimes I wonder if you might not accomplish more for labour's cause should you do less primping and seek less public plaudit. It may do you well to know and remember that in my day labour organizers went about carrying not fine leather brief cases but a 'rock in the sock'."

At Big Jim's funeral in Sturgeon Falls on August 21, 1964, Nels Thibault, then president of Sudbury Local 598, delivered the funeral oration and the traditional Mine Mill ritual.

✄

The Big Jim McGuire story follows:

"In June of 1907 Cobalt Local 146, Western Federation of Miners, decided to put on a full time local union organizer, in addition to the secretary, and elected me to the job — when they did, they started something. I had worked about two weeks as a local organizer but the progress I was making was entirely too slow to suit me so I took advantage of the fact that the Nipissing Mines was introducing a phony bonus system into their mines. Although only a green kid at the time, I realized then what the facts have since borne out as to what the outcome of this bonus system would be — speed-ups and exploitation.

"Accordingly, on the Monday morning that the bonus system was to go into effect, I went over to the Nipissing Mine and, without authority from the international or the local or any person else, I called all the miners out on strike. And, believe it or not, although many of them did not belong to the union, all of them came out. I know this is going to sound fantastic to a modern labour leader but that is exactly what happened.

"Of course the men who came out on strike all came up to the union hall and joined the union. At least that was a good day's organizing. At the next Sunday's meeting, the union drew up a wage schedule for the whole camp demanding a base wage increase of 25 cents a day, and on the following morning we called the whole camp out on strike to enforce our demands. Some of the smaller mines immediately met the union's demands, but most of the larger mines decided to fight it out to a finish.

"Since we still had no competent speakers in our ranks we got a man named Bob Rhodehouse to do our talking for us — a combination of Big Bill Haywood and Joe Hill. Of all the rough-and-tumble orators I ever heard, Bob was easily the best. He spoke every night on the Cobalt square in front of the strike-bearers, bankers, mine managers, businessmen and speculators, and what have you, and held them all spellbound for from one to two hours every evening for over two months. I say a man who can do that is a wizard of words with a dynamic personality to boot — that was Bob.

"In the meantime I had been charged with violating the Industrial Disputes and Investigation Act which was a Dominion law strongly enforced. I was convicted and fined $500 or six months in jail. Of course the union appealed the conviction to a higher court and, after a considerable time elapsed, judgement was handed down. The conviction was sustained but the sentence was reduced from six to three months. However, due to some technical error on the part of the judge in adjourning the case, there was no legal means of returning me back into court to enforce the sentence. That

act has since been declared unconstitutional by the Judicial Committee of the Privy Council; but that was not the only lawsuit our union was in by any means — we had lots of them.

"The mine managers succeeded in getting out court injunctions restraining us from doing everything but breathing. However, it took more than a mere court injunction to stop our union from functioning and Bob Rhodehouse from speaking. We went right on with our meetings and he went right on with his speaking.

"One day the managers placed a stenographer at a window of a building where the union was holding a meeting and took a report of the proceedings. We were of course charged with violating the injunction act and were brought to court and, after many delays, the case came up before Chief Justice Meredith in Toronto. When the justice asked the crown prosecution to show him where the injunction had been violated, the prosecutor started to read quotations from Rhodehouse's speech, to which the judge commented, 'It is all so much rant and Rhodehouse' and asked the prosecutor to show him the real violation. The prosecutor was unable to do so, and the injunction was quashed and the case dismissed.

"It was in the early part of that strike that I first recall seeing and hearing 'Long Angus' MacDonald, who later became an executive board member of Local 146 and a Member of Parliament for Temiskaming riding. Being a thorough Scotsman, he gave us a thorough tongue lashing for our extravagance in handling union funds, and what a tongue lashing he could give!"

✄

A Minor Skirmish

"One evening about midway through the strike the Union advertised a public meeting on a vacant lot at Haileybury; it rained that afternoon and we cancelled the meeting. One of the local newspapers, *The Silver City News*, came out later that afternoon with a report that the union had learned that 'a group of citizens' were coming to get us with rotten eggs and tomatoes, etc. When we heard this we immediately advertised another meeting and invited the trouble makers and company stooges to come on. Rhodehouse of course was our principal speaker, and I was chairman of the meeting. The meeting no sooner got underway when a swarm of young lads, and some not so young, began blowing whistles and ringing bells and everything else to drown out the speaker. It didn't stop Rhodehouse; he went right on talking and, after he was going for approximately half an hour, I was advised that there were several men approaching with eggs and tomatoes.

"Knowing there would likely be trouble my first thought was to get the kids out of the way so they would not get hurt. I put my hand on one little fellow's shoulder and told him that he had better get out because there was going to be trouble. As I touched him I was grabbed by a man named Gallagher, a stooge dressed up in civilian clothing, who afterwards stated in court that he was a special constable. Of course as soon as he grabbed me I struck him and almost instantaneously five or six stooges closed in on me and the fight was on.

"It was a damn good fight while it lasted, but the odds were too great and they overpowered me and landed me in jail. I was charged with assaulting Gallagher and the Chief of Police, Jack McCall. The fellows with the eggs and tomatoes never got a chance, however, to throw them at the speaker. When they reached the outskirts of the crowd, they ran into union secretary Mickey D'Wyre and, to borrow a phrase from baseball, Mickey dropped them 'one, two, three, in order.' The fellows who saw the fight wondered where Mickey got his punch. Of course, Mickey was an Irishman and might have a rock in a sock.

"When I appeared in court the next day, I had attorney Arthur Slaght defend me. What a monkey Slaght made out of Gallagher under cross examination. The charge against me was eventually dropped from the lower court and I was committed for trial at the fall assizes in North Bay on the charge of assaulting police officer McCall. We found out afterwards it was the police committee of the town of Haileybury that had organized the disturbance. It was proved in court when the case came up that it was the police committee themselves that were guilty of the disturbance and not the union. I was therefore acquitted by the jury.

"The strike was lost in two months and of course should have been called off much sooner than it was, but at that time the old Western Federation of Miners carried out a practice of never calling off a strike unless they had won."

Political Action

"In the spring of 1908 the Ontario elections were coming up and we learned by that time that striking was a pretty tough and costly proposition. We noticed also that the lawyers and mine operators, who had a much more solidly organized union than we had, had gone into politics and organized the laws so that the police did their picketing.

"Accordingly, we thought there would be no harm in trying a little political action of our own and so, in the summer of 1908 when the Liberals called a convention in Cobalt to elect delegates to their own national convention, a bunch of us went over from the union hall and nominated each other in the hope that in this way some of us might get elected as delegates.

"We asked the candidates seeking nomination if they would support the union program for the 8-hour day law for miners, the Workmen's Compensation Act, widows' allowance, old age pensions, and other legislation. They told us bluntly that they would not consider such nonsense and that if we wanted such crazy legislation we should get out and organize a party of our own. There was one delegate, however, who thought our proposition should at least be considered. His name was Attorney Arthur Roebuck, who many years later, during the 1937 Oshawa General Motors strike, established his reputation as a consistent supporter of labour and civil liberties issues. At the time of the strike, as Attorney General in the Mitchell Hepburn Ontario government, together with Labour Minister David Croll,

he left the Ontario Cabinet declaring they preferred to 'walk with the workers than ride with General Motors.'

"We took them at their word and organized a local branch of the old Socialist Party and nominated secretary Art Botley as our candidate. We, of course, had no organization outside of Cobalt and while Art got a very good representative vote from among the miners he scarcely got any vote elsewhere in the riding. However, in the tradition of the policy of the old WFM we voted for whom and what we wanted anyway.

"An interesting sidelight: On August 19, 1908, the first hand steel drilling contest in Cobalt was held. Up to that time our enemies had argued that 'good miners don't belong to the miners' union.' To prove otherwise, Jack Welsh, who was then president of Local 146, and myself, a former president, drilled as a team and won first prize — thus proving that union men, even union presidents, could do a bit of practical mining. There were many drilling contests in after years, and they were all won by union men.

"Apart from the establishment of several local unions and a few local strikes and skirmishes, nothing of importance took place in the district to affect our union or the course of organized labour until 1911."

A Provincial Election Candidate

"In the fall of 1911, a provincial election was called. I had been previously nominated by the union as candidate on the Socialist Party ticket. The first gun fired in the campaign, and, incidently, the first real public debate of my life, was a debate with Senator Arthur Roebuck, who was a Liberal candidate at that time. Or at least it was advertised as a debate. I think that he agreed to the joint meeting and debate knowing that he would get a larger audience that way than to hold a meeting by himself. The theatre was packed.

"We conducted a really lively campaign. Among other things, I walked every square mile of the farm country from New Liskeard to the verge of the mining country north of Englehart and as far east and west as the constituency was inhabited. The mere fact that a parliamentary candidate would do all that walking and carry a pack of literature sufficient to distribute in each home made more of an impression on the farmers than I or any person could say or do. Most of my literature was socialistic and WFM material.

"Of course we had no hope of winning the election but we did roll up a sufficiently large enough vote to make the old parties take notice of our union's demand for the 8-hour day. The union had Pete McCauley to do the work that would now be done by a paid official enumerator. After considerable time and trouble, without pay, Pete completed a list which consisted of some 4,000 names of eligible voters. At that time such a list had to be validated by a judge and 30 days elapsed from the date of validation before it could be used as a voters list in an election.

"The Ontario government pulled a fast one on us by calling the election just three days before the list became registered and validated. The results were that we voted on a list that was a year and a half old. Such a list in a country with a floating population like Northern Ontario at that time meant that about half of the men who should have had the right to vote were disenfranchised. Out of some 2,000 members of the Cobalt miners' union there were only 12 names on this list.

"At a protest meeting which was attended by all four candidates, Roebuck, F. H. Eland, Clement Foster and myself, all four were elected as a delegation to go to Toronto for the purpose of interviewing Sir James Whitney, who was then Premier of the Province of Ontario, to try to have the election in that riding postponed until the new list could be used.

"An interesting point. The other fellows all addressed Sir James in the diplomatic language of politics but when my turn came, I was not too diplomatic, nor was Sir James. I addressed him in good old WFM language and in no time we were into it hammer and tongs. The *Toronto Star* came out with big headlines which read like this: 'Man of North Beards Lion in His Den and He Roars Old Whitney Style.' The *Toronto Telegram* published a cartoon on its front page showing Sir James leaping high in the air and smashing a picture on my head with the words below, 'You rough neck miners from up north think the people down Toronto way are mild and soft spoken yapps.' Needless to say, Sir James refused to change the election date and told us, among a lot of other things, to 'go back up north and blow your horns and be damned.'

"In view of this situation, I realized then that I could not even make a representative showing in the Temiskaming riding, so, at my own suggestion, and the approval of the union, I withdrew and ran in the riding of South Waterloo. Here there was little organization and I did not have much of a chance. In the meantime Roebuck had accepted the 8-hour day program of our union as a plank in his program and I advised all my supporters in Cobalt to vote for him in the hope that he might be elected and we would have at least someone in the legislature to get the bill for the 8-hour day on the floor of the House with a champion to support it. Roebuck was defeated by a very small majority by the Conservative candidate, Bob Shillington."

◄────►

Workmen's Compensation Act

"Our agitation and work started to pay off. In the early part of 1912 the Ontario government appointed Chief Justice Meredith to the office of Royal Commission with the power to take evidence on the advisability of passing the Workmen's Compensation Act. Justice Meredith held hearings in Cobalt. Both the union and the mine operators were present and presented briefs and verbal viewpoints on the subject. Art Botley, Local 146 secretary, led off for the union but had hardly got started when the managers jumped on him on the ground that he was not a miner. Art had worked around the mines for a number of years but had never worked underground.

"At this point the judge called on me to present the case for the miners. By that time I was so mad that I was bad, and when I was bad I was good, and I opened up with everything I had. It was later openly and freely conceded by all who heard the hearings that the union's argument was far superior to any others presented at the hearing. This had quite a bearing on the passage of the present Workmen's Compensation Act. But the fight was not over by any means."

◄────►

The Eight-hour Day

"A little later on in 1912, Bill Thompson's representative of the Porcupine local, Charley Lothien from Silver Centre Local, and myself from Cobalt were sent to Toronto by the union to lobby the legislature on behalf of the 8-hour day law for miners and other such labour legislation.

"The Honourable A. C. McKay gave notice of motion that he was going to introduce an amendment to the Mining Act. When the amendment was presented it meant that he was introducing an 8-hour day law of his own. However, we found out that it was the intention of the government to let the bill die on the order paper and since it was usual parliamentary procedure it had precedent over Mr. McKay's bill and accordingly his bill would die also.

"When we got that bit of inside information, the union delegation went to Mr. McKay and told him what we had heard. He was pretty smart too, for he looked up an old rule of the House that had not been in use for years that gave him the right to force his bill onto the floor notwithstanding Sir James' amendment. This he did, and by so doing we got the first 8-hour day bill before the House. A great victory for the miners and our union. However, Honourable William Hurst, who was then Minister of Mines, moved to give the bill the well known six months hoist. Since the government had a majority, Mr. Hurst's motion carried, which meant that there would be no more action on the bill for at least another year.

"In the meantime, as a result of the union's constant bombardment, the government decided to submit the question of the 8-hour day to a referendum vote of the miners of Ontario. They knew that the miners of Cobalt, Silver Centre and further points north would vote for the 8-hour day, but hoped to defeat it at the Helen Mines of Michipicoten. The workers of that mine were largely Finnish and not too familiar with Canadian laws. I immediately left Cobalt for the area and managed to get a job organizing for the old Socialist Party at Port Arthur. The Finns were then publishing a daily Finnish newspaper which had a wide circulation among the Finns of the country. Of course I had no way of knowing what the Finnish editors wrote in their paper, but I was whispering in their ears all during the campaign leading up to the referendum vote. The Helen miners voted 97 per cent for the 8-hour law. Hence the 8-hour day became law.

"The most important event which occurred in our union and the mining country was the 1912 Porcupine strike. However I have no first hand knowledge of this bitter battle as I was in Port Arthur at the time. It should be noted that I left Cobalt in 1912 and did not return until the latter part of 1914, and, therefore, have no first hand knowledge of events in that section of the country during that period. Apart from the 50 cents a day wage increase won by our union in the Cobalt camp in 1917 that was paid all the miners to prevent a strike, no important events occurred in the mines or in our union until 1919.''

The One Big Union

"In April of 1919, the Cobalt Miners Union received a communication, an unforgettable bit of communication, from the general secretary of the One Big Union at Winnipeg, a national industrial organization much along the same lines as the CIO or the CCL, inviting the local to 'break away from the IUMM&SW and join the OBU.' Executive Board member 'Long Angus' MacDonald moved that this communication be filed. The motion was duly seconded and, following considerable discussion, was so filed that most of us thought this was all there would be to it. Jim Cluney had different ideas, for he immediately started a campaign within the organization to have us send our IUMM&SW charter back to Denver and affiliate with the OBU.

"Speaking of democracy, we were so democratic in Local 146 that union funds were used to buy and distribute a lot of OBU literature which soon was to play a large part in our own undoing and downfall. Let me emphasize this point: we were strictly democratic in all our dealings in this local, as it will be very important to know this later on.

"From here on I will have to deal somewhat unkindly with Jim Cluney. And I do not like to do it for he was a friend of mine for many years and I still believe that he was always honest and a sincere union man as he saw things, but at some time or other in Jim's life he must have come under the influence of the anarchist philosophy of life, that is to say, 'destruction is creation.' He was also the self-proclaimed leader of the opposition in the miners union at that time. Once in an argument he told me that he had learned his radicalism from me. To this I replied by paraphrasing a famous poet, 'My thoughts so passed through you no longer are the same as the food taken in, they have changed to another name.' ''

The Cobalt Strike

"In the later part of 1919, I contracted small pox and therefore was confined to an isolation hospital for more than 25 days. While I was so confined the union drew up a series of demands, the most important of which was a demand for a 50 cents a day increase in the base wage and recognition of the union. These demands were sent out to the mine operators in a manner that amounted to an immediate ultimatum.

"If I had been at that meeting that ultimatum would never have gone out if I could have prevented it, and I certainly think I could have. For it was almost certain to lead to a strike and I would have opposed such action at that time, not because the strike was not morally justified — in my way of thinking so long as a man is exploited by his fellow man a strike is always morally justified — but because it is bad judgement in my opinion for a body of men to go out on strike when they do not have a reasonable chance to win. And I figure that we didn't have a reasonable chance to win a strike at that time.

"Here are the facts: Our local treasury was badly drained as a result of the 'flu epidemic which occurred in the latter part of 1918, during which period of time each member, while off sick, received $2 a day from the union. Furthermore, the international organization had not yet recovered financially from the results of the extremely long and costly strikes which occurred between 1912 and 1914, one in Black Hill, Dakota, and the other in the copper country of Michigan. In view of these facts it will be clearly seen that neither the local nor the international union had the necessary funds to finance a prolonged strike.

"As was expected, the mine operators ignored our demands which left us with no other choice but to strike or eat crow. If we had to eat crow because of our financial weakness, this supplied our OBU advocates, our avowed enemy, with a first class argument that we should leave the IUMM&SW and affiliate with the OBU. On the other hand, if we went on strike and the strike was lost through lack of funds, the OBU had a ready made argument again. It was a hard decision to make.

"Perhaps I should mention here that during the period I was confined to the hospital, Jim Lord, who was president of the mining division of the AFL, visited Cobalt and made a speech in which he was quoted as saying the United Mine Workers of America would give us the necessary financial assistance if we went out on strike. I want to say that if Jim really made that statement he was only trying to bluff the mine operators for he had no authority to commit the UMW to any such thing.

"However, we took a strike vote and the Cobalt miners voted almost unanimously to strike. The executive committee was appointed as a strike committee. This committee consisted of Pat Redmond as president, Joe O'Gorman as secretary, and John Corn and John Conland. There were others on the committee but I cannot recall their names. John Conland afterwards resigned from this committee over differences of opinion on policy.

"It will be noted that I was not a member of the executive committee or the strike committee and did not hold an official office in the union at that time. The committee, however, invited me to sit in and take part in all of their deliberations. I agreed. After the strike vote was taken and all our attempts to negotiate directly with the companies had failed, the union sent me to Ottawa to interview Senator Robertson who was then the Minister of Labour in the Dominion Government.

"After hearing what we had to say the senator agreed that our demands were quite reasonable and indicated that he thought if he could get representatives of the mines to come to Ottawa he would work out a settlement of the dispute without a strike. He therefore extended an invitation to the mine operators to send a delegation to Ottawa for an interview. This they bluntly refused to do and gave as their reason for refusing that they feared the senator might manoeuver them into a position where they would have to 'discuss the matter with me.' I cannot help referring here to a remark once made by the famous fighter Jack Johnson who once wrote 'when a white boxer refuses to meet with a coloured boxer what he really means is that he will not meet with a good coloured boxer.' There was nothing left for me to do but to return to Cobalt without having accomplished anything for our union.

"On my return to Cobalt I learned that the Kirkland Lake miners were all set to go on strike the following morning: so as soon as we had held a meeting of the Cobalt local they sent me to Kirkland Lake to try to work out a settlement there. By the time I got to Kirkland the miners were already out on what would now be considered a 'wildcat strike.' The main issue here was union recognition and a wage increase. The union did manage to arrange a meeting between a committee appointed by the mine operators and one appointed by the local. I was made a member of the union's committee and spokesman for it.

"After some discussion we worked out what seemed to be a rather reasonable compromise as a basis for settling the strike. We returned to the union hall for a meeting of the miners and put the proposition before them. And they voted to accept. The managers also held a meeting in their club house and many of us thought that they would agree to the settlement also, but there was a fly in the ointment. There was a manager who, it was alleged at the time, had built a mill at his mine, the Hurd Mine, as a stock selling proposition, but who had no ore ready to put through the mill and welcomed the strike as an easy way out of a tough spot. I do not know if the foregoing is a fact but it was the manager of this mine that blocked a settlement and prolonged the strike.

"Nearly two months had elapsed from the time the Cobalt strike vote was taken up to the events we are now recording. During that period most of the Cobalt miners wanted to call the strike immediately, but the executive committee and myself managed to persuade them to wait until we had exercised every possible effort in respect to a settlement short of a strike.

"The Sunday following my return from Ottawa, we held a large special membership meeting and decided that there was no point in asking the miners to withhold strike action any longer. Therefore the executive committee, with my approval, recommended that we strike the following morning.

"If some critic should ask why I had switched my position from my earlier stand on the strike, I can only say that I am somewhat of a disciple of Stephen DeCanter: my policy had always been that I would back the union on any and all issues, whether right or wrong, after it had democratically decided on a given line of action. There was the further point — to back out then would certainly mean the breaking up of our organization and, while our chance of winning the strike was not good, any game fighter always had a chance, and I believe then and still do that most of our members were game.

"Throughout the strike, preachers, politicians, businessmen, and nearly everybody else who thought they could help, were making suggestions of one sort or another as a basis for a settlement. However, when any suggestion was presented to the mine operators they always asked the same question, 'Does Big Jim McGuire approve of this?' If I had, the answer was always 'no' regardless of the merit of the proposition. I record this fact to show how far a bitter, blinding, stupid prejudice will carry an otherwise intelligent people.

"With the limited financial support we received from headquarters, plus the addition of certain amounts of money that we got as a result of organizational appeals from other labour organizations throughout the country, we were able to carry on the strike for approximately two months. By that time our financial resources were completely exhausted, but before we were forced to surrender we got Jim Lord, a very able negotiator, back with us again. Through Jim's efforts and the co-operation of some local men of good will, we finally got the managers to meet and negotiate with the union committee. However, they still refused to meet either Joe O'Gorman or myself, so we waived the right to sit on the committee and appointed one headed up by Leonard Bond.

"The committee reported back to the union with a draft of an agreement which gave the union the 50 cents a day increase in the base wage but rejected formal recognition of the union. I must pause here to explain that at that time miners were receiving $3.75 a day and a bonus of an extra 25 cents a day for every 5 cents that silver sold over 75 cents an ounce. Since silver at that time was selling for $1 an ounce our wages were relatively satisfactory but we wanted union recognition and protection against a possible drop in the price of silver; accordingly we demanded that at least 50 cents of the silver bonus be frozen into our basic wage.

"The companies' argument was one of persistently quoting Senator Pitman. Senator Pitman of the United States had previously stated that silver would not go below $1 an ounce in the foreseeable future. Therefore, the companies argued that I did not know what the price of silver was going to be and had no way of knowing whether Senator Pitman knew either, but if silver was going to remain at a dollar as he and they claimed, there was no justification in resisting the union's demands to have this bonus frozen into the basic wage. As a matter of fact the bottom dropped out of the price of silver about six months after the strike.

"I want to state here that it would have been easy for the executive committee and myself to have given the miners the simple fact that the union owed over $4,000 of immediately pressing bills and had no money in their treasury to pay them and therefore avoid taking the responsibility of recommending that the strike be called off on the basis of the agreement offered by the mine operators. But we knew if that was to be made known or done, the mine's stool pigeons, of whom there were plenty, would report back to them and they would probably refuse to give us any kind of an agreement at all. Therefore the executive committee recommended that the strike be called off on the basis of the agreement which was not quite satisfactory to anybody but the best we could hope to get under the circumstances.

"Admittedly, it was largely my job to persuade the miners to accept that recommendation, but the recommendation was made in the first instance by the executive committee and not by me. Before the final membership meeting started, I called Jim Cluney to one side and asked him to co-operate with a view to saving our union.

"He refused point blank to support the resolution to call off the strike and bitterly opposed the motion when it came before the meeting for debate. That convinced me that Cluney was more interested in breaking up Local 146 and the IUMM&SW itself than he was in trying to save it. Of course his objective was to clear the way for the OBU. The motion to call off the strike, which was vigorously debated, was finally carried by a substantial majority, and the strike was called off.

"When the men went back to work early in September 1919, there was a member by the name of Hiram Hudson who was running an underground hoist at Nipissing Mine before the strike broke who was put back to work temporarily as a surface labourer, until the mine was dewatered, at 50 cents a day less than he was receiving while running the hoist. It came back to the union hall that he had been 'sent back to work for 50 cents a day less than he was receiving when he came out on strike.' This news soon spread to all sections of the camp. Of course as soon as the mine was dewatered, he got his hoisting job back at his former rate of wages plus 50 cents bonus that the union succeeded in having frozen into the basic wage. But this action of his and others started the oft repeated story that 'Big Jim' McGuire sent the miners back to work for 50 cents a day less than they were receiving when they came out.

"Since ours was a democratic organization, neither Jim McGuire nor anybody else had the authority to send the miners back to work under any conditions unless they voted to go back themselves. However, they did not go back to work for less than they were getting when they came out, but for 50 cents a day more. Fifty cents of the previously paid bonus was frozen into the basic wage, which really meant something when silver started to drop in price.

"Shortly after the strike, an election was called to elect delegates to the Convention of the Trades and Labour Congress of Canada to which we were affiliated at that time. Jim Cluney's and my name appeared on the ballot. Jim was elected by a ratio of about five to one over me. I realized then that I had lost the confidence of the miners and that my usefulness to my union and the labour movement had ended, so I called Jim Cluney and some of his friends and told them, 'all right boys, I am through . . . you have a clear field and no opposition as far as I am concerned, so go ahead and see what you can do; do a good job for the workers.' What did they do? I suggest you ask Jim.

"This is the end of my story but not the end of the IUMM&SW; it must and will go on. It's the only union that understands the miners. There never has been, is not now, nor ever will be a substitute for it."

Mrs. and "Big Jim" McGuire in their home in Sturgeon Falls, Ontario during his retirement years. Solski Collection

The One Big Union

By 1919, several organizers of the One Big Union (OBU) had built up beach heads in most of the mining camps of northern Ontario, and before long could claim functioning local unions. Some sections of the membership, especially the Cobalt and Porcupine locals, demanded an immediate transfer from the International Union of Mine, Mill and Smelter Workers (the WFM had changed its name in 1916) to the OBU.

A district union convention to deal with the matter was called in September of 1919, following the Cobalt and Kirkland Lake strikes. With forty delegates present, Jim Cluney supported the move to secede from Mine Mill and go over to the OBU, opposed by Jim McGuire. When delegates voted to secede, meetings were immediately held at the local level, and each of the locals voted to go over to the OBU.

By December 1919, the OBU had completely replaced the IUMMSW throughout the district but, although it had sufficient support to take over from Mine Mill, it was unable to function efficiently and soon lost everything Mine Mill had gained. Local union halls and equipment, paid for and built in the name of the old locals of the WFM and Mine Mill, were turned over to the OBU and later lost through sales for back taxes. By 1922, the OBU had gone out of existence in northern Ontario. From 1919 until 1936 when the IUMMSW was re-established, the mine operators were in control.

Organization Falters

At the end of World War I, the advent of the Russian revolution sent shivers of fear through industrialists and governments everywhere. In the United States, the well publicized Palmer Raids, headed by Edgar Hoover, who later achieved notoriety as head of the infamous FBI, resulted in fierce attacks on trade unions and socialist groups in that country. In Canada, the 1919 Winnipeg General Strike encouraged federal authorities to bear down heavily on union organization, harassing union leaders and deporting many rank-and-file activists.

Furthermore, although there was an economic boom in Ontario during the 1920s, union organization in Canada faltered. The conservative, craft-union-dominated Trades and Labour Congress, which was an affiliate of the AFL, failed to organize workers in the new mass-production industries (such as automobiles, and electrical, rubber and chemical products) even while the TLC's affiliates withdrew to their redoubts. Organization literally died in the period leading up to the disastrous financial crash of 1929, which began the Great Depression.

In 1930, the Workers' Unity League stepped into the vacuum and, through its affiliate, the Mine Workers Union, took up the challenge of organizing the metal miners in northern Ontario. Minimal success was achieved in the three main centres, Sudbury, Kirkland Lake and Timmins. Although sustained effort brought some results in winning small wage increases, significant progress was not possible in face of determined and vicious opposition from companies attempting to head off organization.

In 1935, when a group led by John L. Lewis of the United Mine Workers, formed the Committee for Industrial Organization within the AFL, the WUL withdrew and merged with the TLC. When the IUMMSW returned to northern Ontario in 1936, the Mine Workers Union sent its members into Timmins Mine Mill Local 241, Kirkland Lake Local 240 and Sudbury Local 239.

Hollinger Mine Disaster, February 10, 1928. At 9 a.m., rubbish dumped in stope No. 55A on the 550-foot level of the Hollinger Mine spontaneously combusted, releasing carbon monoxide gases which killed 39 miners working down the No. 11 shaft, 500 feet from the fire. Of more than 450 men who went down the same shaft that day, some worked until late afternoon before they were notified that the mine was on fire; some completed their shifts before finding out. The fire burned for four days, while special fire fighting equipment was rushed in from New York. This old postcard records the burial of eight Finns and one Ukrainian who were buried in a mass grave and shared a tombstone for a monument. Courtesy George Prusila

Timmins Organization
Revives: 1936

Timmins Mine Mill Local 241 made significant progress in organizing from 1936 to 1938. However, in order to deter the spread of the union, the mine owners authorized a wage increase of five cents an hour. Membership did indeed drop substantially, with the exception of membership at the McIntyre Mine, which under its own chartered Local 274, had 80 percent of the miners organized and was prepared to strike for union recognition in 1938. Unfortunately, when the company refused to deal with the union, the decision to organize all the mines and call a strike covering the entire gold industry of northern Ontario resulted in a sharp deterioration of the strength at McIntyre.

Ankerite Local 382 was also on the verge of striking in 1938. However, due to the decision to wait until all the gold mines were organized, membership fell off and it was decided to drop the charters of Locals 274 and 382 and combine the memberships into Local 241.

Not until late in 1943 was a new organizational drive launched in the area by Local 241. In the course of five months, more than 4,000 members were signed up, and in May 1944, application for certification was made for twelve operating mines. After a long delay, certification votes were ordered by the Ontario Labour Relations Board. Local 241 won eleven of the mines; the Dome Mine was lost by a mere three votes out of 421 votes cast. Agreements reached with the companies were reasonable, but under War Labour Board regulations no wage increases were permissible.

Shortly after, with Local 241 firmly established, elements within the local started disruptive actions which in the late 1940s and 1950s resulted in open raids by the Steelworkers, and eventual loss of the local.

⊏━━━⊐

THE BOB MINER STORY

Successful organization of the miners of northern Ontario was the product of the previous generation, and owed much to the likes of veteran hard rock miner and union organizer Bob Miner, who was born in Timmins.

In August 1979, Dr. Wayne Roberts of the Labour Studies Programme at McMaster University, published an interview with Miner, entitled *Miner's Life*, in which he outlines conditions in the Timmins gold fields. Timmins had a death rate from tuberculosis higher than any municipality in Ontario, a work week eight hours longer than the developing Ontario average, and a level of personal income third lowest in Ontario, thirty percent below the rate deemed necessary for decent family living. Moreover, one of the area's largest mines indiscriminately sprayed a treatment for

Timmins Ladies' Auxiliary Local 128, 1944. Seated (L-R): *Jean Maisonneuve, Dorothy MacDonald, ———, Myrtle Walsh, Jessie Kennedy, Flo Larcher, ———, Valerie Vedonic, Faye Stephenson, Val Biloki, Mary Orlich (Butte, Montana), Kay Carlin, Clara Simpson, ———, ———, Margaret Slak, ———.* Photo courtesy Val Biloki

Timmins Mine Mill Local 241 office after the secessionist executive led by president Ivan Vachon and staff representative Buck Behie walked out in 1948, in an attempt to lead the membership out of Mine Mill, first into CCL Local 100, then into Steel. All the furniture was taken and union records dumped, although CCL Local 100 was later forced to return union property by court order. Solski Collection

Local 241 officers in 1949, who fought the Steel raiders. (L-R): Dave Walsh, Alex McKinnon, Oscar Gustavsen, Eugenio Leo, Stan Kremyr, Art Leblanc, Con Fournier, Ernie White, Joe Corless, Adelard Houle (kneeling). Photo courtesy Stan Kremyr

silicosis, condemned by medical authorities as insufficiently tested even on animals, in all change houses. The collective bargaining relationship "provided hardly more than a formal, letter-of-the-law vehicle of protest over wages and other dissatisfactions." The community suffered substandard housing conditions and high unemployment, and offered few jobs for women.

These and other charges concerning the conditions in the Timmins gold mining camps were revealed in a brief to the Special Committee Appointed by the Ontario Legislature to Inquire Into The Socio-Economic Problems of the Goldmining Industry in Ontario in 1954. Some of the companies relied on substandard conditions to subsidize their operations, the brief said, and "are not in business to mine metals, but rather to mine labour and the public; and both must take measures to protect themselves against exploitation."

⬤━━━◆

Miner On Timmins in the 1920s

"Timmins at that time (early 1920s) had about 15,000 people and was definitely a frontier town. Practically any mine that was working had a bunkhouse and cookery because the majority of employees were single. There were people here from practically every country in Europe — Russians, Ukrainians, Germans, French, Belgians, English. The town of Schumacher was practically a solid Yugoslavian town. There were no such things as bars — every second door was a bootleg joint.

"But the bosses really influenced people, and quite understandably too. They controlled everything. Hollinger had a huge townsite, a bunch of tarpaper shacks. You could live there very cheap. Dome had a townsite, Paymaster had a townsite, Buffalo-Ankerite had a townsite, Preston Dome East had a townsite. You worked, ate and slept company.

"The companies controlled absolutely every breath you took. They ran the school board. They used to have school board elections on New Year's Eve, and with a quorum of six or seven would nominate a board. On the high school board they were all appointed, all company officials, all the time.

"They were responsible for recreation as well. Each mine had a hockey team and we had the best amateur hockey league in Canada then. They played for $1.20 or $4.80 a day, what they got for working at the mines. Recreation was big thing. At McIntyre, we used to pay 50 cents a month — we joked that we were paying for the grass down at the ball park. The president of McIntyre was Jack Bickell, who advanced the money to Conn Smythe for Maple Leaf Gardens. Bickell took an active interest in the social welfare of his miners and he built the McIntyre Arena, with a restaurant, bowling alley, curling rink, hockey rink and basketball court. To make it even better, he gave every McIntyre miner thirteen dollars a month in coupons for use in the arena. This was good in a sense, but on the other hand it was meant to keep the men quiet. We used to play hockey when we came off shift at 4:00 in the morning, and when we

Dome Mine in South Porcupine, No. 3 shaft completed in 1913. Mike Farrell

were busy doing that we weren't too busy thinking or organizing a union.

"And the preachers kowtowed to the boss. Happy Longmore, the manager of Hollinger, was a lay preacher for the United Church. If the minister was away, he'd take over.

"The first hospital was the Presbyterian hospital, but the Dome practically ran this. They sank a lot of money into it and sent their maintenance men to do a lot of work there. You have to give them credit for that. Of course, what's the difference? They weren't paying any wages; the least they could do was keep the hospital going."

The Dome Mine Community

"The Dome was something else. It had been running since 1910, and a great number of its employees were from Cornwall, England. People who were class conscious to the extent that they took their caps off whenever they met the boss.

"The Dome had a townsite and supplied the people their coal, light and water. They had their own grocery store

with a system whereby employees could get coupons to cover what they had coming on payday. Fortunately, my uncle lived with us, and he paid forty dollars a month room and board. That was the only cash my mother ever saw.

"But the rent was low, so people were anxious to live on company property, even though the boss was looking down their necks all the time. And they figured that the Dome was the beginning and the end of everything. Without Dome, they just couldn't live. As people used to say, their children went to bed and said, 'God bless mommy, God bless daddy and God bless the Dome.'

"Actually, once they lost a little of their fear, they found out that they resented the paternalism of the company as much as anyone. Nobody wants to be patted on the head instead of paid.

"To look back on it, I am very happy that I grew up here, because growing up in such a cosmopolitan community, you didn't have any prejudices. You grew up with other kids — you'd eat and sleep over at their houses, they'd come over to yours. The different ethnic groups brought their own culture and music with them. There were more choirs and bands than you could shake a stick at . . . . It was nice to be a kid here. We thought we had everything . . . .

72

"I went to work in the Dome office at 15, as an office boy. My sister and brothers all got the mumps, so I lived in the bunkhouse all summer. And this Scotchman came through the bunkhouse, trying to sign men up in the One Big Union. I paid two dollars, signed a card, and he gave me a button, but I never saw anybody after that. It never amounted to anything.

"After they smashed the 1919 strike in Cobalt, I guess it took the wind right out of the sails of the labour movement. Quite a few of the Cobalt miners who were union officers came to Timmins, and many of them became supervisors and captains. The underground superintendent at McIntyre had been secretary of the Cobalt miners' union, and he used to treat me very well after I became president of the union here. He used to let me work graveyard shift when I had meetings, which was a lot better than missing a shift. If he thought I was doing something wrong, he would talk it over. Many times he was right too."

⊷

The Depression

"When the depression came . . . I couldn't get a job in the mine. It was impossible. I rustled Hollinger one morning in 1932. There were 3,000 men outside the gate. Across the lake at McIntyre there were another 800. At the Dome, six or seven miles away, there were 600. One morning we went to the Dome, and the captain came out and said: 'No men today.' We walked away, and got about three-quarters of a mile when a man caught up to us. He said: 'Did you hear about an accident? There's been a man killed at the Dome.' You know, a bunch of us went back to see if we could get that guy's job. No such luck. The man who had been killed was one of us. When the captain said 'no men,' he walked up to the headframe and jumped down the shaft . . . .

"At McIntyre, if you wanted a job you bought it. When I worked for the union, I had seven affidavits in the union safe to the effect that men had paid for their jobs. I just had seven for evidence; I could have got 70 quite easily. I started in the mines at McIntyre in 1932 but I managed to get a job without buying it . . . .

"Seventy per cent of the work underground was done on contract — the incentive bonus system. You received a base rate of 53 cents an hour, and you were supposed to be paid a production bonus. But you had nothing to say about the price — the company had the sole say in that. But you could make six dollars a day on bonus, as I did occasionally. But you couldn't get a job working on bonus unless you paid for it. The same for drilling or development work. Every payday, the shift boss would have his hand out. They were a bunch of bastards, that's the best I can say for them.

"But conditions were not so bad. In fact, I think they were better in many instances than they are now. Everything was done manually. Instead of mechanical loaders, you moved it with a number six Jones shovel. But two men with a shovel didn't stir up half the dust. On top of that, you're working now with diesel equipment, which gives off terrible fumes.

"You only saw the boss for about five minutes a day . . . so you were a pretty free man. Except that you had a worse boss than that. You had yourself driving you, trying to make that little bit of bonus. If you did make a bonus, sometimes they'd give it to you. Then the next month, your rate would be cut. So you'd have to produce, say, 20 per cent more the next month to make the same dollars.

"But then you considered yourself lucky to be working at mines that went on all year without layoffs. If you worked in southern Ontario or in a pulp mill, you were liable to be laid off two or three times a year. The companies here used that as an argument for not paying too much money."

⊷

Joins Mine Mill Local 241

"In the thirties, I knew I could be fired any bloody minute. That used to keep me pretty well in line. I'll tell you quite frankly. I can remember one guy named Jack O'Connell at the McIntyre. He was a cage tender, a Nova Scotian. He had silicosis so bad, he could hardly breathe. He tried to get me to join the union in 1933 or 1934. And I said: 'Jack, what do you expect to gain by this? You can't possibly gain anything.' He said: 'Bob, you might not believe this, but some day miners will make a dollar an hour in this camp.' I said, 'Jack, you've been smoking opium!'

"We should be thankful for the men who kept that little bit of a union flame alive. They attempted to organize every mine individually. It was all done very secretively, because if the slightest word got out there was no argument — you were fired. These were men who'd go on the job and organize. You can have a dozen organizers sitting in the office, and they won't organize anybody. The ones who started the union were just ordinary workers, of every known denomination and nationality. They were definitely class conscious people — after all, the constitution of Mine Mill which came out of the very radical Western Federation of Miners, declares that there is a class struggle.

"There was John Higginbottom from the Hollinger, a lay preacher in the Baptist church, one of the staunchest trade unionists you ever saw in your life. You get a good English unionist, and he's staunch as hell. A Finn named Hajerman was a United Church minister, but there weren't enough Finns around to support his church, so he had to work at Pamour Mines as a labourer to support himself. Stan Jermain was a Ukrainian, and a great man with a Gestetner. Big Angus MacDonald from the Hollinger, great big hands on him. He'd been fishing lobster in Cape Breton since he was knee-high with just a pair of woolen mitts. Then there was Ernie White, who came up to the Porcupine in 1911, and Pete Edlund, a Swede who used to tell me about the time he heard Lenin in Stockholm.

"In 1939, I'd been at McIntyre seven years and I didn't like it. My partner was the Presbyterian minister's son — he was part way through a university degree when he went broke. We were walking down the street one night and saw a sign: 'Local 241, Miners Union.' By this time he had raised enough money to go back to school, and he said: 'You know, Bob, you should get in and join that thing. If you're going to be stuck in the mines, you should belong to the union. Build the damn thing up and force McIntyre to behave decently. Drag them into the twentieth century.' So he talked me into it. I went up and joined. Six months later I was elected president . . . .

"Our membership was in the hundreds, out of a total of 7,300 miners in 13 mines. Local 241 embraced all the mines, but each mine was represented by a mine committee. We didn't have an organizer on the job until after the Kirkland Lake strike in 1942. In Timmins, our hall in 1939-40 was right next to a hotel. The guy that rented us the hall decided to jack up the rent. We couldn't afford to pay more, and we figured we would have to move. The guy that owned the hotel came to me and said: 'Bob, I'll pay the increase in rent. I want the hall to stay right here. Do you realize what a move could do to my business? Anywhere from 50 to 200 men came to a meeting, and where did they go after? Into the hotel.' "

Miners drilling into a raise with a stoper at the Hollinger Mine, Timmins in the early 1940s. Mike Farrell

From Cobalt to Noranda

The following account is taken from the October 1936 issue of the *Union News*.

The Union Must Come Back to Noranda

By Bert Whyte

> You may talk about your cities
> And all the towns you know,
> With trolley cars and pavements hard
> And theatres where you go.
> You can have your little auto
> And carriages so fine,
> But it's hobnail boots and a flannel shirt
> In Cobalt town for mine.

— from traditional Cobalt song

"We used to sing this song of Cobalt, the Silver City, in years gone by. After a hard shift underground a group of miners would drop into a blind pig for a slug of whiskey at fifty cents per slug. ('Drink up Mike, you may get killed tomorrow') and soon someone would begin bellowing the familiar refrain. It never occurred to any of us that the hobnail boots and flannel shirts we eulogized were not worn by the mining magnates we slaved for, or that the things we missed in that barren, rocky land — the pavements, theatres, etc. — were enjoyed by these self-same magnates, who lived in fine homes down south on the money we earned for them, drove limousines and even sported golden toilet bowls.

> We've bet our dough on hockey
> And swore till the air was blue,
> The Cobalt stocks have emptied our socks
> With the dividends cut in two.

"Yes, they used to get us both ways. Playing the stock market was our pastime — 'if you don't speculate you can't accumulate' — and we took a constant trimming. But didn't Noah Timmins make money playing the stock market? And Harry Oakes? A run of luck and our ship would come in, too — yeah.

"Mining towns boom and die. Cobalt was no exception, and as the town shrunk in size and importance, new mining areas grew and developed. The miners from the Silver City scattered far and wide, and today you can run across Cobalt old-timers in Kirkland Lake, Red Lake, Flin Flon, Porcupine, Noranda, Val d'Or, or any mining centre you care to mention. Most of the men are too old to work underground now. They do odd jobs, live a hand-to-mouth existence, and sigh regretfully for the 'good old days.'

"A new generation takes its turn at digging the riches from the bowels of the earth. These lads aren't quite the same breed as their fathers. They do not sing as they work. Wages are lower. Manpower gluts the labour market and a vicious speed-up system is in operation in the mines. A man must work his heart out to keep his job. Speed-up means a slack-down on safety measures. More men are killed than ever before. When a man goes underground he is never sure that he will see daylight again. Such things do not make for song or laughter.

"Sometimes conditions reach a point where men revolt, strike for decent conditions and higher wages, less speed-up and more regard for human lives. When this occurs as at Noranda and Flin Flon in 1934 — the mining operatives are thrown into a panic. Police pour in to defend the company's property, which has never been endangered. Picket lines are brutally attacked, all miners suspected of having encouraged the strike are arrested. Men from other areas are brought in and given jobs. The strike is broken. The arrested leaders are taken before an anti-labour judge and sentenced to long terms in prison. Many foreign born workers are deported.

"Unfortunately (for the company) breaking a strike is not enough. The vicious, inhuman working conditions which caused the strike remain. Short-sighted officials do nothing to rectify these deplorable conditions and soon the very 'scabs' who in their ignorance 'broke' the last strike are themselves grumbling and beginning to murmur about 'the

need for some kind of a union' to struggle for higher wages, shorter hours and better conditions in general.

"This is exactly what is happening today at Noranda Mines Ltd. The men who were instrumental through their 'scab' activities in crushing the miners' strike of 1934 are protesting today about the speed-up system in force. Because Noranda Mines employs a large number of 'stool-pigeons' most of these protests are not voiced openly; yet the discontent is there, and small groups of miners often discuss the question of a union.

"In its campaign to organize the mining centres of the north, the International Union of Mine, Mill and Smelter Workers should not overlook the workers in the Rouyn and Noranda areas. The smelter workers at Noranda work continually in a haze of dust, heat and gas and are forced to wear gas bags at all times. These bags are soaked in sodium chloride and worn like a horse's feed bag. The men are expected to work like horses, too. As Ben Anderson, a former boss at Noranda, once said to me: 'I've worked in 23 smelters in my time, but this Noranda smelter is the dirtiest, stinkingest hole I've ever come across.' "

Northern union conference held in Kirkland Lake in the early 1940s. Seated at first row of tables are (from back to front): Jean Poirier, Noranda; Bill Somers, Sudbury; Lucien Boiselle, Val d'Or; Buck Poitras, Timmins. Seated at the back along stage are (L-R): Leonard Kelly, Noranda; Ivan Vachon, Timmins; Joe Rankin, International representative; Robert Carlin, board member District 8; Nels Thibault, Sudbury.

In front of Carlin and Thibault are Eldon Stobo and Hilliard Shebiski, Sudbury. Mike Solski is second from right. Behind him, along the wall, are (R-L): John Stewart, New Toronto; Laughton McLean, Noranda; Emile Chalifour, Noranda; Charlie Coté, Noranda. Seated in front of Solski is Art Jones, Timmins. Solski Collection

Mine Mill in Quebec

Through the early years of the century, unions from outside Quebec were heavily frowned upon, especially by churchmen, and international unions achieved little success. Rather, workers insistent in their demands for unions joined the church-directed Canadian and Catholic Confederation of Labour after it was formed in 1921. The Western Federation of Miners, because of a reputation for radical and socialistic pronouncements, had very little success in early efforts at organizing in that province. In 1915 the federation had tried, but failed, to organize the Thetford Mines.

It wasn't until the 1940s, under the protection of wartime labour legislation, that Mine Mill was able to establish itself in northwest Quebec, but at one stage, reports from the province following membership drives, revealed a fairly healthy stage of union organization. Noranda Mines Local 688 recorded five small mines organized with a membership of more than 800 out of a potential 1,675. Geraldton and Beardmore Local 669 recorded 110 members. Val d'Or Local 654 reported 200 members out of 220 employees at the Lamaque Mine, 120 out of 240 at Golden Manitou Mines, and 110 out of 170 at Sullivan Mine. Malartic Local 696 reported 246 members.

However, although certification was achieved at a few mines, and bargaining with reluctant managements resulted in some non-monetary gains, wage increases were prohibited by wartime restrictions and union recognition was rare.

At war's end, with labour a provincial jurisdiction, absentee owners, assured of full co-operation from the anti-labour, pro-corporation Duplessis government, unleashed a concerted attack on Mine Mill. In this they found an additional ally in the international disruption organized and carried out by the vanguard of the Steel raiders.

Mine Mill was asked to come in and organize on behalf of the international union in April of 1944. Noranda Local 688 was certified July 1944 under P.C. 1003, federal legislation passed in 1943 as a result of country-wide agitation following the Kirkland Lake strike of 1941-42. P.C. 1003 ordered a vote of workers to signify their preference for a union and obliged the industry to recognize that union and to bargain working conditions with the union.

The first contract with Noranda Mines, signed May 4, 1945, brought considerable improvements for the workers but, because of wartime restrictions, no wage gains could be achieved.

Noranda Strike: 1946

"We lived with that contract for a year and then for eleven months tried to negotiate a new agreement, but without success. We went through all the required procedures, direct bargaining, then lengthy mediation, conciliation, etc., but to no avail. With the war ended and labour under provincial jurisdiction, the company took full advantage of encouragement from an anti-labour government, and, finally, on November 22, 1946, we were forced to take strike action.

"We had a lot of courage — the strike vote was overwhelming — but not much else by way of funds and other such backing . . . and it was cold! Our picket line around the company property was seven miles long. The strike was quiet and peaceful but, before long, the compliant government sent in the provincial police who paraded through the streets with their guns and tear gas equipment in full view — an obvious attempt to intimidate the workers. Tear gas, freely used, disrupted picketing, and then the police declared

JEAN POIRIER RECALLS

According to Jean Poirier, Ladies' Auxiliary member, office secretary of the Noranda Mine Mill Local 688, and active participant in the affairs of the union, organization at the Noranda Mines goes back at least to 1927 when the shaft men, protesting working conditions, struck the mine. Later, in 1934, under the Mine Workers Union of Canada, once again the miners walked out. Here, however, because of a foundering of communication between sections of the workers, the strike was abortive. At that time the non-French Canadian groups walked out, while the French Canadians did not. In order to break the strike, the company recruited from the surrounding farming districts men who were not informed of the issues at stake.

In May 1981, interviewed at her home in Senneterre, Quebec, Jean Poirier recalled that in the late 1930s organization again flourished under the leadership of Bill Lewis who launched a union information bulletin, *Copper Bullet*, encouraged grievance activity by the workers, and carried on a trade union education campaign.

Strikers outside smelter, Noranda Strike (November 22, 1946 — February 10, 1947). Jack McCool

Police use tear gas, Noranda Strike, January 1947. Solski Collection

a 9 p.m. to daylight curfew in Noranda for all inhabitants. Anyone on the Noranda streets after 9 p.m. was stopped and interrogated by the police.

"The strike carried on with tremendous support from all directions, trade unions across the country, church and other groups, and with the Ladies' Auxiliary on a voluntary 24-hour-day assistance .... Finally, with the company offering a few more concessions and a wage increase of 13 cents an hour, the strike ended in early February 1947.

"In many ways it was a well conducted strike. No one went hungry or lost possessions. The financial support was outstanding, to the point where we ended the strike without any debts whatsoever; in fact, we ended with more money in the local treasury than when we started it.

"We carried on for more than a year as a functioning trade union until the Steel raids started and the company refused to recognize us on the pretext that with Steel actively on the scene, they would 'sit it out' until the final outcome.

"With an intensified attack on Local 688, and with the open assistance of government agencies and the company itself, Steel was successful in a certification vote and ousted Mine Mill as the bargaining agent for the Noranda workers. Ironically, today the bargaining agent at Noranda Mine is no longer the Steelworkers but the Confederation of Catholic Trade Unions."

Not long after the Noranda loss, Mine Mill, under constant and increasingly intense attack, lost bargaining rights in other of its units in Quebec.

Eastern Canadian delegates, including Bob Miner, pose with International President Reid Robinson at 41st International Convention in Pittsburgh 1944. Front row (L-R): Kay Carlin, Bob Carlin, Sudbury; ———; Reid Robinson. Second row (L-R); Margaret Fisher, Geraldton; Irene Long, Rouyn; Val Biloki, Timmins. Third row (L-R): J. W. Shannon, Sheridan; Mel Withers, Sudbury; Mae Whitehead, Sudbury; Peter Boychuk, Timmins; Bob Miner, Timmins. Fourth row (L-R): Nels Thibault, Sudbury; Wm. Johnson, Sudbury; Ann Kozloff, Kirkland Lake; Jack McCool, Sudbury. Fifth row (L-R): Carl Neilsen, Sudbury; Bart Hunter, Sudbury; Hamilton Shedden, Port Colborne. Top row (L-R): Melvin Lemay, Geraldton; Stanley Strath, Port Colborne; Mike Solski, Sudbury; Steve Quendek, Sudbury. Solski Collection

CHAPTER IV

Kirkland Lake

A S FAR BACK AS 1919, KIRKLAND LAKE MINE MILL Local 149 had gone out on strike in sympathy with Cobalt silver miners who were fighting a wage-cutting campaign by the mine operators there. Cobalt Local 146, first chartered by the WFM in 1906, had been forced into a strike not only to protect wages, but to defend the existence of the union itself. The Kirkland Lake strike of 1919 lasted six weeks and, although a fifty-cent-a-day wage increase was won, the companies continued to hold out against union recognition. The mining industry of northern Ontario was the fiefdom of mine owners and their over-bearing managers, with the workers their serfs. Wages were low and the work place was inevitably hazardous, since safety was always secondary to profitable production.

The next strike of Kirkland Lake miners led by Mine Mill Local 240, successor to Local 149, took place over twenty years later. Although it was unsuccessful in achieving its immediate aims, the historic gold miners' strike of 1941-42 exposed to the Canadian people the unwillingness of provincial and federal governments to uphold their own laws in face of the arrogant, nose-thumbing mine owners.

Prior to the strike, in response to increasing pressure for a Canadian version of the Wagner Act which had legally provided for recognition of unions in the U.S. in 1933, the newly-elected Mackenzie King government had passed the inadequate order-in-council PC 2685, which was a declaration in favour of unions in principle only. PC 2685 urged voluntary recognition of unions by employers; it said employers *should* have the right to negotiate these collectively, that disputes *should* be resolved by negotiations and conciliation, and that agreements *should* include means for solving grievances. But it did not provide any legislative protection for unions either to organize or to negotiate.

During the eleven weeks of the strike, increasing revelations of the mining companies' brazen defiance of mediation attempts and the powerlessness of government conciliators brought more and more pressure to bear on governments to enact labour legislation. The strike conducted by Local 240 in the Kirkland Lake area, seemingly

a defeat at the time, was actually an important victory for Mine Mill and the whole Canadian labour movement. The example set by the Kirkland Lake miners began the progress toward PC 1003, as unions all across Canada began to put pressure on the government for a Canadian version of the Wagner Act. PC 1003 was the order-in-council issued in 1944 that provided the framework for the post-war law guaranteeing the right of workers to organize and bargain collectively.

Kirkland Lake Local 240: 1936

Kirkland Lake, situated in the fabulously rich "golden mile" with its dozen producing mines, was host to the one Canadian industry that defied the depression of the "hungry thirties." The prospect of work in the gold mines enticed tens of thousands of jobless, able-bodied Canadians into the area seeking dirty, dangerous jobs at the pitiful wages offered. During the thirties, with the jobless clawing at mine gates for a chance to earn a few dollars, the mine operators were in their prime.

The mining of gold, selling at $25 then $35 an ounce at the time, amassed hitherto unheard-of fortunes for arrogant, absentee owners luxuriating in vast estates or castles in Niagara Falls, Toronto, Chicago, New York and the Bahamas. The huge profits provided substantial residences, even for local mine managers. From 1907 to 1944, Ontario gold mines paid out more money in dividends to stockholders than in wages to miners: dividends amounted to $474,000,000, while wages added up to $427,000,000. From incorporation to 1946, just seven of northern Ontario's better known mines paid their owners more than $430,000,000 in dividends and bonuses *(IUMMSW Research Department, 1948).*

In Kirkland Lake, with several operating gold mines where jobs could be had — under certain conditions and unquestioning compliance by desperate breadwinners — the

79

oppression reached such extremes that, despite the threat to jobs, organization was the only recourse. Kirkland Lake Local 240 was chartered in May 1936.

Mike Mokry, a union organizer in Kirkland Lake in the early days, related his experience to a seminar of the Winnipeg Social Action and Research Centre on April 28, 1980:

"For the worker in the mining industry the job was hazardous and unhealthy, with his working life estimated at about 18 years. Miners were paid from $4.25 to $5.25 for an 8-hour day and, with living costs much higher than in most other centres, to save enough during the working years to care for retirement was not a realistic possibility. Workmen's Compensation disbursements were inadequate and some work-induced illnesses, such as silicosis, were not properly covered. In the thirties the miner had to prove he was not responsible for an accident before he could get compensation.

"Job selling by mine bosses was a common practice. Jobs were sold on the basis of a specific payment — a kickback — to a mine official to be made each payday until the specified price for the job was met. The worker would be kept on for six or seven months — longer if he was 'reliable.' Discharge on any plausible pretext was common thereby giving another the opportunity to buy a job. Foreign-born workers were the most frequent victims of this job market.

"I started working on surface at the Wright-Hargreaves Mine. Later I got a job in the mine cookery when I was still in my 'teens and, on turning 21, I got a job underground.

"Miners in northern Ontario started organization in the Western Federation of Miners which later changed its name to the International Union of Mine, Mill and Smelter Workers . . . later still (when the IUMM&SW faded away for a time) the Mine Workers Union of Canada, an affiliate of the old Workers Unity League, recruited the more militant of northern Ontario miners . . . . When I started working underground there were small cells of the MWUC and already signs of firings for membership in the union were visible.

"At a conference in Sudbury in February 1936, it was decided to merge the MWUC into the International Union of Mine, Mill and Smelter Workers . . . . I was a delegate from Kirkland Lake and on returning to work I found a yellow slip with my time card—I was fired. Later I learned that an agent from the Pinkerton Agency worked at Wright-Hargreaves, joined the union, sat on our committees, reported on our meetings and had the information of the Sudbury conference. A number of other MWUC members were also fired at other Kirkland Lake mines.

". . . although they built costly estates in the Bahamas and other places, Harry Oakes of Lake Shore, William Wright, and other absentee Kirkland Lake mine owners refused to pay for oil on the roads of Kirkland Lake covered with the crushed rock from underground, filled with silica dust, so that not only the miners breathed the dangerous dust, their families did so as well. The mine owners escaped surface taxes, and with the exception of pittances for water, sewage, firefighting and some other services supplied by the town, paid nothing to the municipality . . . .

"Some of the men fired for union activity left town, but a group of us decided to challenge the despotic rule of the mine owners. A few of us volunteered to become unpaid organizers and the first thing we did was to announce the

As blacklisted mine workers in 1937, Mike Mokry (left), formerly of the Mine Workers Union of Canada (Workers Unity League), and Nick Rozok (centre) worked as full-time organizers for Mine Mill, along with Tom Church (right), living on donations of meals and clothing before granting themselves five dollars a week pay. When open elections were held for the first time, John Ford, a brave miner still working underground, agreed to be the first president of the local. All other executive positions were filled by the blacklisted union organizers, including Mike Mokry, Sammy Longert and Jack Symons. Tom Church became the first board member representing District 8. Photos courtesy Mike Mokry

existence of the union since, in the summer of 1936, locals of the IUMM&SW had been established in Sudbury, Timmins and South Porcupine.

"At first the work was carried on from homes as we could not afford an office. I became financial secretary, elected by the group transferred from the MWUC. Some two dozen miners joined on the first approach. The number grew. Some, who were not prepared to join, helped with financial contributions, gave organizers the odd meal so that they could continue organizing. With dues coming in and

some donations in addition, we were able to open an office in 1937.

"The mine owners moved against the union. Stool pigeoning intensified, the union office was ransacked at night, and we took turns sleeping in the office. Some union records were kept in homes and they were broken into. Periodically a group of members would be given the walking ticket. During 1937 to mid-1938 we lost three complete executive committees, each made up of 9 to 15 men. Active members were also fired.

Dr. Norman Bethune in Kirkland Lake in 1937 on a fundraising drive to finance his mobile blood bank unit during the Spanish Civil War. Dr. Bethune stayed on in Kirkland Lake to help Mine Mill prepare a report on silicosis in the mines. At the time, silicosis was not considered an industrial disease. (L-R): Mike Mokry, Dr. Bethune, Mrs. Nick Rozok, Nick Rozok, Dan Sokoluk. Photo courtesy Stan Kremyr

The union went into the open with a Two Weeks Holiday With Pay campaign in 1937, a health issue: "Miners living much of their lives without sun and in conditions that did damage beyond normal health undermining of most industries, would be considered to deserve much more" (Mike Mokry, "Some Background Facts on Organization of Miners and Mine Workers in Kirkland Lake, Ontario," Solski Collection.) Photo courtesy Mike Mokry

"It is hard to imagine the fear that spread among the mine workers. From the very beginning they could be visited only at night, while in daytime only the brave ones were visited, while we used unknowns in the mines to pass on information . . . . We started radio broadcasts hitting away at the companies for resisting union organization. Every broadcast was heavily censored, and some were banned altogether. In addition to local speakers, we had broadcasts recorded in the U.S. and sent to us, but even they were censored and banned, although they had been broadcast in the U.S. We were called foreign communist agents, but not from Moscow — from the United States.

"Our main thrust for a time was the demand for vacations with pay. Banners were spread across the main street with this demand; a petition was launched and signatures collected at the mine gates, with members of the union's Ladies' Auxiliary participating in the campaigns.

"By the end of 1938 the union in Kirkland Lake became too large and too strong to have all its members fired. Among the members were key personnel and the mines could not operate without them. We then took a bold step — we started to hold membership meetings in a public hall and that was the beginning of open public work of the Mine Mill Union in Kirkland Lake.

"The union operated openly in Timmins for some time prior to Kirkland Lake's public debut, but Sudbury remained a closed town for some time. Progress that was made justified a Canadian District of the IUMM&SW and the head of the union in Kirkland Lake, Tom Church, became the Board Member. In the municipal election for the 1939 township Council, Tom Church headed the polls, automatically becoming the police commissioner and thus discouraging many actions against the union. With Church's election to the Council, Mickey Maguire, a CCF member, who sat on Council for some time prior to 1939, announced that he, too, was a member of Mine Mill, and thus the union had two of the four councillors. This gave additional strength and public recognition to the union's influence."

Kirkland Lake union members prior to 1941. Solski Collection

Kirkland Lake union representatives meet with Industrial Disputes Investigation board in the Teck-Hughes test case, July 1940. Local 240 had petitioned for the government conciliation board in November 1939 as required by the IDI Act before strike action could be taken. The conciliation process took over six months, while Teck-Hughes fired 47 men (six were re-instated). In its report of June 7, 1940, the board favoured 'voluntary' recognition of unions by companies; however, it recommended a cost-of-living wage adjustment. The company rejected the report and no legislation compelled the company to accept even the board's mild recommendations. The Teck-Hughes test case convinced the union that it was useless to deal with mining companies individually and led directly to the Kirkland Lake strike of 1941-42. For Local 240: seated in the background on the right is Tom Church, District 8 board member; standing are Nick Rozok (right) and John Ford, Local 240 president. Members of the conciliation board, seated (R-L): J. L. Cohen, employees' representative; Justice W. M. Martin, chairman; (?) C. G. Bateman, company representative. Photo courtesy Mike Mokry

Kirkland Lake Ladies' Auxiliary Local 77 celebrates the anniversary of its charter in 1941 with union officers in attendance. (L-R): Local 240 president William Simpson, Myrtle McLeod, International representative Tom McGuire, Mary McCarthy, Olga Whelan, Kitty Jones, Local 240 executive members Robert Carlin and Dan Cuddy. *Photo courtesy Ann Kozloff*

The Forties

The persistence of dedicated rank-and-file organizers and the relentless exploitation by the companies propelled the miners to protect themselves through union organization. Local 240 made steady gains in support not only from the miners but from the community generally.

Early in 1940, Local 240 members perceived the need for experienced assistance and called upon the international union. In June 1940, Thomas F. McGuire, an international representative active in the western U.S., arrived in Kirkland Lake to help the local people administer the union's affairs. Under his leadership, organization expanded rapidly and, by mid-1941, the union was ready to face the industry.

C. "Doc" Ames, a former member of Kirkland Lake Mine Mill Local 240 and Teck Township councillor, related his experiences in the gold mining district prior to and during the 1941-42 strike in a Laurentian University Archives recorded interview. As Lake Shore Mine first-aid room supervisor for some ten years prior to the strike, "Doc" was able to observe conditions in the district mines and to get the feelings and grievances of the men:

"In the thirties if you talked union out loud they would find some reason for firing you. 'Get the drift round out! Get that muck out because if you don't there's plenty of men at the gate who will!' These were the words mostly heard around the mine.

"As far as the industry was concerned men were not as important as machines. Men had no security, no self respect, no dignity because the threat was over them continuously. Safety was secondary, the important thing was

'get that muck out!' Rock bursts were frequent at the Lake Shore. In one night there were as many as 19 rock bursts. Men did not know when they went to work whether they would come out alive . . . . Relationship of the mines with the men was at an all-time low.

"The miners staged a one-day stoppage and the mine management realized that the union was much stronger than they thought . . . . Before long the safety inspector came to me and said we were going to have labour problems and they wanted me to head up an employees' association—a company union. I said 'no way.' I said, 'I think the miners deserve to have their own union.' . . . Tension kept building up and I was told that whether or not I headed up the employees' association, when the strike came I would be expected to do other jobs in the mine or I wouldn't have a job. The office staff, etc., were to be given the loyalty test. After that I went down to the union office and joined Local 240 and when the strike came I took an active part."

When the strike ended, "Doc" along with hundreds of others was fired by Lake Shore. During the strike, he was elected to Teck Township council and was prominent in local politics for some time afterwards.

On July 18, 1941, Local 240 applied for a government conciliation board under the Industrial Disputes Investigation Act. On October 15th, the board, consisting of a government nominee, an employer representative and a labour representative, unanimously recommended in favour of union recognition, but the mine operators still refused to meet with the union.

The *Canadian Mining Reporter* commented on October 31, 1941:

> In the bitter battle of Kirkland Lake between the operators and the miners' union, the sandwiched shareholder is getting one sweet grilling.
>
> Truly the situation is amazing. A unanimous report from the Board of Conciliation that was appointed to hear the dispute recommended that the C.I.O., or as it is otherwise labeled, be recognized as the bargaining agency for the men. We repeat, the report was unanimous. The Chairman of the Board, Mr. Justice McTague, and the nominees of the miners and the operators were unanimous.
>
> Then the operators repudiated the verdict of their nominee. . . .
>
> In the pontifical, arrogant attitude of the operators, the Canadian Mining Reporter re-envisions the black pits of South Wales, the coal pits of benighted England that nearly made a race of moles of its splendid humans.
>
> So the management have less to lose than the employees. Of course they have less to lose. Bulwarked by the vast profits that they have made in the Kirkland Lake area which have permitted the buying of estates in the Bahamas, the acquisition of knighthoods, the ownership of national newspapers. They lost only an unneeded income upon which they might have to pay additional income tax — providing they remain within the country.*

Meanwhile, a new piece of legislation came into play. PC 7307 was passed following a successful strike at McKinnon Industries for a revision of the government's wage control policy there, a situation the government intended to prevent recurring in the future. Under the restrictions of PC 7307, the strike vote had to be held under conditions strictly enforced by the minister of labour and calculated to make it more difficult to strike. For instance, PC 7307 required that the strike vote include all employees who in the opinion of the minister might be affected by a strike; the wording of the strike vote was also determined by the minister. The Kirkland Lake strike was the first time this order was applied. On the other hand, there was no equal compulsion brought to bear on employers to comply with PC 2685. The *Toronto Daily Star* commented on this situation on October 24, 1941:

> The situation is, therefore, that the mine owners of Kirkland Lake are in the position of defying the Dominion government's declared policy when they refuse to recognize or negotiate with the Mine, Mill and Smelter Union. The situation is clearly set out in the conciliation board's report and that report is signed by the employers' own representative as well as by a judge and by the employees' representative—experienced conciliators who had worked together on a conciliation board before. During the McKinnon Industries strike at St. Catharines, much was made of the 'fact' — which turned out to be not a fact at all—that the strikers were acting in defiance of the established policy of the government. Now we have a case in which employers are found by a duly constituted board to be doing that very thing. It will be interesting to see whether those who were quick to criticize the St. Catharines employees will be equally critical of the Kirkland Lake employers.

Throughout the organizational surge in Kirkland Lake, Local 240 members had been under constant attack by the *Northern News*, a paper owned by the same Pearce family that ran the *Northern Miner*, long a mouthpiece for nation-wide mining interests. Union members and community supporters agreed that another media voice was essential to balance the coverage of district affairs. They decided to launch a competing newspaper.

The editorial board consisted of three officers of Local 240 — president William Simpson, past president M. H. MacLeod, and recording secretary Lawrence Sefton — as well as two of Kirkland Lake's small business people, R. E. Acton and P. Waxer. For professional direction, John Smaller, a member of the Toronto Newspaper Guild, CIO, rounded out the management of the newspaper, from whose columns much of the information in this chapter is derived.

The first issue of the *Northern Citizen*, a weekly, appeared November 6, 1941, on the eve of the strike vote. Local 240 President William Simpson announced:

> Local 240 is going down the line to win the strike vote by 90 per cent. This is no idle claim; the local enjoys a membership which exceeds 4,000 of the 4,300 eligible to vote.
>
> Local 240 has always been anxious and ready to settle the dispute by peaceful methods. Our union accepted without reservation the unanimous report of the Board of Conciliation. As late as last Monday the union assured the Department of Labour conciliation officers, who are in Kirkland Lake now, that it would welcome an opportunity to sit around a conference table and settle this dispute amicably. The offer was transmitted to the mining companies by the Labour Department representative and was turned down by the mining companies.
>
> During the months of prolonged proceedings Local 240 has leaned over backwards to give the mining companies the benefit of all doubts in its endeavour to arrive at a peaceful settlement. And all the way through, the companies have rejected any overture that the union has made.
>
> The Conciliation Board brought in a unanimous report. Proof that the case for Local 240 was justified is the fact that even the companies' own nominee on the Board agreed with the decision recommending the companies meet with the union.
>
> Because the mining companies have refused to accept the government's Board of Conciliation recommendations, we have been forced to apply for a strike vote under Order-in-Council 7307, by which a strike vote is conducted under the Department of Labour supervision.

The vote, taken Friday, November 7, 1941, overwhelmingly favoured strike action. Correspondence and discussions between Ottawa and Local 240 followed.

On Wednesday, November 12th, federal labour minister Norman McLarty informed the union that the mine operators had agreed to join him and the executive of Local 240 in a three-way conference in an attempt to solve the dispute. The conference was to take place in Kirkland Lake; however, on Monday, November 17th, the hoped-for settlement failed

---

*Sir Harry Oakes of the Lake Shore Mine fled to the Bahamas in order to escape the wartime excess profits tax. W.H. Wright of Wright-Hargreaves Mine had purchased two Toronto newspapers, the *Globe* and the *Mail and Empire*, which merged into the *Globe and Mail*.

Kirkland Lake strike in the winter of 1941-42. Strikers and supporters assemble for a parade. Jim Tester

to materialize. The mine operators refused to recognize the laws of the country which directed them to deal with the union their employees had selected to represent them. The *Northern News* quoted the Honourable Norman McLarty: "The employers will not recognize or do business with the union in accordance with government policy. The employers refuse to engage in any negotiations directly or indirectly with representatives of the union."

On the anti-union side, the *Northern News* reported Teck Township area MP Walter Little's approach: "Keep those professional agitators out of the country. The men will be all right if they are left alone, but these agitators have been working on them for fifteen months . . . . Between 650 and 700 of the men who voted are not Canadian citizens."

Meanwhile, Mrs. Dorise Nielson, MP for North Battleford, had addressed the Local 240 Ladies' Auxiliary in support of the strike earlier: "The eyes of all Canada are on Kirkland Lake. The whole future of organized labour in this country depends on the outcome of the battle you are waging here. Your men are in the front line trenches of labour. If the owners of the mines persist in their arrogant attitude, if they continue to refuse to deal with the union, then the miners will have to go into the last trenches of democracy — the strike."

The Fellowship for a Christian Social Order commented: "There is a place in Ontario, about 500 miles north of Toronto, which used to be called Swastika. It is in the principal gold producing district of Canada. By rail it is only 5.7 miles west of Kirkland Lake. Today, Swastika is called Winston,

but the spirit of another 'swastika' seems to be hovering around, about 5.7 miles east. For the 'swastika' reminds us of the Nazis. The Nazis do not recognize trade unions nor collective bargaining, and the mine owners of Kirkland Lake do not recognize such things either."

On November 18th, the *Northern News* reported that the Association of Clerical, Supervisory and Technical Workers of the Kirkland Lake Mines decided to actively fight the CIO. President W.E. Johnston was quoted as saying: "Unsettled labour conditions in Kirkland Lake have been brought about solely by the entrance of small groups of C.I.O. agitators. We are strongly oppposed to any union affiliated with the C.I.O. gaining control of labour through the Dominion of Canada, and we will refuse to support any political party which aids and abets them in their activities."

The Strike

On Tuesday, November 18, 1941, just under 4,000 men struck eight gold mines in the Kirkland Lake area in the most significant dispute in Canadian labour history since the memorable 1937 Oshawa General Motors strike which ushered the CIO into the country.

On Wednesday, November 19th, the *Northern Citizen* cited Tom McGuire, district administrator of Mine Mill:

Miners' meeting after the parade.
Jim Tester

"Of more than 3,800 employees affected by the strike, not more than two dozen have passed through the picket lines in all the shifts of a full 24 hours of all the mines combined.

"Picketing has been absolutely peaceful. The mines have either given up any attempt to operate or are closing down their mills which they tried to run with supervisory and technical staffs. No underground work has gone on since the strike was declared."

The *Northern Citizen* also interviewed A. R. Mosher, president of the Canadian Congress of Labour:

"The struggle of the Kirkland Lake miners concerns the whole Canadian Labour movement. If the mine operators can flout Government policy and a unanimous board recommendation, then every anti-union employer will be encouraged to follow a similar line. It is, in the opinion of the Congress, also of grave concern to the whole Canadian people. For industrial democracy is a fundamental part of the British way of life and one of the principles for which we are fighting this war.

"For these reasons the Canadian Congress of Labour calls upon organized labour in Canada to give every possible assistance to the Kirkland Lake miners and itself pledges them the fullest support."

On the strike front, a group of strike breakers had been housed in the Wright-Hargreaves bunkhouse. The minute the strike was called, many of them quit the company property, unable to effectively produce. The mine superintendent was said to have remarked that, despite the elaborate preparation his mine had made for the strike, it would have to close down immediately.

Enter Hepburn's Hussars

Reeve of Teck Township R. J. Carter issued a statement on the policing of the community: "Our police force — regular, voluntary and special — are here for maintenance of law and order, and to protect life and property. We are for the close co-operation of all citizens with these men. As I have previously mentioned on numerous occasions, the unions have conducted their affairs in a legal manner and I look for a continuance of the same attitude in the present situation. We are convinced that no emergency would arise necessitating the calling in of outside police assistance."

Forty members of Local 240 were appointed by the local to act as members of a union patrol whose duty it was to keep a brotherly eye on union members on Kirkland streets. The men of the patrol marched the streets in pairs throughout the day, prepared to look after any over-enthusiastic fellow unionist, but reported that "no rowdyism of any sort is visible on the streets here."

In Toronto, Attorney-General Arthur Conant conferred with Ontario law and labour department officials. It was understood that, in line with the usual procedure in cases of this nature, there would be no interference with the authority of Teck Township. Attending this meeting were Labour Minister Peter Heenan, Deputy Attorney-General C.L. Snyder and the Provincial Police Commissioner W. H. Stringer.

Strikebreaking Provincial Police on parade during
Miners Union Strike, Kirkland Lake, November 18, 1941
to Frebruary 10th, 1942.

The strike was peaceful and orderly. However, despite the assurances of Attorney-General Conant, Premier Mitchell Hepburn apparently had other ideas, more in line with those of his mine-owning friends George McCullagh, William Wright (Wright-Hargreaves, Teck-Hughes), Jules Timmins (Hollinger), Jules Bache, and J. P. Bickell (McIntyre-Porcupine).

A special train pulled into Kirkland Lake and unloaded some two hundred uniformed police. "Hepburn's Hussars" as they were dubbed by some, or by others "Sons of Mitch's," marched in military formation through the main thoroughfare of Kirkland Lake.

On Tuesday, November 25, 1941, the *Northern News* reported that Teck Township Council had strongly protested the action of Attorney-General Conant in sending into Kirkland "unwarranted numbers" of provincial police. A resolution of protest was sponsored by Tom Church, M. T. Maguire and Reeve Carter, with Councillor Anne Shipley opposed.

From Queen's Park in Toronto, Premier Hepburn declared: "Some of our jails and reformatories are yawning for some of John L. Lewis's paid organizers." Harassment of striking miners on the picket line and on town streets began: the authorities were actively looking for violence.

On November 27th, the *Northern Citizen* quoted from affidavits sworn out by a number of Kirkland Lake citizens complaining of treatment by police officers now in the camp. One affidavit described the following situation:

"We, the undersigned, were doing our picket duty at the back gate of the Wright-Hargreaves mine, which adjoins the railroad track, between the hours of 4 p.m. and 7 p.m., when seven or eight more Provincial policemen came to us and ordered us to tear down our tent, to which a picture of the King and Queen was attached, and above which was flying the Union Jack. We didn't like to tear down our tent so the police immediately tore it down damaging the tent and firing the picture of the King and Queen on the ground. Then they ordered us away from this location."

"I, the undersigned," said another affidavit, "while peacefully walking along the sidewalk of Goodfish Road, was unceremoniously accosted by an Inspector of the Provincial Police, and told that I couldn't walk along that particular part of Teck Township. Upon questioning the Inspector's authority regarding the use of said sidewalk, I was definitely told that I would be picked up and charged.

"As a citizen of this town, in good standing, and who has served in His Majesty's Forces in this struggle for democracy, I strongly protest this very undemocratic display of authority and demand that the proper authorities take some definite action regarding this matter."

On November 28th, the *Northern News* printed charges made by Councillors Tommy Church and Hugh Kinniburgh in a Council meeting that provincial police were intimidating strikers, tearing down tents and generally making the job of picketing onerous and extremely difficult. The newspaper report remarked that pickets at the gates of the various mines

Every morning at 8 a.m., the entire contingent of Ontario Provincial Police paraded through the town. Mike Farrell

ONTARIO PROVINCIAL POLICE
ON PARADE IN KIRKLAND LAKE
DURING THE STRIKE.

looked small contrasted with the strong force of provincial police that mounted guard at the mines. At the Wright-Hargreaves mine gate, there were twenty-five husky provincial police, and at every mine gate of the eight mines affected by the strike, the police were stationed.

The Hoary Dynamite Plant

In response to a story issued to the press by Chief of Police R. Pinegar that dynamite had been found near the homes of two strike-breakers, Local 240 officers said:

"There is only one place in Kirkland Lake where you can get dynamite, and that is from behind the mine gates. Local 240 emphatically denies any connection with such an incident, if such an incident did in fact happen. This is another occasion where the mine operators and those assisting them are attempting to frame the members of Local 240 and create an artificial atmosphere of terrorism. Let the police look behind the mine gates for the guilty party. This same trick of planting dynamite and blaming the union is as old as the hills. This alleged incident will probably be an excuse to burden the Township of Teck with even more Provincial Police."

In Toronto, Attorney-General Conant responded: "Drastic and effective action will be taken immediately to deal with terrorism in any form. The suggestion that the dynamite was planted by persons other than C.I.O. agents is too absurd to comment."

In Kirkland Lake for a union leaders' conference on the Mine Mill strike, Silby Barrett, the United Mine Workers' Canadian leader, had this to say: "The United Mine Workers have had the Provincial Police and Royal Canadian Mounted Police sent in to their strike areas in the past and in two instances even the militia was called into Nova Scotia. In a situation like this, police are sent in only to aggravate the situation.

"This strike is a peaceful one and there really was no necessity for such a demonstration of force by this army of policemen. We've had plenty of experience with 'plants.' No matter where you go, the companies always seem to have their stooges."

On December 19th, the *Northern Citizen* reported the arrest of Local 240 vice-president Joseph Rankin on charges of intimidation laid by W. Perry and A. Paquette. On Sunday, December 21st, W. Perry, whose real name was E. Perrier, was arrested by military police for deserting from the army and lodged in the local jail. A. Paquette had been released from jail on the day the alleged intimidation took place, having earlier been found guilty on a charge of drunkenness. He was also found to have a criminal record.

Strike Organization

With the strike declared and in progress, the previously selected strike committees went to work. Picket schedules were arranged, finances scrutinized, a welfare council established, and publicity and public relations planned. Following an agreed-upon interval during which strikers were expected to rely on their own resources, strike relief based upon need was to be made available through a voucher system acceptable to the district merchants.

On November 27th, the *Northern Citizen* covered a meeting of Kirkland Lake merchants at which they pledged co-operation with Local 240 in accepting strike benefit vouchers when issued and in extending credit where practical. Landlords promised that no one would be evicted; hydro payments were to be deferred and power maintained. Winter fuel supplies of coal and oil would be available through dealers and wood through union wood-cutting teams.

But all was not all that auspicious. The wholesale houses, for the most part headquartered in southern Ontario and unmistakably in collusion with the financial and mining interests, precipitously announced that Kirkland Lake merchants, customarily operating on thirty to sixty days credit arrangements, would be required to pay for all supplies on a strict cash basis.

With the exception of a handful of middle-class managers and representatives of large corporation branches and the riding MP, the district was in sympathy with the miners and pledged full support. Even the Kirkland Lake *Northern News*, long-time advocate and apologist for the mining interests, handled the miners and the strike with considerable caution in the first few days. Nation-wide support was generous: public bodies, prominent individuals, church organizations, labour councils and trade unions all supplied financial and other support for the strikers.

The mine owners persisted in flaunting their disdain for the workers and the community by boasting that "gold in the ground doesn't deteriorate." By keeping the gold in the ground, they dodged wartime excess profits tax. They pretended, with the assistance of a handful of scabs and the threatening presence of the provincial police, to be in production. Ottawa still refused to enforce its own laws.

BOB MINER ON KIRKLAND LAKE

Reminiscing on his experiences organizing a union in Timmins during the early forties, Bob Miner recalled: "By the time of the 1941-42 strike in the Kirkland Lake goldmines, one of the most important strikes of the war and a strike waged just for recognition, we had just a handful of members [in Timmins], just a few hundred. The strike in Kirkland Lake helped us increase our membership — we must have had a thousand members. After all, there was action.

"We raised a lot of money to help that strike. We didn't ask for donations of 25 cents, like the Steelworkers. We would accept nothing less than a day's pay. A hotel keeper in Schumacher let us use his hotel for a stag party, and turned the profits over to the Kirkland Lake strikers.

"I went to Kirkland Lake occasionally as president of the union [Timmins Local 241] to represent the local, take down a cheque or help co-ordinate relief work. A local hotel keeper used to put me up 'buckshee' — for free. I took a cheque to Kirkland Lake, to a meeting in the Strand Theatre, the biggest theatre in town. Murray Cotterill from the Steelworkers said he was sorry he didn't bring any money

Picket line duty. Strikers used the tent as shelter from the wind at temperatures of 40 degrees below zero (F), before police tore down the tents and banned mass picketing. Jim Tester

Two-mile-long demonstration of support by wives and children of striking Kirkland Lake miners. Jim Tester

Kirkland Lake Ladies' Auxiliary Local 77, 1941. Seated centre (L-R): ———, *Grace MacDonald, Clara Simpson, Billy McGuire, Marjorie Sloan, Jenny Nankervis, Audrey Clogg, Floss Lockheart, Bridie Hughes, Vina Cassel, Vi Benson.* Seated left row (L-R): *Kitty Jones, Olga Whelan, Mary McCarthy, Myrtle McLeod, Hazel Coffey, — Levinsky, — Levinsky.* Standing first row (L-R): *Louise Hodkins, ———, Dorothy MacDonald, Lil Beneki, Ann Kozloff, Vern Beaton, Jean McDonald, Irene Ames, Eva Lindstrom, Sally Wilson, Grace Turcott, ———, Gloria Rooney, Mrs. Cooley, Francis Cuddy, Mary Casey, Monica Lavalle, Margaret McDonald, Kay McGinnis, Audrey Cain, Lorreta Murnaghan, Maxine Cook, Gertrude Stack.* Standing second row across back of room (L-R): *Betty Greenway, Ann Bates, Alice Burke, Hilda Bentley, Ann Allick, Maude Hill, Mrs. Doney, Mae Kearny, Millie Lee, Lorraine Roy, Olive Spode, Kitty Griffiths, ———, — Neilsen, ———.* Photo courtesy Ann Kozloff

with him, but they had sent 80 pounds of coffee and were selling buttons on the streets of Toronto for 25 cents apiece. Hell, when the chairman announced that the miners in Timmins had sent a cheque for 1000 dollars, they pretty near tore the roof down.

"Kirkland Lake was run by two men. Harry Oakes was the president and major shareholder of Lakeshore Mines, a fabulously wealthy man who moved to the Bahamas to avoid paying income tax. Bill Wright, known as the 'millionaire private' during World War I, owned the other mine and the *Globe and Mail*. They both paid starvation wages. The companies fought back with everything they had. Not only the Kirkland Lake companies — Inco stuck in between two and three million dollars to help pay for the losses . . . .

"When they went on strike, they had a certain amount of strike relief. I've seen Yugoslavs go at each other. If any Yugoslav went to the union hall for strike relief, another Yugoslav would grab him and pretty near kill him. 'Leave that for those goddamned Englishmen. They might go back to work if they don't get any strike relief.' When they started bringing in scabs from Quebec, the Yugoslav women were so militant that they got on the picket line one night without anyone realizing what they were doing, with bags of red pepper. Quite a few guys went to the hospital to get their eyes washed out. Red pepper in the eyes is pretty vicious.

"The type of ore in Kirkland Lake resulted in what were known as 'bumps', rock bursts. During the strike, I happened to be in the union hall, and the hall shook as if some giant had grabbed it and rattled it around. Word came through that it was at the Lakeshore, and they were all scabs working there. Most of the mine rescue squad were out on strike, but they left the union hall, went down, and rescued all those men trapped in the 'bump.' Which gives you some idea of the integrity of miners. Once somebody's trapped, there's no question about it. A mine rescue squad goes through hell and high water to get them out.

"It's considered quite an honour to be a member of a mine rescue squad. They don't get any pay. They train like hell. They have contests every year. It all started after the Hollinger [Timmins] fire in 1927, when 38 men died underground. There was no such thing as a mine rescue squad then. They had to send a special train up from Pennsylvania. After that, it became the law to train mine rescue men here."

An Ottawa Confrontation

"I went with a delegation to Ottawa to see Prime Minister King, to insist that the government support union recognition and collective bargaining at Kirkland Lake. We said: 'Tell us straight, is it or is it not an essential industry? There's a war on. If it's not an essential industry, close the damn thing down and we'll transfer all the miners to base metals.' Unfortunately, we landed there Saturday morning. We were told that King didn't work weekends. I blew my cork. 'Who the hell does Mackenzie King think he is? The biggest war in the history of mankind, millions working seven days a week to produce the necessities for war and home use, men standing on a picket line in 50 below weather

while the boss is in the Bahamas and refusing to recognize their union, and Mackenzie King says he only works five days a week?' Someone asked, 'Who is this young whippersnapper?' J. L. Cohen, our lawyer, said: "This man is typical of those he's talking about.' That's the way it was before we got certification rights. The government wouldn't require the owners to recognize a union supported by a majority of the men, and the men were starved back to work.

"I always said that the Kirkland Lake strike was one of the most advantageous, for the working class as a whole, that ever took place. As a result of what took place there, we obtained labor legislation which made recognition of unions compulsory once a majority backed the union.

"For the workers who participated in it, it was pretty well disastrous. They lost their jobs, their homes, everything. I remember Oscar Gustavson, a Norwegian — 250 pounds, and hard as a keg of nails and one of the best soccer players in the country. He went all through the Kirkland Lake strike. About five years later, I had to distribute some leaflets in Timmins one morning, and Oscar helped me after he finished night shift. After, I said: 'Well, you'll probably catch hell when you get home for being out late.' 'Oh, no,' he said, 'the old lady's down in Kirkland Lake.' And I asked: 'She finally got wise and left you?' 'No, no, no. To pay off the last of the bills from the Kirkland Lake strike.' Five years later, she went down to pay the last of the bills from the Kirkland Lake strike.

"We had to support it whether we liked it or not. They were putting up a fight for everybody. There was no pro-union labor legislation in this province. There was a wartime labor relations board in Ottawa, but that didn't mean a helluva lot. They were fighting for recognition. If they could get it, we could get it. And, of course, when the strike was defeated, it had the reverse effect. A lot of people couldn't see any future at all. In Timmins, we gave them everything we had, and by the time the strike was over, we were flat too. Our membership just dropped and dropped and dropped after the strike. Everybody took a dim view of the whole thing, said this was the worst defeat ever handed to labor in the history of Canada.

"We also lost membership because we took the attitude that if Kirkland Lake gold camp was not declared essential, and subject to wartime regulations requiring recognition of unions supported by a majority of employees, no gold mine was essential. We transferred as many of our members as we could to base metals, essential to the war effort.

"The government strengthened that notion by insisting that goldmines couldn't hire men or buy equipment during the war. A couple of mines tried to get around it. I can remember McIntyre taking all its machines underground. As long as it was underground, the government couldn't confiscate it. Hollinger had a little copper project and decided to mine copper, an essential metal. They got a little extra equipment for that. Hell, there wasn't enough copper there to put in your teeth. Now, Texas Gulf has one of the biggest copper projects in the world, and it was sitting right in Hollinger's and McIntyre's backyard, but they never had enough gumption to find it. It's ironic."

Support Undiminished

In Niagara Falls, Ontario, Colonel George Drew, Ontario Conservative Party leader, commented that the Kirkland Lake strike "obviously starts with the fact that the Dominion Government has permitted, approved and recognized the course which the workers have followed . . . (and) now has washed its hands of the situation . . . that is not responsible government. That is the sort of thing that can destroy democracy in Canada even if we are completely successful in our military effort." Colonel Drew urged the government to call a conference of representatives of federal and provincial governments, organized labour and employers in an effort to settle the dispute.

On December 5th, the *Northern News* reported that the AFL Building Trades Council voted financial assistance to the Mine Mill union in Kirkland Lake and quoted its president P. J. Healy: "In a matter of this sort we are united in one common course . . . . We feel that in this case all labour organizations should lend assistance."

On December 9th, the newspaper carried a report of a telegram to Prime Minister Mackenzie King from Silby Barrett, urging that he "should get mine operators of Kirkland Lake to recognize the democratic rights of the workers or resign as premier of Canada." He signed as District 26, International Board member of the United Mine Workers. He was also regional director of the Steelworkers Organizing Committee.

At a meeting of Teck Township Council on Tuesday, December 9th, councillors criticized the attitude of the mine operators to council's suggestion that they agree to submit the local labour dispute to an arbitration board. The operators' reply, which was signed by M. W. Hotchkin, manager of the Toburn mine and spokesman for the eight mines on strike, was an insult to the council, Reeve R. J. Carter declared. The letter "questioned the good faith of the present municipal council of Teck Township in passing such a resolution, seeing that a majority of its members have actively encouraged the agitation that resulted in the unfortunate and unnecessary strike at the eight mines. Also we are not forgetting that we are on the eve of a municipal election."

Reeve R. J. Carter had opened a drugstore in the town in 1923. He had served his first terms as reeve in 1926, 1927 and 1928, and was re-elected reeve in 1935, which position he held until 1942. Reeve Carter retaliated against the mine owners in their own terms. From the council meeting:

Reeve Carter: "I and other members of Council strongly object to being taken to task by this group of men whose letter is signed by a man who is not a Canadian citizen."

Councillor M. T. Maguire: "As a corporate body this Council has done everything in its power to avert a strike,

even going so far as to send a delegation to the Minister of Labour . . . . I deny the veracity of the statement made by that non-British subject."

Councillor Anne Shipley: (later defeated in a bid to unseat Reeve Carter): "Only one of the operators is not British."

Councillor Maguire: "Do you know that definitely?"

Councillor Shipley: "Are there others?"

Councillor Maguire: "I don't know. I was merely asking that information. I thought you would be in a position to know."

On December 10th, delegates to a meeting of the Association of Mining Municipalities of Northern Ontario in Timmins unanimously endorsed a resolution calling on Prime Minister King to end the Kirkland Lake strike.

On December 24th, in his address to the weekly luncheon of the Optimist Club, Reverend E. S. Garvey, C.B.S., Professor of Philosophy at Assumption College, upheld labour's right to organize, deplored the backwardness of Canada's labour legislation, and declared the policies of the CIO would help bring about a more Christian social order. He further commented: "Striking gold miners in Kirkland Lake are fighting for a principle that is justified by the common good," and remarked that "the decisions of the recent CIO convention in Detroit are in agreement with Papal encyclicals."

The United Church Committee on Evangelism and Social Service called on "the Dominion Government to take such action on the Kirkland Lake strike as will make good the promise that the right of collective bargaining through organizations of labour's own choice will be made effective."

Meanwhile, the *Northern Miner* reported on December 30th that the Kirkland Lake gold mines "this week issued figures on the strikers' national origin."

On January 5, 1942, Winnipeg City council voted eleven to five for a resolution calling on the federal government "without delay to exercise the authority with which it is now invested, and to insist . . . that the owners of the Kirkland Lake gold mines . . . participate in collective bargaining with the representatives of the union." Winnipeg's executive body pointed out that the failure of the federal government to deal with "this flouting of its own declared policy is undermining the confidence of Canadian labour in the Government's labour policy, with repercussions through the country which cannot but be inimical to Canada's war effort." The resolution was forwarded to Prime Minister Mackenzie King and the new Minister of Labour Humphrey Mitchell. The appointment of Humphrey Mitchell to succeed Norman McLarty as Minister of Labour did not reassure the union. Mitchell had been chairman of the Industrial Disputes Inquiry Commission (IDIC) throughout the strike.

New Assessment of Strike

As the strike wore on, widespread support continued undiminished, and the determination of the miners to carry on to victory did not flag. But a qualitative change in the wartime climate in Canada called for a new assessment of the dispute within the labour movement at large, within Mine Mill, and especially within Local 240.

Three critical problems had escalated to paramount importance. One, the mine owners were not to be moved from their intransigent position—they had nothing to lose from the strike, precisely because of the war. If the mines remained closed for the duration of the war, the unneeded income from continued production could readily be deferred in light of savings from the wartime excess profits tax.

Secondly, the federal government, for reasons not altogether obscure — the desire to curb labour's demands in the post-war era — appeared unlikely to enforce its declared policy of encouraging collective bargaining.

Thirdly, the union was not unmindful of the fear expressed by the Winnipeg city council that the strike, with its cumulative anger and frustration among workers, would result in "repercussions throughout the country inimical to Canada's war effort."

On December 31, 1941, a petition signed by more than 2,000 striking gold miners was forwarded to Prime Minister King asking him to clarify whether gold mining was an essential war industry. Signed by Local 240 president William Simpson, the petition set out new terms for government to deal with the strike:

> When we sought to bring union conditions to the mines, all the impediments and restrictions of wartime labour laws were placed in our way. We accepted in good faith all the proceedings necessary in our attempt to maintain industrial harmony and peace in Kirkland Lake during wartime. We were told we were a war industry and therefore we abided by all wartime requirements.
>
> The mine operators of Kirkland Lake have been trying to confuse the issue of the strike, which is for the enforcement of recommendations of your government's board of conciliation, by suggesting that gold mining is not a vital industry today.
>
> In this propaganda they have been assisted by the Member of Parliament for this constituency, Walter Little, a supporter of your Liberal Party, who has allowed himself to be quoted in the press to the effect that the Minister of Mines and Resources, Honourable T. A. Crerar, has declared gold mining is not regarded as an essential wartime industry by your government. We ask you to clarify this issue.
>
> We ask it for the one reason above all, we are anxious to be engaged in production that will assist the war effort of our nation. We want to do our full share in crushing Hitlerism and all varieties of fascism forever. Therefore, if gold mining is not a war industry we ask to be transferred to a bona fide war industry in the base metal fields with the provision that the mines here be closed for the duration of the war and not worked by other labour.

From Ottawa, the Prime Minister's reply signified nothing. To the union's request that Ottawa state emphati-cally whether gold mining was an essential wartime industry, King replied: "It is not possible until all the complicated factors involved have been carefully weighed to give a categorical answer to the representation of the petition."

Referring to the request to transfer striking miners to other industries, the Prime Minister hedged: "The problem of labour transference cannot be considered in relation solely to one particular industry. It must necessarily be integrated with the general manpower policy of the Government to which urgent consideration is now being given."

Arbitration?

First broached by the Teck Township Council, the suggestion that arbitration of the dispute could resolve the deadlock captured the attention of Labour Minister Humphrey Mitchell. He proposed to the parties in the dispute that the issue be arbitrated by the National War Labour Board with the decision to be binding on both miners and mine owners. Teck Township community spokesmen immediately expressed approval of the government's proposal, and Local 240 officially announced acceptance and willingness to abide by the board's decisions.

However, on Friday, January 23, 1942, K. C. Gray, mine owners' spokesman, took to the airwaves to announce in blunt terms that the government's arbitration proposal was emphatically rejected. He said: "When will the strike end? I do not know. The mines are getting along very nicely and are prepared to continue at the present rate indefinitely."

Now was the time for the government to exercise the power vested in it and compel the mine owners to submit to the laws of the country. But it did nothing; it did not even respond to the challenge.

With the refusal of the mine owners to co-operate in any manner to end the strike, and the continued refusal of the government to use its power to end the dispute, the miners were faced with the necessity to decide the outcome alone. They declared that, as of February 11, 1942, the strike was officially ended and the men would return to work, hopefully with the assistance of the authorities and without discrimination against any of the unionists.

Strike Called Off

On February 12, 1942, the *Northern Citizen* reprinted this statement by Local 240:

> The strike called against eight gold mines in the Kirkland Lake area on November 11, 1941, after a strike vote was duly conducted by the Federal Department of Labour under Order-in-Council 7307, is hereby officially declared to be over. With the primary issue of union recognition unsettled, this action is taken in the interest of national unity of the Canadian nation in time of war.

The Government has not yet acted upon the union's request for co-operation in preventing discrimination in connection with the resumption of work. It is hoped this will be forthcoming, and that the mine operators, having accomplished their purpose of maintaining the open shop, will place men on a seniority basis, and will co-operate in restoring normalcy in the community without unnecessary delay.

Committees of employees who have been on strike will endeavour to consult with the respective mine managers in order to assist in necessary preliminary arrangements.

In the event of discrimination against men for union activities, which is illegal under Section 502A of the Criminal Code of Canada, proper appeal to the Government will be made.

A resolution calling on the Department of Labour to appoint an official of that department to assist in the return of men on strike to their former employment was passed unanimously by Teck Township Council.

<hr/>

Discrimination and Speed-Up

But discrimination against union leaders and rank-and-file activists was immediately manifest. Foremost in the public eye was the lock-out of some 300 mine workers at the Teck-Hughes mines where the company refused to rehire any men who were on strike. President of Local 240 William Simpson was told by the superintendent of Lake Shore Mines that he had been fired on November 16, 1941, two days before the strike began. Simpson was informed that the cause of his dismissal was "loss of time" while attending a pre-strike conference in Ottawa called by the Honourable Norman McLarty, then Minister of Labour.

On February 26, 1942, fifteen days after the strike ended, a preliminary survey revealed that less that twenty-five percent of the hard rock miners (excluding the 300 miners locked out by Teck-Hughes) had been returned to their jobs.

Reports from those back underground disclosed that a vicious speed-up was in progress. Formerly, machine men drilled seven holes and used steel up to six feet in length. Now these men were forced to drill fourteen holes using steel much longer than the customary six feet in the same length of time.

Very few of the miners were back on their old jobs at their former rates of pay. The practice carried out by vindictive mine operators was to put men who had been rehired on a different job at a lower rate of pay.

Another practice followed by most mines was to hire single miners who had been employed for only a short time prior to the strike and with no stakes in the community, leaving men who had from five to fifteen years of service unemployed. The operators reasoned that, even though unemployed, these long-service miners would stay in the community where they had their homes and owned property, thus providing a surplus of labour. As of mid-March, there were approximately 1,000 miners in Kirkland Lake still not re-hired by the local mines.

Union Growth and PC 1003

In the event of discrimination against men for union activities, which is illegal under Section 502A of the Criminal Code of Canada, proper appeal to the Government will be made.

—*Local 240 statement calling off strike, Feb. 12, 1942*

The Kirkland Lake miners had received the unstinting support of the growing Canadian labour movement and public support across the country, yet they could not get the arrogant and uncompromising mine owners to meet with them. The mine owners sought to hide behind the argument that the gold mining industry was not essential to the war effort. The three-month strike in the dead of winter and its aftermath publicly exposed a government unwilling to enforce declared wartime policies affecting labour.

The Kirkland Lake miners, having lost everything they had, pulled up stakes and began an exodus from Kirkland Lake to industries essential to the war effort. They went to such industrial centres as Windsor, Hamilton, Sarnia and Oshawa in southern Ontario and to the nickel mines of Sudbury. It is one of the greatest ironies in Canadian history that the Kirkland Lake mine operators did more to encourage the spread of industrial unionism in other parts of the province than to defeat it.

As an editorial in the February 12, 1942, issue of the *Northern Citizen* predicted:

> the miners have succeeded in bringing to the fore the problem of labour relations in Canada and the need for a Labour Relations Act in our country similar to that in other democracies. That such an Act will come, and very soon, there is no doubt. Kirkland Lake has shown the need.

In a summation of the strike delivered to the Good Roads Convention in Toronto on February 25, 1942, Teck Township Reeve R.J. Carter pinpointed the significance of the Kirkland Lake strike: "The reason we were selected for the battleground would indicate of itself the need for organization of workers existed.

"Some mining districts have gone a lot further in employer-employee relations than Kirkland Lake. Despite the fact that our district was one of the richest and that our municipality includes producing gold mines from which millions of dollars have been paid annually in dividends, for many years we were a way behind other areas in these things and only a few of the local mines took any considerable interest in their employees once they left the mine gates . . . during the depression years in Southern Ontario we saw our biggest boom and at times there were more than 500 men waiting at the gates of the different mines for employment. This was a very satisfactory set-up for the mine operators with only costs and tonnage to contend with. Unfortunately, when this condition changed, their attitude did not change quickly enough to avoid the trouble that had been brewing for a long time as a result of a number of real grievances.

For community and employees had no contact with the non-resident owners to right the grievances.

"The Dominion Government by its enunciation of labour policy encouraged the men to organize, but when this was done and men sought recognition of the union of their choice, it was found that this labour policy was no more than the expression of a pious wish on the part of the Dominion Government. The absolute bankruptcy of the Dominion Government labour policy was shown when, after all means of conciliation provided by the Government were exhausted, and the Conciliation Board of the Government brought in a unanimous decision, a strike still resulted.

"My observation is that the employers should realize that we cannot educate and encourage men to believe in the democratic process in every phase of life, and continue to deny it to them in their industrial relations, the most important of all. Until the Government realizes this and institutes a fair and effective labour policy and puts definite responsibilities on both employer and employee organizations, we are only storing up troubles for ourselves in Canada.

"In Kirkland Lake our strike is officially over. Never had a group of men such an opportunity as the mining operators have today to enlist their workers in a spirit of co-operation letting by-gones be by-gones, turn over a new leaf, and right the existing grievances. If, as maintained by the mine operators, the organization for which recognition was sought is not needed for protection of their employees, they have a glorious chance now to prove that they were right."

On February 26, 1942, Local 240 presented a petition to the Speaker of the House of Commons, calling upon the government to appropriate sufficient funds to assist miners who had been discriminated against by the gold mine operators to move to other industrial centres where they might work in the production of munitions and other wartime materials.

Also on February 26th, the *Northern Citizen* reported that, in answer to a question from Clarie Gillis, CCF MP for Cape Breton South with respect to discriminatory hiring practices, Labour Minister Humphrey Mitchell responded: "The strikers returned to work unconditionally."

The newspaper pointed out the comparison to unconditional surrender evoked by Mitchell's words.

Immediate reaction was a tremendous surge of organization by metal miners in northern Ontario and in British Columbia. Organization of the nickel mining workers in the Sudbury region advanced at an amazing pace, reaching membership of some 6,000 workers in less than one year. In British Columbia the union, although smaller than in northern Ontario, grew with equal speed.

In 1943, pressure from unions for collective bargaining became a powerful movement. Resistance by employers continued unabated. Labour-management relations had become a major problem for governments. Shortages of workers became so acute the federal government National Selective Service was forced to conscript workers for essential war industries.

In this critical political atmosphere, the legislature of British Columbia decided to take action in the summer of 1943: collective bargaining was made compulsory by law. A month later, similar legislation was enacted in the province of Ontario. In both of those provinces, the CCF had made major gains.

The federal government finally felt compelled to act. In 1943, it set up a public inquiry to investigate "the present causes of labour unrest in this critical period." The majority report suggested the biggest cause of labour unrest was the lack of legal guarantees for collective bargaining. In addition, it stated that company unions set up to keep out bona fide unions were part of the problem.

Government recognition of the role of freely-selected labour organizations in a democratic society came in February 1944, with the enactment of order-in-council PC 1003, which guaranteed the right of workers to choose the union they wanted to represent them without outside interference and directed the employer to bargain in good faith with the union.

PC 1003 was applied across Canada in war industries that came under wartime emergency regulations. Most of these industries, such as the Sudbury nickel operations, reverted to provincial labour regulations when the war ended, but at the time, PC 1003 was a potent legal force that cleared the way for a new era for unions in Canada.

CHAPTER V

Sudbury Local 598

I N ITS HEYDAY, SUDBURY LOCAL 598 WAS NOT ONLY THE largest, most successful local in the International Union of Mine, Mill and Smelter Workers, it was the largest trade union local in Canada. The early history of the area shows how many years of struggle to build the union made the Sudbury local strong, not only in terms of its size, but also in terms of its commitment to the principles of unionism advocated first by the WFM and then by Mine Mill.

Early History

In the aggressively entrepreneurial atmosphere of the early 1900s, owners of mining companies considered the right to make profits the only universal right. For them, the Sudbury basin represented an area rich in nickel, copper and precious metals, waiting to be mined, smelted, refined and converted into incalculable wealth for those with the finances necessary to build the structure that would make it all possible. The right to decent working conditions was not even considered. People who had nothing to barter but their labour were driven by need to work hard, long hours at near starvation wages in extremely hazardous surroundings. John F. Thompson, former president and chairman of the board of Inco, recalled conditions in the reduction plant in 1906:

> The work week for everybody on shift was eighty-four hours. We worked ten-hour days one week, fourteen-hour nights the next week and, to accomplish the shift changes, twenty-four hours on Sunday, with twenty-four hours off the following Sunday. That was the work schedule that had been in existence for many years in the metal industry.[1]

In the mines and offices, he wrote: "The workday for people in the mines was twelve hours — from 6 a.m. to 6 p.m.; for office workers, ten and one-half hours, from 7:45 a.m. to 6:15 p.m. Overtime was frequent." On top of this, Thompson recalls, most men "preferred to walk along the railroad tracks between Sudbury and Copper Cliff rather than take the stage coach."

Jim Tester, Sudbury labour historian, questions whether most men actually preferred to walk:

> Why would they prefer to walk the two miles to Sudbury along the railroad tracks, after having worked a 10-hour day, or a 14-hour shift? The answer isn't too difficult to figure out. A miner earned the princely sum of $1.75 a day. A labourer earned a daily wage of $1.00, foreman $2.00, machinist $2.25 and blacksmith $2.50. The stage-coach fare was 25 cents. Who could afford to ride it?[2]

In contrast, far from the mining camps, on New York's Wall Street, decisions governing miners' lives were being made by such men as Colonel Robert Means Thompson, Inco's first chairman . . .

> an Annapolis alumnus, he never missed an Army-Navy football game. From hobnobbing around Europe with the Kaiser, the Rothschilds, the Prince of Wales, he'd return to the States each season, charter a special train, deck it in Navy colours, and ferry his friends to the event. Then, in top hat and cane, he'd lead the team onto the football field.[3]

Inevitably, unbearable conditions forced the workers to consider means of inducing the industry's owners to ameliorate conditions and to establish decent living wages, security of employment, and safer work places.

---

[1]John F. Thompson and Norman Beasley, *For the Years to Come: A Story of International Nickel of Canada*, Toronto, 1960.

[2]Jim Tester, *The Shaping of Sudbury: A Labour View, An address to a public meeting of The Sudbury & District Historical Society* (pamphlet), published by Mine Mill Local 598, April, 1980, p. 13.

[3]"The Arrogance of Inco," *Canadian Business*, May, 1979.

Miners at Victoria Mine, Mond Nickel Co., east of Sudbury in 1903. Nickel Centre Coniston
Branch Library

Smelter workers at Victoria Mine 1903. Nickel Centre Coniston Branch Library

GARSON WFM LOCAL 182: 1913

The earliest available data on worker organization in the Sudbury area is contained in the translation from *Suomalaiset Nikkelialueella (Finns in the Nickel Basin)*, a commemorative booklet published by Vapaus Publishing Co. in 1937 on the 25th anniversary of the founding of the Finnish Organization Local 16 in Sudbury.

> Nearly 30 years ago, in 1909, the miners at Garson Mine, with a show of solidarity, were able to thwart the employer's attempt to "lower the boom."
>
> What had happened is that during blasting operations underground, a drill, which Gus Viitasaari had buried under some loose ore nearby, had been damaged. The practice then and in later years was to cover the equipment near the working area and not to drag or carry them a great distance before blasting, and thirty years ago drills were a great deal heavier.
>
> Despite all the precautions that had been taken to assure that the tools were protected, a drill was damaged. The supervision of Garson Mine (Mond Nickel) demanded that Gus pay for the damaged drill. Naturally he did not agree to this.
>
> Gus had been working on the night shift and as soon as the news of the company position became known to the miners on the day shift they understood that this was of grave importance to them all because it was not unusual for tools to break or disappear in the underground workings. And if they should give in this time there would be a possibility of recurring cuts in pay for the future.
>
> Despite the fact that there was no union in the area the miners had a deep sense of solidarity and co-operation. On the basis of the discussions on the issues involved, the day shift went on strike with the demand that Gus would be taken back to work and he need not pay for the damaged drill.
>
> Because of the solid front put up by the miners, the Company had no alternative but to take Gus back to work under the conditions laid down by the miners.

> The first strike at Garson Mine, and perhaps of the whole Sudbury basin, did not last a whole day and ended as honourably as possible — with full victory for the miners. And an indication of the spirit that prevailed in Garson in those early years is the fact that the Western Federation of Miners were able to establish their first union local in the Sudbury basin — in Garson.

WFM Local 182 was chartered in Garson on March 9, 1913. However, because of overwhelming pressure from management, this first local in the Sudbury basin lasted only one year, its membership hounded out of the industry.

SUDBURY DISTRICT WFM LOCAL 183: 1913

Nevertheless, organization continued, and from Garson the union movement spread to other Mond mines at Stobie, Gertrude and Worthington. Workers for the Canadian Copper Company in Creighton, Crean Hill and Copper Cliff also joined the union. On April 18, 1913, Sudbury District Local 183 was chartered.

As the union showed signs of growth, the companies went into action with the notorious Pinkerton spy agency imported from the U.S. Little by little, union men lost their jobs, and a vicious blacklisting system came into being in the district.

When the union still persevered, the union offices in Garson and Sudbury were ransacked in 1915; the safe was opened, and union material, including membership lists, was stolen. As a result of these activities, union members, the majority of whom were Finnish miners, were blacklisted and the local collapsed during the years 1915-1916. The local's membership minutes, in the Finnish language, were deposited with the Western Federation of Miners.

The Finnish president and secretary of Western Federation of Miners Local 182 in Garson 1913.
Solski Collection

Bird's eye view of the Canadian Copper Company smelter at Copper Cliff 1913. Public Archives of Canada PA-30015

CONISTON MINE MILL LOCAL 116: 1919

Local 116 was chartered in Coniston in 1919, this time by WFM successor IUMMSW, and lasted until 1920. In 1933, the Workers Unity League attempted to organize Sudbury miners into the Mine Workers Union of Canada, but withdrew in 1934.

By 1933, some 340 men worked at the smelter in Coniston, but only 116 company houses existed. The new housing in the immigrant community was, of course, smaller and of lesser quality than that of management, but, nevertheless, reasonable housing of a private nature was built at a time when the average labourer's wage was only 45 cents an hour. Boarding houses were used to accommodate the additional men the smelter required. Because only three or four existed, the famous system of "hot bedding" was used, whereby men slept in shifts in their respective beds according to their rotating schedule at the smelter.

Coniston Village 1913: company homes provided for supervisors, foremen and skilled tradesmen, who were mainly Anglo-Saxons. Photo courtesy Nickel Centre Coniston Branch Library

Roastyard at the Copper Cliff mine 1913. The high sulphur content of the Sudbury nickel-copper ore was burned off by heap roasting in order to produce standard matte. Cars running on trestles carried 2-3,000 tons of ore to sites where cordwood and dead pine had been laid down; the heap was set afire and sulphur burned off for three to four months. The effect of sulphur dioxide fumes on vegetation was disastrous, but was not found to be unhealthy for the men. Photo by H. N. Topley from the Geological Collection in the Public Archives of Canada

Polock Town, Coniston: area occupied by immigrant Ukrainian and Polish workers. Photo courtesy Nickel Centre Coniston Branch Library

The Thirties

Nick Stempien, a retired Frood miner interviewed in 1981, summarized working conditions in Sudbury in the thirties: "Conditions in the mine were terrible in the early days. Very hot and men were driven like slaves. Safety? There was no such thing. There was at least one man killed a week. I personally helped to dig out three men in one day. They fired men for no reason at all. One poor fellow, a family man with seven kids, pleaded with them not to let him go but to no avail. He ended up blowing himself up with a stick of dynamite at the city dump on Frood Road. That's the kind of pension he got for his hard work."*

SUDBURY LOCAL 239: 1936

In the mid 1930s, George "Scotty" Anderson and his younger brother Hugh, both employees of Falconbridge Mines, launched a new organizing campaign. Sudbury Mine Mill Local 239 was chartered March 31, 1936. Hugh, secretary of Local 239, took on the editorship of one of the first union papers in the district, the *Union News*, whose pages reported conditions then prevailing.**

The first public meeting of Mine Mill Local 239 was held at St. Anne's Parish Hall in Sudbury, in April 1936. Greetings were delivered by Mayor W. J. Cullen and Leo Gauthier, later federal Member of Parliament for one of the Sudbury ridings. By May, Local 239 had 150 members. In September of 1936, George Anderson was appointed international representative of the IUMMSW, the sole organizer on the union payroll for the Sudbury area.

Inco's response to the presence of the union indicated it would not tolerate any attempts to interfere with its tyrannical rule over its workers. George Anderson was molested by thugs and the union office wrecked. As was normal practice, spies were hired.

In September 1936, the *Union News* reported that Mr. I. N. Petelka, in a statement sworn before a Notary Public in Sudbury, admitted having received a letter of introduction from Mr. Paul L. Keller, head of the Auxiliary Company of Canada (a private detective agency, but more familiarly known as a stool pigeon agency in the employ of big mining companies) addressed to Mr. Donald McAskil, general

manager of Inco. The purpose of the letter was to get Mr. Petelka a job in the Copper Cliff smelter under the assumed name of Ivan Pavlew, so as to enable him to enter the membership of Sudbury Local 239 and secure its membership lists and plans. After that, he would be dismissed by the company, ostensibly because of Red sympathies, in order to avoid any suspicions of union members and officials falling on him. Many years later, George related the following:

"During the organizational campaign in the 'hungry thirties' we had a meeting in the Grand Theatre in Sudbury. Inco threw a free booze party in the afternoon, transported over 300 intoxicated potential goons to the meeting. We didn't get a chance to speak. We were howled and booed beyond any opportunity to convey the union message to the workers of Sudbury. The city police stood by and laughed, ignoring the most foul and filthy language being screamed at us, no matter that many women were in the audience.

"We protested bitterly to the then Attorney General of Ontario, Arthur Roebuck, who gave us good advice: 'Go back and build your union. Only then will you successfully beat the company and their hirelings.' "

In September 1936, Inco and Falconbridge announced voluntary wage increases of five percent, a further attempt to stall development of the union.[4] Further increases of ten percent were announced in the March 1937 issue of the *Union News*, along with formation of a company union for Inco's 10,000 employees and establishment of a Workman's Council at Falconbridge Nickel Mines. These increases indicated that the union had partially succeeded in challenging the mining companies, but union organizers still faced many obstacles before a secure union would be built.

International headquarters was unable to provide assistance. Due to lack of funds, George Anderson was removed from the international payroll in December 1937, and was elected local secretary. An appeal for financial aid from Anderson to international secretary John Sherwood received the following reply: "At this time I cannot take up the donation as I am broke like the rest of us are no doubt, but I will send this to you after pay day and make it as much as I can." The correspondence also revealed other appeals to headquarters:

"The Toronto papers state that John L. Lewis is coming to Toronto for May Day. If it is at all possible we would like to get him here . . . with the amount of men working in this industry in Sudbury it would be one of the best places in Ontario he could possibly come to . . . we will prepare well for it and guarantee good results. This is one of the largest campaigns being conducted in Canada at the present time.

"The situation here is still tough. We cannot secure a hall or theatre to hold meetings in, but we expect the settlement of the Oshawa strike to help us on this."

With the chronic shortage of funds and the loss of George Anderson as full-time organizer, membership declined. By August 1938, only 29 members remained. The local was dissolved in 1939.

---

*The February 1937 issue of the *Union News* reported that Edward Daulut, 59, father of seven children, committed suicide by holding a stick of dynamite in his teeth and lighting the fuse. After eighteen years of service at Inco's Frood and Garson mines, he had been fired from the Frood mine and had been unable to get his job back.

**The first Sudbury district union paper was published during the organizing effort of the Mine Workers Union of Canada and was edited by Neilo Makela, who later joined the Mackenzie-Papineau Battalion of the International Brigades. He died in Spain, fighting the Fascist uprising. In his turn, Hugh Anderson died in Sicily, an infantryman in the Canadian forces, fighting the Hitler-Mussolini fascists.

[4]*Union News*, October 1936.

FALCONBRIDGE LOCAL 361: 1937

Mine Mill Local 361, covering Falconbridge mine workers, was chartered in July 1937. Harold Lewis, secretary of Local 361 in the late 1930s, recalled that they organized the union in small cells to protect themselves from informers. In a June 1981 interview, he said union meetings were held in his house on Church Street in Garson with the men entering one at a time to avoid detection. When a company informer appeared at the front of the house, the men would leave by the back door into the bush through Mr. Lucas' farm. "We kept the union alive until the big organizing push in the early 1940s. Jock Davidson and I signed up over 200 members in three weeks in the Garson area." Local 361 was dissolved in 1938.

Vapaus office on Elm Street circa 1929. George Prusila

The Forties

Although physical violence against unionists by bullies was ignored by law enforcement agencies, and despite continued company espionage and firings for suspected union membership, organization continued secretly, but unabated. When Locals 239 and 361 foundered, determined unionists continued spreading the union message and began organizing into a new unit.

SUDBURY LOCAL 598: 1942

In 1941, secret meetings were held in miners' homes and a year later Mine Mill went public with its organizing campaign when it opened an office on Durham Street in Sudbury. On February 24, 1942, a dozen goons ransacked the office in broad daylight, beating union workers Forrest Emerson and Jack Whelahan so badly they had to be hospitalized. A former union officer said of Jack Whelahan, "His face was like an old piece of liver."[5]

In response, Mine Mill secretly distributed 10,000 handbills protesting this outrageous act of terrorism by the company and revealing the names of some of the attackers, several of whom were Inco shift bosses apparently at work at the time of the attack.

Sudbury's police, established presumably to protect citizens in their lawful activities, did not interfere with the vicious destruction of the union office and serious injury to

two unionists in broad daylight, on a major city street. Rather, police apprehended Jack McCool and Mine Mill representative Robert Carlin for distributing the handbill, and at the police station warned them they were breaking a city by-law prohibiting littering.

McCool, later financial secretary of Local 598, recalls that at the time of the smashing of the union office in 1942, his wife kept a baseball bat at the door in case these goons, who were reported looking for Jack, came calling.

In the wake of the brutal attack on union officials, condoned by the police and the Sudbury media, Mine Millers were forced to keep their activities secret, but they continued to sign up sympathetic workers in small, independent groups or cells. Public meetings were rare, as contracts for leases would suddenly be cancelled at the last moment. Out-of-town organizers found it equally difficult to obtain accommodation, although Robert Carlin, brought in from Kirkland Lake, eventually found lodging at the Frontenac Hotel, where he held meetings.

In these circumstances, Sudbury Local 598 was chartered on April 21, 1942, with the following as the first executive board:

President	Mel Withers
Vice-President	Archie Smith
Financial Secretary	John Billoki
Recording Secretary	Joseph More
Conductor	Larry Bennett
Warden	Grant Cranston
Trustees	Robert Miner
	James Kidd
	Angelo Barbisan

Following the time-honoured procedure of big mining companies and the practice recommended by Mackenzie King, Inco attempted to forestall the accomplishments

---

[5]Jim Tester, p. 25.

MURDER WILL OUT!

To all citizens and workers of Sudbury we present the true facts concerning the murderous, storm-trooper raid on the Durham Street office which took place Tuesday, February 24th. Behind it was the fascist hand of INCO - - - as we all have suspected. Where did we get the truth? From two of the degenerates who sold out all principle, all honor, all Canadianism, to INCO, and stooped beneath the level of Huns - - - from two of the "loyal workers" who took part in the attempted massacre of two union organizers.

The affair was engineered by Harry Smith, Superintendent of the Frood Mine - - - establishing the whole thing as a viscious INCO plot. Here are seven of the Frood scum who made the raid. There were twelve altogether - - - against two peaceful men in a quiet office. Two of these seven have talked.

GORCE, Louis	**STILLMAC, Stinky**
FORAN, Jack	**O'MALLEY, George**
McKAY, Neil	**LINDSEY, Tom**
JOHNSTON, Jack	

Fuehrer Harry Smith told the above - - - and note the stope bosses - - - to "go the limit" in wrecking the office and everything in it. He told them to "do a good job on the organizers". He told them "not to worry about broken bones or smashed teeth or anything like hospital bills". He told them they wouldn't get caught "because the police would be someplace else at the time". He told them "not to worry about getting back on the job - - - your pay will continue". This is the violence that INCO and their blowzy prostitute "Sudbury Star" blame on the union.

And, as a Sudbury policeman - - - a "guardian of law and order" - - - later remarked, "they sure did a GOOD job". Well, Hitler would call it good - - - it's what he ordered. Whelehan - - - a citizen of Sudbury for over fifteen years - - - was beaten unmercifully with fists and furniture. Emerson - - - an American citizen of Canadian parentage - - - had his head laid open with a cudgel and was beaten with anything they could pick up. Both got the boots when they were half unconcious and bleeding profusely on the floor. Either could have been killed.

The unspeakable "Sudbury Star" has been editorially demanding why the men don't go into court and prove it. The answer is that the men who did this dirty work between 5:15 and 5:30 p.m. were punched in at the mine for the four o'clock shift. INCO had nice alibis all prepared.

This may be what INCO wants - - - it may be what the Star wants - - - but it is not what we want, and not what Sudbury wants. We are not going to stand for this kind of a deal. We are fighting for democracy abroad. We do not propose to accept fascism here in Canada and the above is plain Hitler fascism, and nothing else.

We want better wages, hours and working conditions. We want security and seniority recognition on the job. We want a lot of things so far denied to us by INCO - - - and, ABOVE ALL, we want decency and democracy in Canada. Neither INCO nor anybody else can prevent us from being true Canadians - - - and fighting for what we know is right.

THIS BETTER NOT HAPPEN AGAIN

Rank and File Sudbury Miners and Smeltermen

A photocopy of the handbill that was distributed door-to-door following the Inco-inspired attack on the union office on Durham Street in Sudbury on Tuesday, February 24, 1942. Ten thousand copies were distributed secretly at night to workers' homes. Courtesy John Biloki.

of the union by setting up its own company union. The United Copper-Nickel Workers (UCNW) was established in November 1942. A true company union, it was financed by Inco at a cost of $68,000 and had its office on Inco property.[6] Without any consultation with the rank-and-file, a contract was drawn up by company lawyers, signed by the officers of the UCNW, and distributed in book form to all Inco employees. Miners called it the "Nickel Rash," after the nickel dust that got into the pores of their skin and caused an irritating rash. Needless to say, the Nickel Rash found little support among workers, while Mine Mill continued to grow.

COMING OUT INTO THE OPEN: 1943

During this time, the local media took every opportunity to attack the principle of unionism and support the policies of the mining companies. In the case of the *Sudbury Daily Star*, its bias was so blatant that it was popularly dubbed the *Inco Star*. In the past, Mine Mill had explained the union's objectives in the form of handbills distributed in

---

[6]Local 598's "Brief to the National War Labour Board," May 28, 1943, reprinted in the *Sudbury Beacon*, June 1943.

utmost secrecy. Now, with membership rapidly increasing, the union began publishing its own weekly paper. The first issue of the *Sudbury Beacon* appeared in January 1943; 5,000 copies were printed by the Vapaus Publishing Company. Mine Mill also obtained offices and a meeting hall on Lisgar Street. This was to be the union hall until 1949, when a new hall was built on Regent Street.

The campaign to establish a union in Sudbury was now out in the open. Much use was made of the hall for membership meetings and rallies, during which labour leaders from other unions were brought in to speak. Clarie Gillis, M.P., prominent labour leader from Cape Breton, N.S., was the first of these.

Among the archival collection is a report on the first anniversary of Local 598's charter by an anonymous historian:

> To mark the first anniversary of Local 598 and to commemorate the charter, a gala banquet and dance was held in the Nickel Range Hotel on April 30, 1943.
>
> A parade was to follow this affair but the weather proved unfavourable and instead the union hall was packed the next day and entertainment was provided by the Coniston Band and the Sudbury Band. At times both were playing at opposite ends of the hall.
>
> One of the highlights of the parade was to have been a demonstration of mining procedure in the timbered stopes of Frood Mine. A group of miners decked out in complete miners garb arranged to put up square sets and drill off a round. Not to be

MELVIN WITHERS
President

JOE T. MORE
Recording Secretary

JOHN BILLOKI
Financial Secretary

ARCHIE K. SMITH
Vice-President

ROBERT G. MINER
Trustee

GRANT CRANSTON
Warden

ANGELO BARBISAN
Trustee

JAMES KIDD
Trustee

LARRY BENNETT
Conductor

First executive of Mine Mill Local 598 in 1942. Solski Collection

International president Reid Robinson addressing union rally outside the Mine Mill office on Lisgar Street, May 1st, 1943.
Solski Collection

Reid Robinson (Mel Withers, seated). Solski Collection

outsmarted by the rain and dressed in oilers at any rate these miners were determined to go ahead with the job, so not only once but many times the square set was erected, blocked and timber logged to the platform of a truck and the drill set up ready to go. Thus mining was brought right down town in Sudbury, and I believe the "boys" preferred this day to those spent in the mine because after each "set up" of the timber they set up a few at a nearby tavern.

The open air meeting in the evening in front of the union hall turned the day into a red letter day for Local 598. The P.A. system was installed at strategic points on the street with microphones mounted on the platform of a truck. Despite the rain, thousands thronged to this meeting to hear International President Reid Robinson, Vice-President Ralph Rasmussen, and speakers from Port Colborne and Kirkland Lake. The meeting was a great success and although the throng which filled the street from Elm to Borgia was tense with sheer excitement there were no disturbances of any kind. The workers were glad that their union had at last "come out into the open."

The Canadian Conference of Metal Miners, consisting of delegates from all Mine Mill locals in Canada, met in Sudbury on July 3 and 4, 1943. Delegates voted to press the government to pass labour legislation that would recognize the right of workers to bargain collectively. The conference criticized both the government and the nickel industry for refusing to implement Elliot Little's plan to relocate experienced miners from Kirkland Lake to Sudbury.* Despite the wartime labour shortage, discrimination against union members continued.

---

*Elliot Little resigned as director of selective service in November 1942, partly because of the government's failure to implement his plan to relocate the gold miners to essential war industries.

By this time, Bob Miner had come to Sudbury from Timmins, and his account describes conditions at Inco, which he termed "a literal hellhole."

"The government sent a man to Timmins to recruit men for Sudbury. I think he got 14 or 16 men in about six weeks. The union had been watching this campaign very closely, and in 1942 we passed a resolution that the president of Local 241 should offer his services to help transfer miners to Sudbury. So I did, and the Timmins agent called Elliot Little, the minister in charge of national selective service — it was just coincidental that as a student, he had worked for my father at Iroquois Falls. . . .

"Elliot Little took responsibility for a speech I gave over the radio, without giving the usual 48 hours notice or any censorship rights to the radio station. As a result of our campaign, we got about 1600 men for Sudbury.

"Little offered me a couple of jobs, but I turned them down. I told him I had to go to Sudbury, or my name would be mud with the miners I sent. He warned me: 'The company will kill you in Sudbury. But rest assured that I'll keep an eye on you.' So I went to Sudbury — left my family in Porcupine because it was very difficult to get places to live in Sudbury.

"I couldn't go through the normal channels in getting hired on in Sudbury. They sent me right to Ralph Parker, the general superintendent. A very well educated, very intelligent mining man, probably one of the best in the world. And as ignorant as a pig. He was so reactionary that he set up the Bedaux system in Inco, the infamous system that was instituted in the Krupp works in Germany. There was a steady stream of shift bosses, stope bosses, captains, and assistant bosses, and even these men were insecure in their jobs. No smoking in the mines, even though they were wet — you might take a few minutes away from the company. Bonuses to hurry you up, and then they'd dock your pay for violating some minor rule.

"Well, Mr. Parker was practically frothing at the mouth. He hated me so much, it was just coming out of his eyes. He said: 'I hope these men you're sending down are better than that goddamned scum we got from Kirkland Lake.' I said: 'You can bet your boots on it. I know every man that came from Timmins. They're all members of Local 241.

Wage and Policy Conference in Sudbury, July 3-4, 1943.
Front (L-R): *O. Breton (Sudbury), Melvin Withers (president Local 598), C. Mathieu (Creighton Mine), James Russell (International representative), Archie McArthur (Falconbridge smelter), Lloyd Houser (Port Colborne), Alex Kostyniuk (Levack Mine), Bart Hunter (Copper Cliff refinery). Middle (L-R): J. J. Caprani (Geraldton), Peter Boychuk (Timmins), George King (Port Colborne), Wm. "Bill" Simpson (International representative, Port Colborne), Nathan Witt (International legal counsel), Chase Powers (International board member District 7), Reid Robinson (International president), R. H. Carlin (International board member District 8), J. W. Simpson (Timmins), Paul Dioguardi (Timmins). Back* (L-R): *C. Hopkins (Garson), Larry Bennett (International representative), Mike Solski (Coniston smelter), Mischa Karol (Timmins), Jack Ogbourne (Copper Mountain, B.C.), Louis Fabian (Port Colborne), Duke Hyssop (Kimberley, B.C.), Wm. "Bill" Whitehead (Copper Cliff smelter), Fred Henne (Trail, B.C.), Joe Peltola (Local 598 Nordale Construction), Doc Ames (Kirkland Lake), Benny Doherty (Kirkland Lake), Lloyd Foster (Falconbridge Mine), Harvey Murphy (International representative), Nick Rozok (Timmins), Jack McCool (Sudbury), William Kennedy (Frood Mine), Joe Rankin (International representative, northern Quebec). Solski Collection*

I don't know most of them from Kirkland Lake, but I do know that about 90 percent are ex-scabs. I don't know why you should get so excited because, after all, you and Inco paid for those scabs in the first place. Now they're dumped in your lap because they don't need scabs in Kirkland Lake anymore.' Well, my God! It was practically an explosion. The language! Thirty or 40 girls in that office, and he was using language that you wouldn't use to a mule.

"I went to work at Creighton Mine the next day. We had to go to work on a train. It took about 13 hours to put in a shift. At night, I'd try to find a place to live. I'd find a vacancy, have a look at it, and the landlord would get out his receipt book. 'And what's your name?' 'Bob Miner.' 'Oh, Jesus, I should have told you. I rented that yesterday.' Dozens of times. Inco had the whole city in its pocket. Then, one of the biggest businessmen in Sudbury, who was independent of Inco and owned a building downtown, agreed to rent me an apartment — the business agent for the union was already living there. Boy! Bedbugs and cockroaches. What a place! It was indescribable.

"By that time I didn't have any money. So, I phoned a bank in Timmins and arranged for a hundred dollar loan for my wife, and phoned my brother-in-law to back the note. When I got to work that afternoon, the captain was waiting for me. 'Miner, you don't know who your friends are, do you? Why the hell did you waste your time phoning Timmins to borrow money?' I pretty near went through the floor.

"He said: 'Bob, all you had to do was come to me. We need shift bosses, captains, all sorts of supervisory staff. You know, we have 35 new houses built on the townsite for bosses.' The government subsidized that company for 35 million dollars, and they were supposed to build houses for the workers. He said: 'We want you to be a mine captain. And on top of that, I'll make it possible for you to make 15,000 dollars a year. How does that sound?' I asked why he was picking me for the special treatment. 'That's simple. We buy your services as a miner. We want to buy your services as an organizer. All you have to do is go out and organize a union for us. And forget this goddamned CIO business.' The company was trying to organize a company union, which we called 'the nickel rash.' 'Well,' I said, 'then it's going to cost you a lot more money, because you'll have to hire an army to protect me from the honest workers in this camp.' Well, I left him with a rather long face.

"The next day I came to work, and my card was pulled. At Inco, everybody had to punch a card. If your card wasn't there, you couldn't work — you had to find out what happened to that card. So I went through the whole shebang, from the time-keeper to the manager. Nobody knew where my card was. For the next two weeks, day after day, nobody knew where my card was. And then my card was back."[7]

Despite the success of Local 598 in signing up members, Inco steadfastly refused to recognize Mine Mill and asserted that it had an agreement with the UCNW. For an outsider's view of the labour situation in Sudbury in the summer of 1943, Allan May, producer of a program on Sudbury for CBC's "Production Front," commented that, whereas the UCNW's offices were almost deserted, Local 598's hall was a "hive of activity" with members "literally swarming about the premises all day long."[8]

The period prior to the 1944 certification victory of Mine Mill was filled with an enthusiastic acceleration of organization. The campaign reached dizzying heights when more than 3,000 Inco workers were inducted into the union in a single month. Efforts to stem the tide with feeble and futile company unions were decisively smothered.

To cap it all off, in the provincial election held August 4, 1943, Bob Carlin, running for the CCF, won by a landslide, a further vote of confidence for Mine Mill in the Sudbury area. That year, the CCF formed the official opposition in Ontario. The growing strength of the labour movement and the CCF's popularity in the polls forced the passage of the Trade Union Act by the Ontario Liberals in 1943.

CERTIFICATION: 1944

Local 598 began procedures to achieve certification through the newly established Ontario Labour Court in August. In December 1943, the certification vote was taken, with Local 598 winning by a 70 per cent majority of all employees, and 80 per cent of all those who voted.

At Inco, 8,184 out of 10,050 of those eligible had voted; 6,913 voted for Mine Mill, 1,187 voted for the UCNW, and 675 voted for no union. At Falconbridge, 959 out of 1,090 of those eligible had voted; 765 voted for Mine Mill, 194 voted for the plant council, and three ballots were spoiled. The Ontario Labour Court certified Sudbury Mine, Mill and Smelter Workers Union, Local 598, as the collective bargaining agent for employees of Inco on February 4, 1944, and for employees of Falconbridge on March 8, 1944.

Local 598 had finally succeeded in taming a ferocious management that had made Sudbury a source of strike breakers for U.S. mines at the turn of the century, and in challenging the 'company town' stigma by bringing unionism to Sudbury.

Once certification was announced, things moved with speed unequalled in later years. Following a letter to Inco on February 10th asking the company to meet, the first contract was concluded and signed March 10, 1944.

The first Local 598 negotiating committee chosen to bargain with Inco was chaired by Tom McGuire, veteran union organizer and negotiator who had been assigned by the international union to the post of District Director. Of the other members of this first negotiating committee, Nels Thibault and Mike Solski later became presidents of Local 598 and played leading roles in the union throughout Canada.

---

[7]*Miner's Life*, pp. 8, 9.

[8]A transcript of this program was reprinted in the *Sudbury Beacon*, September 1943.

Although wartime legislation prohibited wage increases, bargaining in other areas was highly successful. Major gains were made in terms of working conditions and union recognition, and a firm foundation was laid for union security based on a revocable check-off. A positive grievance procedure and the principle of seniority over-all within departments were established, along with recall rights on a seniority basis for employees laid off. Hours of work and overtime pay were spelled out; the eight-hour day "collar to collar" for underground miners was won. Before that, as Bob Miner said, "You worked eight hours on the face. You went underground on your own time, ate lunch on your own time, and came up on your own time." Scale of hourly wage rates was guaranteed for the duration of the agreement; a provision was made to reopen the contract after six months if laws and regulations permitting negotiations on wage increases were changed.

The second contract, concluded May 1, 1945, brought further gains, including irrevocable check-off in the union security clause, an improved grievance procedure, job posting, War Labour Board approved classification increases, and elimination of the fourth class in the trades.

The 1946 contract achieved a substantial advance in union security with institution of the Roach Formula, which required all hourly rated employees to pay union dues on the check-off system with no obligation to join the union.* Shift premiums for the afternoon and graveyard shifts were established for the first time in the company's history. Wage increases were implemented, vacations improved to two

---

*Justice Roach was the chairman of the conciliation board in the Inco negotiations; his formula on union security was an improvement on what had been recommended in the Ford Motor conciliation by Justice Rand.

weeks' vacation after two years, and third class was abolished in the trades.

Subsequent contracts made further improvements, with the hours of work per week reduced to 44 in 1950 and to 40 hours in 1951. Wage increases were included in all contracts as well as further gains in holidays, vacations, contract bonus agreements, medical provisions, insurance plans, etc.

Speed of action also characterized Local 598's first dealings with Falconbridge Nickel Mines. After certification on March 8, 1944, the first agreement was reached on March 15th. The Falconbridge contract paralleled the Inco pact in most issues, with only minor differences. As members of Local 598, the Falconbridge workers participated fully in all aspects of the union's activities in all referendums, but as could be expected because of the predominance of Inco in the district, negotiations always followed the Inco bargaining.

PORT COLBORNE ORGANIZED

Port Colborne, the site of Inco's other large Ontario operation, had its beginnings in the public outcry that occurred during World War I, when it was disclosed that Inco was selling nickel to Germany from its refineries in the neutral United States. Prior to WW I, Port Colborne was a quiet, pleasant town adjacent to the Great Lakes, divided into two parts by the Welland Canal with its constant stream of freighters moving from Lake Erie to Lake Ontario and on to inland ports in Canada and the United States. Events

Local 598 bargaining team, first agreement with Falconbridge Nickel Mines, March 15, 1944. Seated (L-R): Lloyd Foster; Tom McGuire, International regional director and union spokesman; Mel Withers, president Local 598; Bill Roworth, vice-president Local 598. Standing (L-R): Lawson Rae; Archie McArthur; Joe Rankin, International representative; Jock Davidson. Solski Collection

during the war were responsible for bringing Canada's first nickel refinery into the area, and Inco became the district's largest employer.

The armaments industry has always played a prime role in the development of the nickel industry. In 1890, the U.S. Navy began testing nickel as a military material, and the strength of nickel-steel armour plate on its ships during the Spanish-American War of 1898 increased this market for nickel. At the start of World War I, the nickel industry boomed; between 1914 and 1918, the output of the Sudbury area mines more than doubled. By 1913, 40 percent of Inco's entire output was shipped to Germany,[9] and during the war years the public reaction against Inco was intense. The press demanded public ownership of the industry and a refinery in Canada that would have control over export of the product.* The *Toronto Telegram* stormed, "not an Ontario boy goes into action except at the risk of having to face bullets barbed with the nickel of which his own province has a monopoly."[10]

Then, in 1916, the year before the U.S. entered the war, it was learned that the German submarine *Deutschland* had made two trips transporting nickel from the U.S. to Germany. Only then, amid demands for expropriation of Inco's assets, did Inco announce plans to create a Canadian refinery at Port Colborne.

Previously, it had been Inco's policy, confirmed by Col. Robert Means Thompson, "to extract Canadian ore and refine it in New Jersey . . . ore would be mined and smelted in Canada, the matte then shipped to New Jersey for refining, and its fate decided at the company's New Jersey head-quarters."[11]

The Port Colborne refinery drew entirely upon Sudbury for its supply of raw materials. In both Inco operations, the practices of pitting ethnic minority and Anglo-Saxon groups against each other, job selling, intimidation, espionage and anti-union firings paralleled those used in Sudbury. When a welfare association and later a full-fledged company union was formed in an attempt to divert unionism in Sudbury, the same procedure was followed in Port Colborne.

During the depression years, when thousands crowded the Inco hiring gates in Sudbury, hundreds did likewise in Port Colborne. And when, in the early 1940s, labour legislation following the Kirkland Lake strike made union organization possible in Sudbury, the refinery was also organized.

The decision to organize a legitimate trade union resulted from the complete inadequacy of the company union, the Port Colborne Inco Employees' Welfare Association. By early 1942, membership in the Welfare Association had dropped to less than half its original numbers. Even when the company allowed the fifteen members of the association's board of directors time off at full pay to solicit members within the plant and reduced membership fees to 50 cents a year, this failed to produce results. Some members of the welfare board refused to serve a second term because of its failure to achieve improvements for the workers.

In 1942, a group of a dozen workers started meeting secretly to discuss organizing a trade union. Contact was made with the Canadian Congress of Labour (CCL) for assistance. A CCL representative met with this small group and a card-signing campaign was started. Within one week, 350 men were signed up.

---

[9]John Deverell and the Latin American Working Group, *Falconbridge: Portrait of a Canadian Mining Multinational*, James Lorimer & Company, Publishers, Toronto, 1975, p. 31.

*Some twenty years later, in the mid 1930s, John Foster Dulles, U.S. Secretary of State, chief architect of the Cold War and high profile Inco board member, "is said to have wept openly for the loss of substantial profits when his law firm decided to close its German law offices; happily for the business-conscious lawyer, his nickel firm continued to supply Nazi stockpiles until late in the 1930s." ("The Arrogance of INCO," *Canadian Business*, May 1979.)

[10]*Toronto Telegram*, Dec. 27, 1914.

[11]"The Arrogance of INCO," *Canadian Business*, May 1979.

First joint bargaining team of Sudbury Local 598 and Port Colborne Local 637 during negotiations with Inco in 1945. Seated (L-R): George Black, Local 598; A. S. Murray, Local 637; Mel Withers, president Local 598; Al Lachance, Local 598 staff organizer; Tom McGuire, International regional director and union spokesman; Lloyd Houser, president Local 637; William Johnson, Local 598; Gavin (Bill) Cowper, Local 637. Standing (L-R): Bart Hunter, Jack McCool, Nels Thibault, Rolly Galipeau, Bill Whitehead, Hilliard Shebeski, S. E. Harrison, T. Tammi, all Local 598. Back row (L-R): William Santala, Mike Solski, Hastie Martin, all Local 598. Solski Collection

Blood donors from the Frood Mine. Solski Collection

On a return visit, the CCL representative advised the group that the Inco employees in the Sudbury district were joining the International Union of Mine, Mill and Smelter Workers. At a second meeting, the decision to affiliate with Mine Mill resulted in the arrival of international representative Bill Simpson to assist in the organizational drive. By early December, 750 cards were signed; Local 637, IUMMSW, was chartered January 15, 1943.

After certification of Port Colborne Local 637 on September 27, 1943, the first contract was signed on March 17, 1944, following the conclusion of Local 598's bargaining for the Sudbury Inco workers. In 1945 and 1946, joint bargaining with Local 598 was conducted at Inco's Copper Cliff offices. However, during the 1946 bargaining, a so-called dissident group in Local 637's leadership created a division between the two locals. In that year, Local 637 signed a separate agreement for an eight-cent wage increase, while Local 598 went into conciliation and won a ten-cent wage raise and implementation of the Roach Formula for improved union security. Pressure from Local 598 induced Inco to bring the Local 637 settlement to the Sudbury level.

Separate negotiations continued in 1947, and Port Colborne was forced into a strike vote and ultimate joint conciliation with Local 598 before achieving a contract. In 1948, joint bargaining was again established and an agreement with Inco concluded.

Local 598's Community Work

For Local 598, as for other unions, annual contract bargaining was the major event of the year and it, together with the policing of the agreements by an alert and informed stewards' body, kept union officers and staff fully occupied. However, in addition to its specific union activity, the local turned its attention to its obligations as a prominent force for social and cultural development of Sudbury as a community. In the tradition of the Western Federation of Miners, prevailing opinion in the union's leadership stressed the need to spread activities beyond the exclusive focus on wages and working conditions within the industry and to concentrate on broader community concerns.

Roots of the union's concern for community affairs were evident early in its organizational days, even before its certification as the bargaining agent for the nickel workers. The records show that in March 1943, Local 598 donated $325 to the Red Cross, as well as organizing a blood bank for the Red Cross. On October 15th, Local 598 received a letter of thanks from the Sudbury Children's Aid Society for a donation of $200. Vigorous union support was also given to the wartime Victory Loan Campaign.

The year 1945 found Local 598 prominent in the Sudbury Full Employment Committee, seeking to establish new post-war industries. J. P. McCool, Local 598 financial secretary, was chairman of the Sudbury Post War Planning Committee.

In 1949, Local 598 actively supported the Sudbury Arena Fund Drive, with 598 President Nels Thibault co-chairman of the Community Recreation Centre. Union representatives attempted to ensure that the arena would serve the needs of the whole community, but gradually the arena which the union and the workers of Sudbury helped build was controlled by a select group.

Local 598 carried on the WFM's concern for improved medical services to the community. Early on, it developed its own welfare fund to aid workers and their families in need as a result of non-compensable sickness or accident. At first, members contributed an additional 50 cents a month to the welfare fund. By 1953, more than $300,000 had been distributed to Local 598 members since the inception of the fund. As well as maintaining its wartime blood donor clinic, the local helped raise money for the Red Feather Campaign by supporting a check-off program at Inco and Falconbridge.

In keeping with the importance the local placed on such issues, Local 598 board member Carl Nielsen was appointed full-time staff officer responsible for handling welfare and compensation matters in January 1951.

In October 1951, the local donated an iron lung, at a cost of $1,900, to the Sudbury General Hospital. In November 1952, Local 598 presented the Sudbury district with a mobile therapy unit for the Canadian Arthritis and Rheumatism Society and undertook full costs of its operation.

UNION HALLS

Local 598 also continued the WFM tradition of building halls that would serve as a focus for community activities. Beginning in 1946, the membership put aside 50 cents additional monthly dues for the purpose of building a new union hall and, after two years of saving, construction was begun on Regent Street in Sudbury. The new hall was partially opened June 4, 1949, while the official opening of the completed hall was held September 30, 1952. Thereafter, the building fund was used to construct Mine Mill halls in the surrounding centres of Garson (1953), Coniston (1956), Creighton (now Lively) (1957), and Chelmsford (1959). A similar building fund in Port Colborne saw the opening of the first unit of their new union hall in 1953. These halls served, not only as meeting places for members of the union, but sometimes as the only community centres these towns had which were available for the use of the whole family.

In a 1950 report, President Nels Thibault described some of the activities launched with the opening of the hall in Sudbury:

> First we launched projects for the members and wives. Dances, weekly and mid-week, turned out hundreds, and before long Mine Mill dances were so many that it required additional dances during the week to siphon off the crowds. With the facilities provided by the new hall, Christmas, 1949, saw more than 5,000 kiddies in the building during the day at shows and in receipt of gifts.

Local 598 donates an iron lung to the Sudbury General Hospital, October 1951. (L-R): Nels Thibault, president Local 598; Sudbury Mayor W. S. Beaton; Carl Neilsen, Local 598 welfare and compensation committee; Sudbury Board of Health officials Ms. R. J. Callaghan, E. A. Martin, Rodger Mitchell; sanitary inspector Frank Rothery and assistant William MacDonald; Mike Solski, financial secretary Local 598; Dr. J. B. Cook, Sudbury Medical Officer of Health. Solski Collection

Carl Neilsen, chairman of Local 598's welfare centre, presents a mobile therapy unit to Dorothy Meusen, recently-hired physiotherapist of the Canadian Arthritis and Rheumatism Society, as part of Local 598's community assistance program, February 1953. Solski Collection

Gala opening of the completed Mine Mill hall on Regent Street, September 20, 1952, Local 598 president Mike Solski presiding. Solski Collection

Regularly scheduled banquets and social affairs for the various union committees proved highly successful, with the annual stewards' banquet the highlight of the season's activities. For the kiddies there were free Saturday morning movies with almost 1,000 in the hall each week. Last winter we launched a Wednesday afternoon event for mothers and pre-school children. During the summer months the children went in for outdoor events, hikes and picnics in the country.

The second phase was the bringing into the union hall the diverse organizations which make up the entire community. The various fraternal, cultural, sport, and religious organizations soon learned they were welcome.

First major group to make its home in our hall was the Roman Catholic Parish of St. Eugene which has been conducting church services in our hall for the past year while their new church is being built. In addition there have been gatherings of the Orange Lodge, other church groups including the St. Mary's Ukrainian Church, the Watchtower Bible and Tract Society, and other fraternal and social groups. Most recently the Separate (Parochial) School Teachers Association held their convention in our Mine Mill Hall. Today,

Wives and staff at gala opening of the completed Mine Mill hall, September 20, 1952. Seated (L-R): Frankie Wilson, Henrietta Jaques, Kay Carlin, Isabel Murphy, Jenny Neilsen, ———, Dorothy MacDonald, Babes Coutts, Lil King. Standing (L-R): Kay Kopinak, Isabel Smaller, Ruth Reid, Jessie Kennedy, Nancy Coombs, Leona Lalonde, Adeline Pavan, Mary Casas, Mary Bardeggia, Gail Larson, Irene Solski, June Liska, Ruth Robinson, Marie Thibault. Solski Collection

in addition to being the trade union of the people of Sudbury, Mine Mill is also the pivotal organization around which all other organizations in the community now revolve.

For the past two seasons the Mine Mill men's softball team headed the Sudbury district league and twice was runner-up for the Ontario championships. This past season the Union sponsored a ladies' softball team and it, too, was the district champion and lost out only in the final for the provincial championship. The Mine Mill bowling team won many championship cups which are displayed in the Union Hall, and have participated in Dominion championship games. Our sports activities have proved successful with the Mine Mill name and insignia now well-known not only in Sudbury but in the many communities throughout the province where our teams competed.

During this year's Steel raid in Port Colborne, our ladies' softball team played an exhibition game in that city with all proceeds going to a new hospital fund there. While in Port Colborne the women assisted in the campaign against Steel.

Sports activities sponsored by Local 598 also included hockey and basketball teams, and establishment of a boxing club in the Sudbury hall. Not to be outdone, long-time member Tony Landry and his team of Siberian huskies carried the Mine Mill colours in the International Dog Derby in January 1951.

The women's baseball team from Sudbury Local 598 went down to Port Colborne to hand out flyers during the Steel raid in the summer of 1950. Front: Isabel O'Rielly. Second row (L-R): Vickey Dagenais, Deva Cler, Iris Wallace, Angie Charbonneau, Chea Medina, Peggy Currie. Back row (L-R): Ida Johnson (manager), Irene Solski, Rose DiPietro, Rose Konichkowsky, Pat Doyle, Ruth Constable, Jerry Pappin, Jim Nemis (coach). Solski Collection

CHILDREN'S CAMP ON RICHARD LAKE

A unique venture undertaken by Local 598 was its campground on a 160-acre property on Richard Lake, about eight miles south of Sudbury. Begun in 1951, it offered a children's day-camp for Mine Mill members, and the beach and picnic facilities were available to other community groups. Each year the facilities were improved: volunteers improved the grounds and landscaping, and a main lodge and dormitories were constructed. Architects Fabbro and Townend received an award for the design of the main lodge. At the end of the first resident summer camp program in 1953, full-time recreation director Weir Reid reported that 1,500 youngsters had attended in two-week intervals. Rates were held down to $9.00 a week so that no child would be denied the benefit of the camp because of the cost.

CULTURAL PROGRAM

On March 17, 1952, Weir Reid, former program director for the central YMCA in Toronto, was appointed to the Local 598 staff in order to orchestrate general cultural and sports activities, as well as to run the Mine Mill camp on Richard Lake. Under Weir Reid, Local 598's cultural program flourished, and residents of Sudbury were able to enjoy and participate in cultural activities previously considered suitable only for the elite of society.

Conducting such a program for Mine Mill was not easy in the McCarthyist atmosphere of the fifties. For instance, the internationally famous Royal Winnipeg Ballet had been booked to perform at the Sudbury union hall January 29 and 30, 1954. With all seats sold, a week before the scheduled concerts, the ballet company suddenly cancelled its appearance for spurious reasons. Later, it was revealed that the cancellation had resulted from U.S. State Department pressure: the company's American tour had been threatened if it chose to perform in a Mine Mill hall in its own country.

Nevertheless, in the fighting spirit of its predecessors, Local 598 persevered. In defiance of the cold war pressures, it hosted Soviet artists, headed by internationally acclaimed violinist Leonid Kogan, in April 1954.

Among its innovations, Local 598 ran a dance school under the direction of Nancy Lima Dent, and later Barbara Cook, teaching children ballet, folk and tap dancing out of the area's union halls. Furthermore, Weir Reid produced and directed plays for the local's theatre group, composed of union members, and the Haywood Players regularly competed in the Quanta Drama Festival.

In April 1954, Sudburians were able to view Mine Mill's feature film, *Salt of the Earth*, at a local movie house. This film, based on the militant strike of unskilled Mexican-American workers in Mine Mill Local 890 against Empire Zinc in Bayard, New Mexico, portrays the triumph of labour, minorities and women over seemingly insurmountable

Main lodge, Mine Mill camp on Richard Lake, eight miles south of Sudbury. No child was denied the benefit of the camp because of cost. Solski Collection

Ruth Reid, director of the summer camp program, with summer staff in 1956. Standing (L-R): Dale Jones, Ruth Reid, Ted Loyst, Jean Galbraith, Ellen MacKinnon, Irene Mihalcin, Gordon McCandless, Steve Bell, Dale Loyst, Joan Racicot, Stan Racicot Local 598 executive camp liaison officer. Front (L-R): ———, Gary Gauthier, Sonny Gawalko, Elliot Posen, Pat Gibson, George ——— (the cook), Marjory Young, Mary Mihalcin, Wally Dittburner, Barbara Verri. Photo courtesy Ruth Reid

Weir Reid with the Haywood Players cast of The Man Who Never Died, *a dramatization of the life of Joe Hill. Standing (L-R): Weir Reid (director), John Grant, Ron Allen, Oswald Ouimette, Eric Johansson, Vern Haluschak, John Wolfe, Don "Popeye" Henry. Seated (L-R): Otto Koivula, Rolly Bodson, Jim Tester, Carol Lepage, Lawrie Bertrand (on floor), Ann Buda, Pearl Chytuk, Tony Bertrand, Gordon T. Young, Cecil Ralph. Solski Collection*

Steward schools were conducted regularly at Richard Lake camp. Attending the August 1953 school conducted by Research Associates of Montreal were (front row L-R): *Gilbert Walsh, Bill Petryshen, George Spears, Herb Wright, –––, Allen Moorby, W. Ed Stephens, –––.* Second row (L-R): *Mickey Stahan, –––, –––, Bill Milks, Roger Favretto, –––, Mike Pailey, Dan Monstead, Rusty Gainer, Bob Cooney.* Third row (L-R): *Mike Solski, Vern Haluschak, Jack Galbraith, Tony Blanchard, Basil Jennings, Ron Allen, Albert Langlade, Ray Stevenson, John Keen, Buster Martel, Karl Kudla, Jack MacDonald, –––.* Fourth row (L-R): *Joe Pachota, Walter Caba, Gilles Henault, Leo Roeback of Research Associates, –––, –––, Paul Mihalchuk, Bill Cryderman, Lynn MacLean.* Solski Collection

Matti Stelmakovich (left) and Tony Paraskake compete in a mucking contest at Richard Lake camp. Solski Collection

Nancy Lima Dent's last appearance, June 1957. (Front row top to bottom): *Linda McKeagan, Chickie Haluschak, Lillian Lemanis, Sharon McDougall.* (Back row top to bottom): *Leslie Hoffman, dance instructor Nancy Lima Dent, Margaret Klassen.* Solski Collection

opposition. Eight months into the strike, in June 1951, an injunction preventing picketing had been issued against the miners. The local's Ladies' Auxiliary put women on the picket line, and added to the list of union demands hot running water and toilets like in the Anglo miners' company housing. Despite injunctions, goons and scabs, the men and women of Local 890 won their strike in January 1952.

The fact that *Salt of the Earth* was made was in itself a triumph. With Screen Actors Guild president Ronald Reagan and the House Committee on Un-American Activities typical of the climate in Hollywood, the total opposition of the movie industry included refusal to make available any of the usual crews. Those professionals who worked on the film did so entirely at their own risk. Filmed on location in New Mexico, most of the roles were played by miners and their families; Mine Mill organizer Clinton Jencks and his wife played themselves.* Services such as film processing, soundtrack, dubbing and editing facilities were also refused. Nevertheless, the film was completed in 1954.

Salt of the Earth, although refused screening in Canada by the U.S.-controlled Projectionists Union and refused distribution by the commercial companies, did get released through persistent efforts of Mine Mill locals and film societies throughout the country.

The late Nathan Cohen, noted theatre critic, reviewed the film on CBC's "Critically Speaking" program August 22, 1954:

> *Salt of the Earth* has a naked emotion and pile driving power. It grinds a special axe with energy and authority. The acting is controlled and spare. In the leading parts, Rosaura Revueltas, one of the five professionals in the cast, and Juan Chacon, in actual life a union leader, are brilliantly projective. They bring to their personal scenes a quality to which that banal phrase wonderfully sensitive is honestly applicable.
>
> I said that *Salt of the Earth* is an American movie. This may seem to contradict my earlier remarks about Hollywood, so I'd better explain now it was not made by Hollywood but independently by a group of blacklisted screen people in collaboration with the International Union of Mine, Mill and Smelter Workers, a union expelled from the CIO. Various efforts were made to disrupt the production. Miss Revueltas, a distinguished Mexican star, was detained as an alien, crew members were attacked by vigilantes, and it took six months longer than planned to finish the film. Since then, attempts have been made to prevent its being shown to the general public, and not just in the U.S. Here in Toronto, members of the Projectionists Union were advised not to screen the movie and a special screening for the critics was cancelled. However, it is now playing in a local theatre and I am told it will be shown in the communities too.
>
> If it plays in your town, by all means see it. Whatever the political affiliations of its makers, the worst thing you can say against it is that it is strongly pro-labour.

---

*Clinton Jencks was hounded by charges brought against him under the Taft Hartley Act. A long, costly legal battle in the U.S. Supreme Court resulted in complete acquittal when the chief state witness, Harvey Matusow, testified that his original statements had been perjured under direction of the FBI. Matusow's book *False Witness* was later made available to Sudbury members at cost price through Local 598.

A scene from Salt of the Earth, *released in 1954. In the foreground (L-R): Clinton Jencks as Frank, Juan Chacon as Ramon (Chacon later became president of Local 890). Solski Collection*

Cinematically, *Salt of the Earth* is an exciting experience, a deeply human drama in the documentary manner perfected by the Italians in such masterpieces as *Open City* and *Shoe Shine*.

Popular entertainment hosted by Mine Mill during the fifties included Doc Williams and Wheeling Jamboree shows, the Barnard and Barry Circus, Pete Seeger, the Travellers, and, on February 29, 1956, Paul Robeson. The local also ran a popular program on local radio. *Mine Mill on the Air* first ran on Sudbury station CHNO, then on station CKSO, but it was banned by each station in turn for being "too controversial."

Paul Robeson gave his first performance outside the U.S. in Local 598's Regent Street hall after the travel ban imposed on him in 1952 was lifted. "My art . . . is a weapon in the struggle for my people's freedom and for the freedom of all people," he told the convention. "And I want you to know that your understanding and courage and friendship during these years have helped sustain my strength and courage." Robeson poses with Local 598 officers at the 8th Annual Canadian Convention in Sudbury, February 29, 1956 (L-R): Mike Solski, Paul Robeson, Nels Thibault, Lawrence Brown. Solski Collection

SUPPORT OF THE UNION MOVEMENT

Fellow unionists in need of support, financial or otherwise, always found Local 598 members ready and willing to contribute. Financial support, either from the local's treasury as authorized by membership votes, or from collections gathered by volunteer unionists, speeded its way to strike-bound workers. Local 598 delegates, strongly supportive of the union movement, attended labour conferences and conventions throughout the country and reported back on the actions and decisions of these assemblies.

Early in its development, a Local 598 resolution to the 1943 annual convention sought "to achieve unity and co-operation with all unions and other trade union centres and their affiliates in Canada . . . between CIO and AFL, Anglo and Soviet trade union committees with a view to setting up a United Nations trade union central body."

Also in 1943, Local 598 sponsored the Sudbury Workers Organizing Committee to organize all non-nickel industry workers into the CCL.

Among the records of help to other unions, the following provides an interesting reading list in light of subsequent events:

January 29, 1944: Donation of $100 to striking Steelworkers in Galt, Ontario.

March, 1950: Local 598 responds to Steelworkers' request to help them organize Timmins gold miners. They do not red-bait or talk about Mine Mill being bankrupt at this time, but ask Sudbury workers to help bring the conditions of Timmins miners up to Mine Mill standards.

June 2, 1952: Local 598 contributes $1,000 per week to the Quebec Textile Workers strike.

November 10, 1952: Financial secretary Norman Jaques announces that, for the first ten months of the year, Local 598 has donated $22,629.19 to trade unions in Nova Scotia, Quebec, Ontario, British Columbia and the U.S., and that these include CIO, AFL, CCL and independent unions.

September 27, 1954: Philip Kearns, president of Local 539, United Auto Workers, appeals for Local 598 assistance in the Massey-Harris strike.

December 21, 1954: Local 598 sends $1,000 to the UAW Local 200 strikers at the Ford plant in Windsor, Ontario.

October 5, 1955: Local 598 sends $1,000 to the DeHavilland strikers in UAW Local 112.

February 26, 1957: Scottish mine union delegates visit Local 598.

President Nels Thibault summarized Mine Mill Local 598's achievements in this way in his 1950 report:

> We have proven ourselves in a solid, well-established organization functioning in the interests of the nickel industry workers in employer-employee relations, and we have established ourselves as an organization functioning in the interest of the entire community; we are the acknowledged organization that has raised and maintained and extended the standard of life for all the people of Sudbury.

Celebration of a breakthrough in the company town stigma with two of four union candidates elected to office in the Sudbury municipal elections in 1953. In the centre Albert Gravel and Stan Racicot, elected, are flanked by Dave Purdy and Nick Skakoon, who made a good showing at the polls. They are surrounded by campaign workers Weir Reid, Fred and Pete Rewega, Lynn MacLean, Joe Doucette, Ed Charleau, Ted Grabish, Mike Solski, Nels Thibault, Angelo Barbeson, Billy Hywarren and others. Solski Collection

Photo courtesy Manfred Hoffman

MINE MILL LOCAL 902

In September 1943, Local 598 sponsored the Sudbury Workers Organizing Committee to bring non-nickel industry workers into Canadian Congress of Labour unions. Mine Mill volunteer organizers were highly successful, and Sudbury district workers in secondary industries and service occupations were soon affiliated with the CCL. The Congress, however, did little or nothing to service these groups, and in time the organization drifted to the point where complete disintegration was imminent.

Then, late in 1948, with the start of unconcealed raids on Mine Mill, several Steelworkers' staff people, posing as CCL organizers, appeared on the scene. Since servicing of CCL union members in Sudbury was a rarity, the intention to establish a base from which to attack Mine Mill was obvious. Mine Mill solved both problems by providing Sudbury's general workers with a union that would enhance its members' welfare and at the same time remove the raiders' base.

In October 1949, Mine Mill General Workers Union Local 902 was chartered. By the end of 1950, it held 24 contracts, and by 1956, 55 contracts, with hundreds of workers enjoying wages and working conditions unequalled in similar occupations elsewhere. With no membership to speak of, the CCL "staffers" withdrew from the district,

presumably to prepare for another assault under different auspices.

In an interview in 1981, Cliff Mathieu, veteran member of Local 598 and later president of Local 902, recalled that when he left the nickel industry in 1945 to work as a bartender, he became a member of the union when it was in the CCL. He said that, even in those early days, the CCL staff member servicing the union was hinting that Mine Mill could soon become part of the Steel union.

With the decision to establish the Mine Mill General Workers Union, Mathieu succeeded in having the Sudbury local of the bartenders' union join the new organization. As an active and popular volunteer organizer for Local 902, he was elected president and held that office for many years, always a working bartender.

Taxi drivers were among the first to join Local 902. When the taxi companies began dismissing pro-union employees, Local 902 led a strike that resulted in a satisfactory settlement.

On December 15, 1950, Local 902 signed a contract with Sudbury Brewing. The company put the Mine Mill label on its bottles and Sudbury's workers rejoiced with Mine Mill beer.

Members of Local 902 also included many women, as Mine Mill proceeded to sign up clerks working at the new Dominion Stores grocery chain in Sudbury. In October 1952, Local 902 obtained the union shop and successfully negotiated a raise in the basic wage from $24.25 to $31.50 a week for clerks and cashiers. Local 902 was also the first union to successfully organize at Loblaws supermarkets in Ontario.

The local grew rapidly, and with the many contracts requiring constant servicing, the need for full-time staff became pressing. Al Lachance, a former Mine Mill organizer, was persuaded to return as business agent for Local 902. He remained in that office until the Mine Mill merger with Steel in 1967, when Local 902 membership affiliated with the International Retail, Wholesale and Department Store Workers Union.

William Kennedy, another veteran Mine Mill member and organizer, later elected to various offices in the Canadian section of the international union, spent some time as international representative with Local 902. Kennedy has fond memories of that period. "This is perhaps the most satisfying period of my life in the trade union movement," he said in a recent interview. "As I recall, I think we built up an organization there that was composed of 55 different groups of workers who knew the effectiveness of Mine Mill at Inco and Falconbridge and wanted to be union members of Mine Mill as well. Mine Mill established wages and working conditions that became the example for unions in every part of eastern Canada."

When Local 902 came under the fraudulent Gillis administration in 1959, one of the first moves in the conspiracy to destabilize Mine Mill was to evict Local 902 from occupancy of office space in the Sudbury union hall and to sabotage the work of the local and undermine its leadership.

In the same pattern, the Inco-Falcon Credit Union, functioning in the Sudbury district on behalf of Local 598 members since receiving its provincial charter in 1944, was the next target of the Gillis administration. First, it withdrew a $10,000 deposit which drew normal interest and assisted credit union members in making loans. Then, the credit union was evicted from its office in the Sudbury union hall.

Next on the destabilizers' hit-list was the Ladies' Auxiliary. First, the Gillis administration mounted a sustained slanderous and disparaging attack on the organization and its activities, and then it banned the organization from the Mine Mill halls throughout the district.

THE LADIES' AUXILIARY

From the earliest days of the Western Federation of Miners, women in the isolated mining camps invariably formed themselves into auxiliaries of the union. Because women were not employed in the industry, except in wartime, in the early days auxiliary members filled the role of social workers. They visited households in distress and in many instances provided primary education for the children. In time, the Ladies' Auxiliary became a constitutional adjunct and integral part of the union itself, and participated fully in the life of the organization.

Auxiliaries had their own chartered locals and were autonomous. Women voted as auxiliary members at the local level and at conventions within their own group. The Canadian Constitution of Mine Mill stated:

> It shall be the aim and purpose of this Union to advance and promote the organization of Ladies' Auxiliaries. It shall be the duty of the officers of this Union both National and Local to assist the Auxiliaries in any manner possible including organization and chartering of branches in Local Unions, or in Local Union areas. It shall be the right of the Auxiliaries to send delegates to all Conventions of the Union, to attend Local Union meetings and be free to express their opinions and make recommendations to these bodies.

Records of the WFM and of Mine Mill tell of times when the women marched shoulder-to-shoulder with the men on many picket lines, took over the picket line when courts

Mine Mill Local 902 executive in 1953 with union officers and staff. Seated (L-R): *Einar Johnson, vice-president; William Kennedy, International representative; Al Lachance, business agent; Nels Thibault, District 8 board member; Cliff Mathieu, president; Jack Yrcha and Felix Belanger, trustees.* Standing (L-R): *Sexton Anderson, conductor; William Cadger, warden; Vic St. Germain, trustee; Harvey Murphy, Western regional director; Carewood White, trustee. Solski Collection*

Sudbury Ladies' Auxiliary Local 117 in the 1950s. "A union without the women is only half organized"—Mine Mill slogan. Seated (L-R): Betty Gunter, Selmi Laakso, June Liska, Dorothy MacDonald, Marie Thibault, Lily Johnson, Janet Kennedy, Pearl Chytuk, Ann Buda, Mary Philips, Sarah Collison, Lena Petroff. Standing (L-R): Bea Stevenson, Ruth Reid, Billie Kozman, Rita Proulx, Isabel Grant, Ann More, Agnes Gauthier, Karen Swanson, Mary Hywarren, Jennie Neilsen, Donna Hugli, Irene Solski, Muriel Quennville, Flo Johansson, Millie McQuaid, Rose Crouch, Ann Barylski. Solski Collection

issued injunctions against the men occupying it, and defied scabs and strike-breakers. Between periods of conflict, they performed innumerable tasks necessary to the functioning of the union.

Auxiliary lights blazed brightly during union organization drives, strikes and the frequent community projects and campaigns. During the memorable Kirkland Lake strike of 1941-42, the Local 240 Ladies' Auxiliary undertook most of the welfare responsibilities, shored up faltering home-makers, and arranged recreational facilities. When Hepburn's "Hussars" staged intimidating parades through Kirkland Lake streets, the women retaliated by leading mile-long parades of striking miners. One militant auxiliary member faced court action for having allegedly thrown red pepper into the eyes of police-protected scabs crossing a picket line.

In Sudbury, during the historic organizational drive in 1942-43, the Local 598 Ladies' Auxiliary canvassed the homes of potential union members, encouraged wives to persuade their husbands to join the union, and distributed handbills from house to house and, at times, plant gates. In the heyday of Local 598's recreational, cultural and children's camp programs, the Ladies' Auxiliary was prominent in every phase. Auxiliary members were on hand as volunteer camp mothers and dietitians throughout the summer, and in the winter they held programs in Mine Mill halls for adults and children.

During the 1958 Inco strike, they played a leading role in all phases of the three-month walkout, notably in exposing and blocking the efforts of district politicians to start a back-to-work, strike-breaking movement among district women. Throughout the intense struggle of Mine Mill against the extended, prolonged and vicious Steelworkers raids, auxiliary women rendered yeoman service in the battle to preserve the integrity of the union.

Pearl Chytuk, a member of the Local 598 Ladies' Auxiliary from its earliest days, talked to Jim Tester in an interview recorded in 1978.

Of a Saskatchewan farm family, Pearl was desperately in search of steady employment during the 1930s depression. Temporary jobs at lunch counters, housework and similar short-term employment were the best she could find. After she was married in 1939, she and her husband Dan decided to try their luck in the east, with an underground job for Dan at Inco's Garson mine. Shortly after came a transfer to the Creighton mine where, with a new-born infant, they settled for a time before moving to Sudbury.

With Dan an early member of Local 598, Pearl joined the Ladies' Auxiliary and became an active member. When Inco started hiring women to replace men who joined the armed forces in 1943, Pearl applied and was put to work in the Copper Cliff smelter. "I joined Local 598 then," she explained, "and I couldn't be active in the auxiliary, but I

122

Ladies' Auxiliary delegates at 1966 convention in Trail, B.C. Seated (L-R): ———, Mary Kelly, Edna Carter, Lorena Skinner, ———, Olga St. Jean, Pearl Moir, Helen Morley. Standing (L-R): Verona Christensen, Doreen Moen, ———, Ann Eastcott, Rose Patterson, Muriel Gendron. (Unidentified: Grace Faurot, Ann Lukey, Charlotte Berg.) Photo courtesy Tillie Belanger

Ladies' Auxiliary delegates at the B.C. District Mine Mill Convention, Vancouver 1961. (L-R): Julia Rigby, Laura Nelsen, Margaret Bystrom, Helen Walton, Rose Patterson, Betty Donaldson, Beryl Kelley, Margaret Moffatt, Verona Christensen, Dot Ratcliffe (three men Alex Fergus, Bill Hammond, Bill Booth). Photo courtesy Tillie Belanger

Some members of Trail Ladies' Auxiliary Local 131. Seated (L-R): Verona Christensen, Helen Larmor, Margaret Bystrom, Inesse Gattrell, Eva York, Dulcie Warrington, Helen Gwillim, Mary Unger. Standing (L-R): Tillie Belanger, Jean McIntyre, Emma Pontius, Dot Ratcliffe, Mary Kelly, Ann Eastcott. Photo courtesy Tillie Belanger

Trail Ladies' Auxiliary Local 131 caters for a labour school in Rossland, B.C. (L-R): Alice Petrunia, Ilda Morandini, Ann Eastcott, Donna Dosen, Kay Dosen, ———, Nora Hughes, Marlene Penson, Evelyn Louis, Emma Penson, Dora Grieves, Dot Ratcliffe. Photo courtesy Tillie Belanger

kept my dues paid up and when the women were laid off after the war I returned to full membership in the auxiliary."

As a three-shift smelter worker, Pearl was an active organizer for Local 598. "I signed up 36 people out of 52 in our department, and it was hard at times . . . we didn't have ballpoint pens, only little stubs of pencils," she joked. "Some people were hesitant . . . they remembered when many were fired for even talking union . . . but we women, many of us from the west where we always felt more free, just laughed when Nickel Rash people tried to get us to join their outfit."

She recalled when she and Charles McClure, then editor of the Local 598 *Beacon*, were distributing leaflets from door to door, and were picked up by the police: "We were taken to the police station, and we were told we could phone home, but we didn't have a phone at our house. . . ."

Accidents were common to the smelter: "people got burned . . . and I remember a young fellow, a high school student . . . there was an elevator that brought things to us, and he got his head cut off . . . his head just dropped and we got sick to our stomachs and the foreman tried to get us back to work while they tried to wake up some doctor . . . we were on graveyard shift . . . there were lots of accidents but we were discouraged from reporting them."

With the Local 598 victory over the Nickel Rash in the Inco certification vote, and even before that when the union was growing stronger every day, "everybody started feeling like human beings . . . no longer afraid."

At war's end, the women at Inco were laid off. Pearl returned to the Ladies' Auxiliary where she participated fully in its activities and held several offices in the organization throughout the succeeding years.

Concluding her reminiscences, she observed that, "today things are different, there's too much 'what's in it for me?' The young fellows are born into the union, there is already a union when they go to work."

Ladies' Auxiliary delegates at the Eighth Annual Convention, Sudbury, February 27, 1956. Front row (L-R): Maude Deline, Marjorie Torok, Millie McQuaid, William Longridge (National secretary), Lily Johnson, Dorothy MacDonald (Chairperson, Ladies' Auxiliaries), Lena Petroff. Back row (L-R): Frances Kowalski, Ann Mack, May Smith, Alice Petrunia, Tillie Belanger, John Clark (International president), Betty Gunther, Donna Hugli, Lucy Barthol. Solski Collection

Background to the Raids

HOT WAR ENDS — COLD WAR STARTS

World War I had ended with the world split into two contending factions, with uprising and revolutionary movements threatening the very ramparts of private enterprise everywhere. World War II ended with the emergence of two super powers, with two opposing political and industrial systems, and the Cold War began, laden with an underlying threat of becoming hot.

With the guns silenced on the European battlefields and in the Pacific Ocean, where the Japanese armada was forced back into its home ports, the U.S. establishment turned its attention to assuring that the post-war world would stabilize in its image. In the U.S., now the western world's leader, external relations were characterized by emergence of the Truman Doctrine, the Marshall Plan, and by the creation of NATO.

Internally, the successful prosecution of the conflict called for the dispersal and silencing of all dissent. As a first step, anti labour and civil liberties legislation, dormant since the outbreak of war, was revived and new restrictive laws promulgated. The McGarren-Warren Act, a new piece of legislation, denied the issuance of visas to anyone who would 'prejudice the public interest.' The Taft Hartley Act demanded that elected union leaders sign pledges affirming their anti-Communism.

The first targets in the labour field were the militant trade unions within the CIO, foremost of which was the International Union of Mine, Mill and Smelter Workers. The sequence of events that led to the open raids on Mine Mill started with the U.S. laws that virtually outlawed the U.S. Communist Party. Following rapidly was the charge that Mine Mill was a "Communist-controlled" union, and accusation and indictment of International Mine Mill leaders for allegedly violating the non-Communist affidavit section of the Taft Hartley Act. For the labour bureaucracy in the U.S. and Canada, that was the "go" signal, and the international conspiracy between the U.S. and Canada began to unfold and reveal itself.

The next step was to secure the full co-operation of the big, bureaucratic labour organizations. Apart from the well-defined political and industrial concessions, the offers made to the top labour bureaucrats which they couldn't refuse can only be surmised. Although intimations of the desire of Philip Murray, president of the United Steelworkers of America, and Charles Millard, its Canadian director, to number all metal mine workers in their ranks had always been discernable, direct action was withheld until the signal came from the Cold War architects.

In May 1947, the first indication that the CIO was to embrace the U.S. administration's Cold War program came with the report of a CIO investigation committee, chaired by Philip Murray, to mediate a dispute within the IUMMSW in the United States. The CIO report called for the resignation of Maurice Travis from the presidency of Mine Mill,* for an administrator to conduct the affairs of the union, and for new executive elections under CIO supervision. Mine Mill, as would any self-respecting union, refused to accept these recommendations and declared it could govern its own affairs.

THE KING GOVERNMENT

Compliance by the King government showed the subservience of Canadian policy makers to Cold War hysteria promoters U.S. Secretary of State (also Inco director) John Foster Dulles and the notorious Senator Joseph McCarthy.

At the 1947 International Mine Mill Convention, it had been decided that, following the 1946 strike in Noranda, Quebec, attention be given to the gold fields of Northern Ontario and Quebec. There, Mine Mill organization and years of struggle had been unable to achieve appreciable material gains or union security in face of adamant and inflexible absentee owners. International vice-president Reid Robinson was put in charge of the campaign to build the union's strength in the gold industry.

Immediately, a media campaign against the presence of U.S. organizers in Canada sprang up in Kirkland Lake, and the *Globe and Mail, Northern Miner* and *Financial Post* followed suit, demanding the deportation of Reid Robinson. In February 1948, a speech by Senator Taft was widely reported, which claimed that these organizers, who had always been present at organizing drives and bargaining sessions of Canadian locals, were fleeing the United States as a result of his bill. As John Lang points out in his excellent unpublished thesis: "No one ever made any attempt to explain how this process occurred; its validity was conceded without question."[12]

Prime Minister King did not wait long to consider the question. Shortly after King announced that the presence of International Mine Mill organizers in Canada was under study, international representative Harlow Wildman was refused an extension of his visa. On March 23, 1948, Reid Robinson was deported from Canada on the grounds of seeking to overthrow the Canadian government and destruction of private property. The same fate met two other veteran Mine Mill organizers.

---

*Maurice Travis was eventually forced to resign as Secretary Treasurer of the International union in the face of court action taken against him for violation of the Taft Hartley Act. After a lengthy, debilitating legal battle in the U.S. Supreme Court, he was acquitted.

[12]John Lang, *A Lion in A Den of Daniels: A History of the International Union of Mine Mill and Smelter Workers in Sudbury 1942-1962*, A thesis presented to the University of Guelph for the degree of Master of Arts, January 1970, p. 109.

The Boring From Within Tactic

The deportations gave the signal for raiding to begin in earnest, with Charles Millard of the Steelworkers leading the way for the CCL and the CCF.

Judging the two major bastions of Mine Mill, CM&S operations in the west and Inco in the east, impregnable, CCL-Steel strategists ordered forays into the gold mining areas of northern Ontario and Quebec. For propaganda purposes primarily, Steel expended huge sums in bribery and manpower to succeed in displacing Mine Mill in the gold fields.

Early on in the 1947 campaign in the gold fields, the Timmins Local 241 leadership began secessionist activities under Ralph Carlin, Joe Rankin and James Russell. These men acted under the guise of being loyal Mine Mill members, but it was not long before the real nature of their activities emerged when they all joined Steel to work against Mine Mill.

The 'boring from within' tactic was high in the strategy to destroy Mine Mill as a union and take over its membership. The subornation of executive boards was a measure that proved successful in Timmins Local 241 and was also to be used against Mine Mill in Port Colborne Local 637 and at the Anaconda Brass Local 811 in New Toronto in 1949, in Trail Local 480 in 1950, and eventually in Sudbury Local 598 in 1959.

The similarity of procedure followed by the conspirators indicated a central planning and directing body. First, executive boards purporting to act on behalf of Mine Mill members created issues of dissent with International convention and conference decisions; next, they withheld per capita payments; and, finally, they withdrew from Mine Mill, attempting to take the local membership either into the CCL or directly into the Steelworkers. John Lang's analysis of this process indicates the source of monetary incentives for such actions by these dissident executive members: "Because this method depended on convincing established local leaders to switch their allegiance, and since Steel had at its disposal such a huge patronage system, this strategy tended to have a corrupting influence on local labour leaders."[13]

Northern Ontario and Quebec propaganda against Mine Mill in full swing, Ralph Carlin, Russell and Rankin now turned their attention to organizing the dissidents in other locals of Mine Mill.

Delegates from Mine Mill locals in District 8, assembled in Sudbury for a Wage Policy Conference, April 3 and 4, 1948, were hampered in their efforts to hammer out a unified approach in contract negotiations. A small group persisted in attempting to introduce the CCL action in support of the expulsion from Canada of Mine Mill organizers. Defeated in bringing the action forward by the conference, the group walked out and set up a Provisional Committee of those supporting the CCL position.

Following the conference, renegade executive boards at Port Colborne Local 637, Local 811 at Anaconda Brass in New Toronto, and Local 819 at the carborundum plant in Niagara Falls withheld per capita dues payable to the international union and paid them instead to the Provisional Committee.

The CCF Joins the Conspiracy

At this stage, the CCF leadership made its first open move against Mine Mill. So thoroughly involved was that leadership in the Steel effort to capture Mine Mill that it performed the classic exercise of self-immolation of the party in the Sudbury district.

In 1943, Sudbury district workers and farmers had elected CCF candidate Robert Carlin, then District 8 Board Member for the IUMMSW, to the provincial legislature with the highest majority of any MPP. He had been re-elected in 1945 with a similar majority, despite heavy losses for the party elsewhere in the province.

However, in the 1948 election, in a desperate effort to discredit Mine Mill, the CCF refused to endorse Carlin as a CCF candidate unless he would join in supporting the CCL position on deportation proceedings against Mine Mill organizers. Carlin refused to do this, and the CCF ran an opposition candidate, knowing full well that even if Carlin were defeated, their man couldn't possibly win. The result was a prophecy fulfilled: the riding went to the Tories. The CCF in Sudbury, which had had the largest membership of any constituency in the whole of Canada, was destroyed for many years.*

The CCL Expels Mine Mill: Port Colborne Raid 1949

In October 1948, dissidents who had been active in Port Colborne Local 637 for the past two years, succeeded in splitting the ranks of the union when the entire executive board led an open move to secede from Mine Mill. The ground for this act had been prepared by the CCL's suspension of Mine Mill at its October convention.

On the basis of a referendum vote held by this executive board, with International President John Clark refused

---

[13]Lang, p. 129.

*In 1953, a similar situation developed in British Columbia. During the provincial election that year, CCF leaders participated actively in the Steel raids against Mine Mill in that province. The election results were as follows: Social Credit 20; CCF 19. Three constituencies where Mine Mill predominated, which had consistently voted CCF, had voted Social Credit because of the raids. Thus, the CCF lost the opportunity of forming the government in B.C. that year.

admittance into Canada to defend the position of the international, the executive board applied for a charter from the CCL, which was immediately granted. The group, however, changed its mind and applied for a charter from the Steelworkers with apparent approval of the CCL.

On January 9, 1949, a vote conducted by the Ontario Labour Relations Board resulted in a victory for Mine Mill, and Local 637 was re-instated bargaining agent for Port Colborne.

Things then moved quickly. On January 11, 1949, the CCL ordered both Mine Mill and Steel to vacate Port Colborne and Timmins. Mine Mill turned down what it considered a preposterous and outrageous proposal, that it surrender its jurisdiction in the face of a raid. In February 1949, the CCL Executive Council expelled Mine Mill for failing to comply with its order; the expulsion of Mine Mill was ratified at the next convention of the CCL, in October 1949.

Encouraged by the dissension within the union, Inco held the Local 637 check-off dues in trust and refused to negotiate with Local 598 if International President John Clark were on the bargaining committee. As John Lang points out: "For the first time, Local 598 leaders would be left on their own to negotiate a contract. The interests of the raiders and the company were complementary."[14]

A new local union leadership emerged after the defection of the majority of the old executive to the Steelworkers, and for some time after Mike Kopinak led the local as president and Gavin (Bill) Cowper was the financial secretary. Cowper had been part of the first leadership of Local 637 and was one of the few that remained loyal to Mine Mill during the first raid. Many others also came forward, such as Louis Brema, Fred Houde, Rolly Methot, John Tronko, Mickey Pine, Dragan Sesto and Yves Lemay, and played a role in that local until it went out of existence in the raid in 1963.

The CCL applied for certification of the Port Colborne workers on April 1, 1949, and the Ontario Labour Relations Board ordered a vote for June 2nd and 3rd. The usual Steel campaign of vilification and red-baiting started and it was reported that the church moved into action a day or two before the vote and that nuns visited workers' homes to influence them against Mine Mill. The vote again sustained Mine Mill as bargaining agent. On September 14, 1949, the Ontario Supreme Court ruled strongly in favour of Mine Mill in awarding the $16,000 in dues money withheld by Inco to Local 637.

The 1949 raid on Port Colborne strengthened Inco's hand and worked to the detriment of the Port Colborne employees, who lost the Roach Formula check-off granted to Sudbury Local 598 that year. However, in 1950 the Roach Formula was regained by Local 637 in joint bargaining with Local 598.

The concluding episode of the year showed that CCL had no intention of respecting the victories awarded to Mine Mill in OLRB-conducted votes and in the courts in 1949,

as the CCL awarded Mine Mill's jurisdiction to Steel for $50,000. As John Lang summarizes:

> The culmination of Millard's strategy was unveiled on November 15, 1949 when the United Steelworkers of America made application for Mine Mill's jurisdiction. At its meeting on January 19, 1950, the C.C.L. Executive Council studied this application and granted it. It was decided that the Steelworkers would "reimburse the Congress for the expenses incurred in the organization of the workers in this jurisdiction during the past year." In this manner, Millard acquired the jurisdictional rights over the mine, mill and smelter workers of Canada for the meagre sum of $50,000.00.[15]

STEEL RAIDS: TRAIL 1950

In Mine Mill's western district, Steelworkers raided Local 480 members employed at the Consolidated Mining and Smelting Company operations in Trail. The tried-and-tested technique of winning over the executive board was used there too. The board, in majority supporters of CM&S company unions of old, announced its defection to Steel on February 9, 1950. Quick membership action brought in a new ('Blitz') leadership with Al King as president, confusion spread by the renegades was overcome, and before long contract negotiations with the company were concluded and a new agreement signed on May 31st.

It took another two years before the Steelworkers were decisively and permanently defeated in a certification vote in Trail, but the raids in the west were not ended. While Mine Mill continued its major task of organizing the many mining camps, Steel staff members trailed Mine Mill organizers, spreading confusion and attempting to prevent organization. It was not until the 1967 merger with Steel that raiding was finally stopped.

Although Steelworker raids were of uniform intensity throughout Canada, it was in the Inco operations in Ontario and Manitoba and to a lesser degree the uranium mines of Elliot Lake that the full force of the conspiracy in all its manifestations was felt.

INCO OPERATIONS TARGETED: PORT COLBORNE 1950

Encouraged by the relatively close vote in the Port Colborne CCL attempt of 1949, the first Steel organizer turned up in Port Colborne early in March of 1950. Before long, between twenty and thirty raiders, accompanied by

---

[14]Lang, p. 133.

[15]Lang, p. 122.

Local 598 sent a busload of campaign workers from Sudbury to assist in fighting off the first open Steel raid on Port Colborne, summer of 1950. Standing (L-R): Jake Collison, Hugh Kennedy, Art Michel, Nels Thibault, William Sproule, Norman Jaques, Jack Quennville, Jack McCool, Charlie Michael, Wally Gorham, Mike Kopinak, Mike Solski, Robert Carlin (board member District 8), Steve Wilson, Tom English. In bus (L-R): Oliver Ellis, Henry Labrose, Geno Sartor. Organizers of campaign at left (L-R): John (Jack) Smaller, publicity director; Nels Thibault, president Local 598; Mike Kopinak, president Local 637; Mike Solski, vice-president Local 598. Solski Collection

Mine Mill victory celebration after the 1950 Steel raid: Port Colborne members and wives, with campaign workers from Sudbury and Buffalo. Solski Collection

Oliver Breton, a new renegade whom Steel had won over, appeared on the scene. Breton, a long-time Mine Mill staff member, had been assigned to Local 637 prior to and during the CCL raid the previous year. The defence of Mine Mill was left up to Local 598.

On the other hand, dismayed and angered by the unprincipled actions of the Steelworkers, some of the most vocal members opposed to the Mine Mill leadership joined in the effort to defeat the raiders. In the OLRB vote conducted on October 4 and 5, 1950, Steel suffered a decisive defeat.

While Local 598 had successfully defended Mine Mill in the Inco operations at Port Colborne, continuing raids in the Timmins area finally resulted in Steel capturing Local 241. By October 1950, Mine Mill had been displaced in the area. Steel, however, having trumpeted their victory throughout the country, did little to obtain contract gains for the workers, despite promises and despite their vaunted size, power and wealth. In some instances, Steel simply allowed contracts to lapse.

SUDBURY RAID: 1950

Meanwhile in Sudbury, where some 13,000 Inco employees were members of Local 598, James Kidd, discredited former president, had previously attempted a futile United Mine Workers raid on the Canadian Industries Limited workers, also members of Local 598. Within the membership as a whole there had been indications of preparations for a Steel raid.

As part of Millard's tactic to suborn an executive board to take over a local from within, the White Bloc, organized and nurtured by James Russell posing as a CCF representative in Sudbury, had attempted to unseat the Local 598 leadership headed by president Nels Thibault and vice-president Mike Solski in the December 1948 elections. The tactic had failed miserably in a more than two-to-one vote. The defeat destroyed any organization the White Bloc had achieved.

A short period of calm was broken when Millard, in desperation at the defeat of his prized tactic, launched an open raid in Sudbury in January 1950. The Steelworkers held their first "public" meeting in a small hotel room addressed by William Sefton and William Mahoney, Millard's assistant director. An office was established in Sudbury and a squad of raiders imported. By April, the raid was a dead issue and, except for a vacant office optimistically leased for a year, there was no sign of the raiders.

Reminiscing on the days when open raiding of Mine Mill started, Nels Thibault, former president of Local 598 and later elected to several offices in the international and national union, in a 1981 interview, recalled that a number of Steelworkers "led by Larry Bennett, Jim Russell and Joe Rankin, who had defected by that time to the Steelworkers, came in and they set up an office on Elm Street and housed their troops in a hotel in Gatchell . . . that was when we

formed the first effective defence committee of Local 598, a group of leading activists in the local who said we are going to be the guardians of the union and no Steelworkers are going to interfere with this community . . . and we used to take some pretty bold marches around looking for raiders — we popularized the term raiders — and at one time we actually caught up with some of them and they didn't bother us much after that . . . we had relative peace for a while."

Decisively defeated at the CM&S operations in the west and the Inco mines and plants in the east, the open raid tactic in these areas was mothballed for the time. Emphasis was placed on hampering new Mine Mill organization and nurturing and subsidizing dissident groups within firmly established Mine Mill locals.

Although relative quiet prevailed overall, there were incidents that reminded the membership that threatening currents could break through the surface calm.

In the 1952 elections for the executive of Local 598, so-called dissidents coalesced in a "Rank and File Movement" to create dissension within the local. Although the Rank and File slate outwardly contested the election as sincere Mine Mill members, their real connections were suspect. As John Lang points out:

> The hand of Millard, and the intention to use this movement as a base to spring a raid on Local 598 can be seen in the method by which the movement recruited new members. A $1.00 donation was solicited to assist in election expenses, and the donor was requested to sign a card, the wording of which would be acceptable to the O.L.R.B. in its certification proceedings.[16]

In 1954 Inco shift boss James Kidd was demoted to the hourly-rated ranks to make him eligible for union membership. Recalling his disruptive activities in the past, a membership meeting rejected his application. The *Sudbury Star* publicized the issue and Kidd picketed the union hall, an act which was prominently covered by the *Toronto Star*. In an interview with John Lang in 1968, Kidd admitted that Murray Cotterill, public relations director of the Steelworkers, concocted the ploy and arranged for the *Toronto Star* reporter to record the incident.[17]

Re-admitted to membership in Local 598, Kidd immediately took over the leadership of opposition groups and, on his own admission to John Lang, sought the assistance of the Roman Catholic clergy. Meeting rooms for his followers were provided by Father M. T. Mulcahy in St. Charles College.

Then came the opening for the Ontario Labour Relations Board and its chairman, Professor Finkleman, to get into the conspiracy.

[16]Lang, p. 153.
[17]Lang, p. 179.

THE LABOUR BOARD AND CANADIAN AUTONOMY: 1955

Mine Mill was the first international union to grant autonomy to its Canadian membership. For many years, in addition to representation on the board of the international union, annual Canadian conventions had been held to discuss and unite policies in Canadian matters. In 1953, the Canadian Mine Mill Council had been formed to direct the administration and organizational work of the union in Canada. An amendment to the constitution to provide for Canadian autonomy was passed at the International Mine Mill Convention in March 1955, and later ratified in a referendum vote by both Canadian and American members. Finally, a convention for the Canadian membership at Rossland, B.C. on July 18th, 1955 drew up the Canadian constitution and nominated a Canadian executive board, both of which were ratified by a Canadian referendum on November 29th.

Meanwhile, in November 1955, Mine Mill had applied for certification at the Algom Uranium Mines in Elliot Lake, Ontario. Ever on the alert to hamper and impede Mine Mill organization, the Steelworkers intervened and presented the OLRB with an argument that the advent of Canadian autonomy meant that Mine Mill was a new legal entity and therefore not entitled to certification.

A few days later, at a hearing before the same board on Mine Mill's application for certification at the Port Colborne Hospital, Chairman Finkleman concurred with the Steelworkers that certification depended upon the question of whether Mine Mill was a new legal entity. The OLRB then ruled the signed application cards invalid on the grounds that the Canadian organization was an entirely different entity, and dismissed Mine Mill's application. Two other Mine Mill applications were later dismissed on the same grounds.

Now it really snowballed! Mine Mill Local 889 had been certified for the employees of the Deloro Smelting and Refining Company at Marmora, Ontario, and had held a one-year contract with the company since December 20, 1954. The Steelworkers had raided the operation and were applying for certification. Finkleman argued that if Local 889 had remained a part of the international organization, it would retain bargaining rights, but if it became a part of the Canadian organization, then it was a "new entity which can establish a claim to act as bargaining agent . . . only if it satisfies the requirements of Section 7 of the Labour Relations Act." This meant that Local 889 would have to go through the procedure of re-signing the members and collecting initiation fees before it could make application to the OLRB. The board then, with incredible cynicism, granted the certification to the Steelworkers without a vote. At the same time, flagrantly biased, the board ordered a vote in an uncontested application by Local 902. Immediately, the media reported that Mine Mill had lost its bargaining rights.

The press reports may have been inaccurate and the contracts between Mine Mill and the many companies legally binding, but the OLRB was on a path aimed at destroying Mine Mill. The board, which was composed of Finkleman as chairman, one representative of industry, and one labour representative who was a member of the CCL unions, refused to recognize Mine Mill as a trade union until it had re-signed a majority of the workers in each plant and had re-applied to the OLRB for certification — meanwhile leaving the field wide open to Steel raids.

In Local 598, Kidd lost no time in spreading further disruption. But his attempts to capitalize on the OLRB's actions were not lost on the local's leadership. On March 26, 1956, the Local 598 *Mine Mill News* warned that "within a few days the *Sudbury Daily Star* will blossom out in advertisements calling on I.N.C.O. to refuse to recognize Mine Mill."

First Canadian Mine Mill Council 1953. Seated (L-R): *Harvey Murphy, B.C. regional director; Nels Thibault, board member District 8; Ken Smith, Council president; Mike Solski, secretary; John Clark, International president; William Longridge, executive secretary.* Standing (L-R): *L. Messmer, Ray Stevenson, Jack Tees, Doug Gold, Robert Michel, Mike Kopinak. Solski Collection*

The prediction was confirmed when, two days later, the *Sudbury Star* published an "open letter" signed by 56 nickel workers, which stated that the OLRB had ruled that Mine Mill "has ceased to exist for purposes of labour relations in this Province," and advising the mining companies not to recognize Mine Mill but to withhold the check-off dues in trust. Years later, Kidd admitted to John Lang that this letter had been drawn up by Murray Cotterill of the Steelworkers.[18] Commenting further on this situation, Lang points out:

> What is most significant, however, is that the Steelworkers and Kidd must have been aware of the contents of the O.L.R.B. decisions before they were released on March 24, 1956. It is not beyond the realm of possibility that the Ontario Labour Relations Board deliberately delayed the release of their March 15, 1956 decisions, in order to give the Steelworkers ten days in which to launch a raid against Local 598.[19]

Referring to the introduction during this period of Section 44(a) as an amendment to the Ontario Labour Relations Act, providing for a declaration of successor rights when unions merged or transferred their bargaining rights to another union, Thibault had this to say: "Look at the time when we established Canadian autonomy, when we got notice that we were a changed entity and the old certification no longer applied. It wasn't by accident that Section 44(a) came into effect. It was because we took the position before Falconbridge and Inco that they recognize the union or no muck came out tomorrow."

[18]Lang, p. 186.
[19]Lang, p. 187.

Meanwhile, taking note of the role played by Kidd throughout this situation, Local 598 once again expelled him from membership in Mine Mill, this time for life. However, Kidd had already become a full-time staff member of the Steelworkers and had established an office in Sudbury to continue his work towards the destruction of Mine Mill.

ELLIOT LAKE RAIDED: 1956

The OLRB decisions had little effect on Mine Mill's membership at the Falconbridge and Inco operations in Sudbury and Port Colborne, or on Local 902. However, they were highly effective in making it virtually impossible for Mine Mill to succeed in organizing in Elliot Lake.

On April 2, 1956, the board rejected Mine Mill's re-application at Algom Mines, in spite of the fact that the union had presented cards for a majority of the Algom workers. It ordered a vote, but with only the Steelworkers and a company union on the ballot, and Steel was certified. Although certification of uranium mines was later declared a function of the Canadian Labour Relations Board, the confusion spread by the OLRB and the Steelworkers, aided by collusion of the companies, resulted in Steel succeeding in the other Elliot Lake mines.

Assessing the ultimate results of the raids in Elliot Lake, Lang makes the following observations:

> It is needless to point out that those who suffered most from such a situation were the workers themselves. . . . With the workers so divided, the companies were free to develop the camps in any manner they pleased. The most basic sanitary precautions were ignored as they crowded the workers — "two men to a bed" — into the bunk-

The Mine Mill convention that established Canadian autonomy in 1955 was held in the union hall in Rossland, B.C., built in 1895 by the Western Federation of Miners.
Solski Collection

houses. . . . Similarly, as the rush to develop these properties continued, and the companies attempted to make the most of their three-year moratorium on taxes, the workers' demands for stricter safety procedures were dismissed as unnecessary. A governmental inquiry was established after fourteen miners were killed between January 1 and May 13, 1958, but clearly, by then it was too late.[20]

For belated recognition of injustice, we have the following from the *Globe and Mail*, April 11, 1963:

Chief Justice J. C. McRuer says David Archer should not have sat as a member of the Ontario Labour Relations Board in a hearing in December involving the International Union of Mine Mill and Smelter Workers. He said that Mr. Archer as chief executive of an organization which had declared a policy of destroying the Mine Mill union should not sit to decide disputes between the two organizations or their affiliates.

The 1958 Inco Strike

The year 1958 is memorable for the growing turbulence that led up to the strike, the first in fifteen years of peaceful relations of Locals 637 and 598 with the International Nickel Company. Forces within and without the union boundaries girded for what they believed could result in the "final solution" for Local 598 and Mine Mill in Canada.

Following an election victory, the Tory Diefenbaker government came through with the first payoff for big business — the Diefenbaker "hold-the-line" dictate to labour. No wage increases in 1958!

Meanwhile, Local 598 had been preparing to negotiate a new contract since conclusion of the two-year contract signed in 1956. Research Associates of Montreal, publisher of the widely circulated monthly *Labour Facts*, was commissioned to prepare a report on collective agreements across Canada for the information of the negotiating committee in 1958 and had also conducted a stewards' school for Local 598 in the autumn of 1957.

Having presented a list of demands to Inco, a series of proposals the membership considered reasonable in light of the company's favourable financial position and of rising living costs, Local 598 prepared to meet the company.

The company, presumably in preparation for its contribution to the final solution for a militant and successful union, had built up a substantial inventory through a year-long speed-up to take care of any eventuality; then it launched a series of provocative actions.

Complementing the company's manoeuvers, members of the union who previously had played no constructive role in union affairs appeared on the scene and began to propose actions which would have put the union in unrealistic and untenable positions, proposals unquestionably in the realm of the *agent provocateur*.

The opening gun in the negotiations was fired by the company on March 5th with a large layoff of 1,000 men in Sudbury and 300 in Port Colborne. Thus, Inco set the tone and atmosphere in which bargaining would proceed.

On April 15th, meetings of the company with the joint Port Colborne Local 637 and Local 598 negotiating committee started and continued through April and May. Throughout these meetings, it became increasingly clear that, unlike in previous years, the company had little intention of concluding an agreement acceptable to both parties. During these preliminary sessions, the company admitted it had piled up substantial inventory and announced a further layoff of 300 men in Sudbury. The union pointed out that, despite layoffs, production had not decreased.

On May 23rd, with no signs of progress, talks were ended and the union applied to the provincial labour department for a conciliator. June 19th, Conciliator R. J. Bradley met the parties for a single day. Faced with stonewalling by the company in its refusal to make a realistic proposal, the conciliator admitted defeat and bowed out, recommending that the labour department establish a conciliation board.

On June 17th, Inco fired its second big gun in the negotiation proceedings by announcing a cutback from 40 to 32 hours of work per week. The union estimated the average loss in wages for each worker to be $17.60 a week, plummeting the take-home pay to the 1950 levels.

On August 11th, a conciliation board made up of chairman Judge D. C. Thomas, union nominee K. C. Woodsworth, and company nominee C. R. Bigelow met in Toronto with union and company negotiators. Four days of intense effort by the board could not move the company from its adamant position. The board called off further sessions and retired to prepare a report.

On September 9th, the report, consisting of majority and minority versions, was brought down, the majority favouring the company to the point where it could not be accepted. The union took the next step, the calling of a strike vote, a procedure normally followed by trade unions for an expression from memberships and a direction for further action.

On September 12th, a strike vote conducted in Sudbury and Port Colborne recorded an overwhelming affirmative: of a total vote of 12,887, 10,662 were for, and 2,185 against strike action, with 40 ballots spoiled. Armed with such membership support, the union called for another meeting with the company.

On September 16th, the bargaining committee met the company in the Copper Cliff offices. From the union's stenographic notes on bargaining sessions:

Company: Well, we're here to listen to what you have to say.

Solski: Your employees are not prepared to accept the majority report. We're ready to use the minority as a basis to bargain; at that it's going a long way from our original

---

[20]Lang, p. 198.

Friday, September 12, 1958 strike vote. The 1958 Inco strike had strong membership support, but Inco was prepared not to bargain. (L-R): John Tronko and Gavin (Bill) Cowper (Local 637); Bill Merrick, Norm Dupuis, Bill Boyuk, William "Red" Sproule, Leo Legault, Les Fitzpatrick. Solski Collection

proposals. We're prepared to start now and continue till we reach a peaceful settlement . . . if you're interested.

Company: . . . we cannot commit the company beyond that which is offered in the majority report.

WILDCAT PROVOCATIONS

The company then referred to what it considered was the inevitability of a strike and sought discussion on procedures to be followed in "an orderly shut-down." Replying to the company's insistence upon discussing shut-down procedure, Solski replied: "We didn't come here to discuss that . . . we were hopeful of doing some bargaining." The company persisted in asking for the date of a strike to be called by the union.

Solski: Beginning on what would normally be the start of the day shift on September 24th — providing there isn't some provocation before then.

Company: Very well.

Solski: I repeat, we're interested in an orderly shut-down, but the provocations . . . some of your bosses are doing a good job of it now.

Company: We'll have to close down if there's wildcat strikes.

Solski: Your bosses, one at Garson provoked it.

Company: We have no intention of operating the mines and plants.

Pacing these discussions, simultaneous, unauthorized and glaringly non-spontaneous walkouts and picketing were taking place at several plants and mines in widely separate areas. Well planned and highly organized through a network whose tentacles surfaced at a crucial time, these provocative actions were condemned by the elected leadership of the union. Officers, stewards and prominent rank-and-filers rushed to and from the various plant gates to urge workers to go to work and stay on their jobs. In every instance, they were met by small groups brandishing commercially prepared "On Strike" placards and armed with clubs and other weapons preventing men from entering the gates.

Still determined to make every effort to settle the dispute peacefully and without resort to a strike, the joint Local 637 and 598 negotiating committee sent Solski to Toronto to persuade Premier Leslie Frost to bring the parties together in continued bargaining. Solski's effort proved successful and the premier arranged a meeting between the parties for September 23, with Labour Minister Charles Daley as mediator.

However, even as these discussions took place, Inco was sending smelter employees home and shutting down its furnaces: it was clear that Inco had no intention of bargaining. At the meeting of company and union committees in the presence of Labour Minister Daley and Deputy Minister J. B. Metzler:

Solski: I made a call to Sudbury and find that we're kidding ourselves. The men were told by management to take their clothes home at 4 p.m. What's the idea?

Metzler: What's the use of dallying? They expect a strike.

Despite this new development, the union committee made a further cut in their last proposals and tried again to move the company. The company refused to consider this latest effort.

Solski: This indicates that no matter what proposal we make they'd refuse.

In a taped interview, recorded some 20 years after these events, Jack Quenneville, representing the Copper Cliff smelter on the 1958 negotiating committee, recalled some of the events:

"I was on the negotiating committee and we were meeting the company in Toronto with the Minister of Labour as mediator, and our boys in Sudbury were told to hold the line and keep solid and stay on the job and we'll try to get the best possible contract. But there were picket lines set up at plants by some people and our leaders went to the various plants to get the workers back and the men were being stopped from going to work and the company ordered the men to take their clothes and go home while we were still in negotiations.

"... it may be hard to say that the company provoked a shutdown but with the help of some of the dissidents they were able to effectively shut down some operations. These same people who after the settlement criticized the agreement were the ones who forced what really turned out to be a lock-out by setting up picket lines before the strike was called by the union ... they were the instigators to assist the company to shut down the operations ... at no time did the company try to keep the operation going ... so I think these people who instigated the early walk-outs had the full blessing of the company. ...."

During 13 full weeks of strike, Inco saved the cost of some $19 million in wages, according to estimates at the time. Furthermore, the company realized savings in continued delivery of nickel and other metals to customers, at no extra cost to the company because its stockpiles were the result of overproduction due to various forms of speed-up. Thus, Inco had its strike, at a substantial profit even for a giant money maker.

THE STRIKE IS CALLED

Faced with the company's determination that a strike would take place, added to the danger that the plot to force a breakdown in the unified and disciplined action of the membership might succeed in creating chaos through sporadic wildcat walkouts, the negotiating committee and officers of both Locals 637 and 598 decided to announce officially that the walkout would take place with the day shift of September 24th.

The strike started on the morning of September 24th in an orderly, well-organized and disciplined manner. Picket lines appeared at the Port Colborne refinery gate and at the many Sudbury area Inco mine and plant gates. With the strike official, and with properly authorized union pickets at the gates, the "pick-handle-and-pipe" bully-boys vanished and went underground to continue their disruption.

The days rolled by, the strike firm and the membership determined to achieve a fair settlement. Union officers continued their efforts through direct approach and through co-operating intermediaries to persuade the company to resume bargaining. Strike relief followed the practice established elsewhere. Calls went out to government agencies to intervene, and appeals were made for moral, political and financial support from other unions. Recalling Mine Mill's unstinting support to unions on strike, trade union locals throughout Canada, including CLC affiliates and independents and unions in the U.S., responded generously.

On the other hand, the commercial print and electronic media railed against the union, denounced its strike, and reviled its leadership. Locally, the *Sudbury Star* led the pack in virulence and fulmination against the union and in unabashed praise and commendation of the company, earning its popular name the *Inco Star*.

Second only to the *Sudbury Star* in its denunciation of the union was the Toronto *Globe and Mail*, ever the spokesman for the mining industry. A piece in that paper by Joan Hollobon, December 14, 1958, was incredibly shameless and ridiculous:

> Communism is being openly cited here as the reason for growing opposition among strikers and their wives to the Mine Mill union executive. . . .
>
> Strikers summoned to a meeting today in the Mine Mill Hall were told in no uncertain terms to bring their wives into line. . . .
>
> If violence does not flare up it will be because rank and file opposition has been crushed by threats against miners' wives. . . .
>
> The man was shaking with fear. His lips trembled as the words tumbled out of his mouth. His hand shook as he lit a cigaret. His phone had rung until 5 a.m. today with continuous calls. His eyes were bloodshot with lack of sleep. He was known to have been among a group trying to organize opposition to the union.
>
> "They'll get me. I know they will. I'm not afraid of dying. I only care about my church and dying in mortal sin. And I'm afraid after my family," he said.

This supposedly from a miner, nameless, of course (lest they get me?) who is accustomed to a job ever threatening to life and limb!

The days grew into weeks and the strike continued with no move by the company to re-open bargaining. The union organized a variety of functions to maintain the morale of the membership and the interest of the public. An auto cavalcade to Queen's Park, the seat of the provincial government, and a picket line around Inco's downtown Toronto offices were highly successful. A shipment of nickel overseas from the Montreal port was picketed by a group of Sudbury strikers, and prominent union personalities visited organizations across Canada bringing them the story of the Inco strike.

Wednesday, December 3, 1958. The auto cavalcade of one thousand Mine Mill members from Port Colborne and Sudbury to Queen's Park in Toronto (above) captured the imagination of the nation and compelled Premier Leslie Frost to meet with union spokesmen in his office for two and a half hours that same day (right). (L-R): Kelso Roberts, Attorney General; William Arthur Goodfellow, Minister of Agriculture; Rheal Belisle, Nickel Belt MPP; James Noble Allan, Treasurer; Gerry Monaghan, Sudbury MPP; Charles Daley, Minister of Labour; Premier Leslie Frost; Rolly Methot, President Local 637; Tom Paradis, Staff Local 598; Mike Solski, President Local 598; Nels Thibault, National President; Ray Stevenson, National Executive. Solski Collection

Local 637 Port Colborne strike committee during the 1958 strike. (L-R): Dragan Sesto, John Tronko, Jack Karpinchick, Alex Davis, Mickey Pine, Louis Brema. UBC Collection

BACK-TO-WORK SCHEME FAILS

On December 10th, 1958, nine hundred women attended a meeting, chaired by Millie McQuaid, in support of the twelve-week-long strike and passed a resolution to march on city hall. However, the *Sudbury Star*'s coverage of the meeting, in keeping with its stance throughout that the strike had no support in the community, highlighted two women who disagreed with the resolution.

Not to be outdone in their support for the company, Sudbury district politicians, elected to their offices by the very people they would harm, moved into action against the union. Sudbury Mayor Joseph Fabbro, Nickel Belt MPP Rheal Belisle, and Sudbury Riding MPP G. J. Monaghan joined forces to organize a "back-to-work" meeting of union members' wives who opposed the strike and the union's leadership. This meeting was not restricted to strikers' wives. It was known that some merchants released their female staff

to bolster the ranks. The meeting in the Sudbury Arena, seen by Mine Mill as a strike breaking effort, received extensive coverage from the local and national media, but failed to achieve its purpose.

The strike ended December 22, 1958. Considering all the forces that were against it, the strike itself was a victory in that the local had remained unified and obtained a final settlement that compared with the Stelco and Algoma settlements that year. Summing up the strike, Mike Solski, who was president of Local 598 in 1958, recalls:

> I think we were the first union to ever lead a motor cavalcade to Toronto to apply pressure. We sure as hell did apply pressure. What did Mayor Fabbro and the rest of the community leaders do? As you know, the pre-strike offer was nothing. It was not till November that they made an offer in the 2nd and 3rd year. The whole thing amounted to 5.5 cents an hour with no fringes at all. The night before the strike was settled, the company offered 1% and 2% and 3%, and some fringes. We were given an ultimatum.

On Wednesday, December 10, 1958, 900 miners' wives attend a meeting at the Mine Mill Hall in support of the men on strike. The meeting, chaired by Millie McQuaid, was either ignored or ridiculed by the media.
Solski Collection

As part of a back-to-work scheme, Sudbury Mayor Joe Fabbro and area politicians address women at the Sudbury Arena, Friday, December 12, 1958. This meeting received extensive media coverage. Solski Collection

Settlement of the strike at the Ministry of Labour, Toronto, Tuesday, December 16, 1958. (R-L): William Longridge, National secretary-treasurer; Orville Larson, International vice-president; Nels Thibault, National president; Mike Solski, Local 598 president; Louis Fine, chief conciliator; Charles Daley, Minister of Labour; Mickey Pine, Local 637; Yves Lemay, Local 637. Solski Collection

We not only took the crap from some civic and spiritual leaders in Sudbury, but Daley, the Minister of Labour, told us point-blank, "You take the offer that the company has given you back to the members, and if you don't, we will."

I was ready to go through the roof! That night we met and agreed. We knew there was no longer any hope of holding on without destroying the union. We also knew we couldn't go to the membership with that government recommendation and survive. So that night we agreed to make one more last effort, behind the back of the government. We sent Orville Larsen to meet the company and we did get a little bit more.

And you know, then we went back the next morning to meet with the Minister, because we wanted his answer. We already knew what the company would accept, which was above what Daley told us we had to accept. So I said to Daley, "Well it's fine but I think they should do this much more, and we would be prepared to recommend."

He hit the ceiling! "No g.d. way!" I saw Louis Fine, the Chief Conciliation Officer, who was sitting beside Daley, kick him in the shins. All of a sudden they realized that we had gone over their heads, so they asked for a recess. That's how it was settled. Right to the last minute, the government was out to cut our throats. Well, it sure was not a normal situation.[21]

If there had not been the union disruption and everything else set up against the union, the 1958 strike might well have been a lesson to the company for future employee relations.

---

[21]Part six of an interview with Mike Solski conducted by Jim Tester, *Local 598 Mine Mill News*, June, 1983, p. 5.

Boring From Within Local 598

Enter Professors Boudreau and Bouvier

Perturbed by the failure of dissidents within Local 598 to achieve perceptible progress in capturing the union despite years of effort, the decision was taken to import specialists in that field.

First on the scene in October 1958 was Alexander J. Boudreau, an alumnus of a Jesuit school, who had arrived at the University of Sudbury as "director of extension courses." The University of Sudbury is the Roman Catholic college of Laurentian University. His main responsibility early in his tenure turned out to be training dissidents within Mine Mill in all aspects of union disruption and in organizing slates of anti-union types to run in Local 598 elections. When the Steel raids finally came out in the open, he functioned openly and actively on behalf of Steel against Mine Mill.

Soon after his arrival, he was joined by the Very Reverend Emile Bouvier, S.J. Bouvier was the 1951 author of *Employers and Employees*, a book thoroughly condemned by Gerard Picard, former president of the Canadian Catholic Confederation of Labour. In a review published in the March 2, 1951 edition of *Le Travail*, Picard said that the "book will not be very well received among workers but it will be more appreciated by employers and it will become a favourite reference book of the provincial police." He concluded his review by pointing out a striking similarity with 'Custos' at the time of the 1949 Asbestos strike in Quebec. "Many pages of the two are identical."

Bouvier came to the University of Sudbury as president. In addition to his reputation as anti-labour, he had an interesting background in international affairs. After receiving his doctor of philosophy degree in economics from Georgetown University in Washington, he had opened a controversial school of "industrial relations" in Mexico City. Later, he had returned to Georgetown to head its department of political economy. Why such a man would interest himself in Sudbury can only be speculated upon, but the November 24, 1980, issue of *Maclean's*, in an article entitled "Academic Cloaks and CIA Daggers" by William Lowther, had this to say about Bouvier's *alma mater:*

> Five blocks from the White House, at the corner of 18th and K streets, stands the discreet "International Club" office building. . . . on the fourth floor are the offices of Georgetown University's Center for Strategic and International Studies. The doors are barred. . . .
>
> The first impression is not of a seat of scholarship, rather of a cloak-and-daggers operation. Second impressions reinforce the first. CSIS, as it likes to be known, has strong links with the CIA. . . .
>
> CSIS was founded in 1962 by the Ivy League Georgetown University, itself administered by the Jesuits, "to foster scholarship and public awareness of emerging international issues." It has an annual budget of about $3.5 million which it raises from "foundations, individuals, corporations and corporate foundations," none of which it names in the annual report. But after U.S. President Reagan's staff appointments from the CSIS had been publicized, CSIS felt it necessary to say in a document released to the press that it "receives a small amount of government funding, . . . but accepts no money from the Central Intelligence Agency and does no classified research."
>
> . . . Its Canadian Studies Program . . . continues to promote "informal exchanges" between Canadians and Americans on "issues in the bilateral relationship."

Boudreau's extension course in spurious labour history misrepresented itself under the dignified appellation, Northern Workers Adult Education Association. In fact, the content of the course centred largely on the characterization of Mine Mill as a Communist menace and included such literature as pamphlets from "The Christian Anti-Communist Crusade," as well as CLC and Steelworkers material. In this context, the instruction offered to class participants in procedural rules governing meetings took on a more sinister motive than that of workers' education.

The course soon progressed to direct teachings of techniques and methods of destabilizing organizations, training union disrupters and subverting the gullible workers who attended classes. Kidd supplied Boudreau with a list of 90 Mine Mill members as possible candidates for the nucleus of an opposition movement; he also suggested to John Lang that the Boudreau course was probably subsidized by the Steelworkers.[22]

Prior to the 1958 Inco strike, Boudreau's prized pupils were prominent among those who suggested provocative contract proposals to the membership. Later, during the tense final days of bargaining, they attempted to initiate

wildcat walkouts thereby disrupting sessions involving the union, company and government, as well as to obstruct preparations for the official and unified strike action.

PROFESSOR BOUDREAU
More than an academic interest. Photo courtesy Michael Dudowich, Sudbury, Ont.

BORING-FROM-WITHIN SUCCEEDS IN LOCAL 598: MARCH 1959

Following the strike, graduates of the Boudreau school moved in to take advantage of the normal reaction among many of the thousands of Inco workers to the strike. The Committee for Democratic and Positive Action suddenly appeared on the scene and set to work within Local 598 at Sudbury area plants, fabricating information that the strike relief fund had been mismanaged and fallaciously attributing much of the blame for the outcome of the strike to Mine Mill's position outside of the CLC. This so-called reform movement was ready with its slate of candidates demanding a change in the leadership of Mine Mill when the election for the Local 598 executive, postponed because of the strike, was called.

From Boudreau's classes, the leading triumvirate, headed by Don Gillis, included Don McNabb, long-time vociferous supporter of the Steelworkers, and Ray Poirier, a hitherto unknown who came in out of the shadows through the Boudreau class.

In the executive election held on March 10, 1959, the Gillis slate defeated President Mike Solski's administration: enough of the "silent majority" who had been taking the union for granted without attending meetings or participating in its activities had been convinced to vote against the incumbent executive and assure its defeat.

After years of effort and lavish expenditures on Local 598 from both sides of the border, the boring-from-within strategy had finally succeeded in a takeover of the executive of Local 598.

---

[22]Lang, p. 223.

Canadian Labour Congress
Congrès du Travail du Canada

81 Lorne St.,
Sudbury, Ont.,
January 6, 1959.

Mr. A.J. Boudreau,
University of Sudbury,
30 Elgin Street,
SUDBURY, Ontario.

Dear Mr. Boudreau:

The following are names of persons that I recommend as participants in your extension course for miners. I have worked with all these men and can speak highly of their interest and capabilities.

I will list them according to occupation, trade and plant in which they are employed. I will also indicate Credit Union experience and national groups as this information may be of some help to you.

With best wishes for the new year and the success of your fine undertaking, I am

Yours fraternally,

James L. Kidd,
Representative,

JLK/sf

United Steelworkers of America
20 SPADINA ROAD
TORONTO, ONTARIO

GOWER H. MARKLE
EDUCATION AND WELFARE DIRECTOR

DATE:
March 18th, 1959

MEMO TO: Prof. A. J. Boudreau, Director of Extension, University of Sudbury,

FROM: Gower Markle

RE: Literature for your Students

We have been waiting for delivery of a supply of some of the literature which you ordered, and which we did not have in stock, so that your order might be completed at once. However, since it has not yet arrived, we are sending you today, by C.N. Express, part of your order, as follows:

150 Discussion Leaders' Manual
100 Officers' Guide to Effective Union Meetings
100 Code of Ethical Practices

24 copies of our Officers and Stewards Handbooks. (I regret that we will not be able to complete your order for this (150) until the sections on legislation which it contains have been revised and reprinted).

With best wishes,

February 18, 1959

Mr. Gower H. Markle
Education and Welfare Director
United Steel Workers of America
20 Spadina Road
Toronto, Ontario

Dear Mr. Markle,

I have received your two cases of educational material, and I also have a letter from Woodsworth House, Ottawa telling me they are shipping at your request two hundred copies of "Who Owns Canada". I want to thank you very sincerely for this great help.

I have, however, a problem of distribution. As you know, we now have a hundred and forty-two student workers and it is as essential that I give to each one of them a copy of the most important materials. It would indeed be a great help if you could possibly complete your generous donation with the following:

Steward's and Officer's Handbook	150
Discussion Leader's Manual	150
Officer's Guide to Effective Union Meetings	100
Labor Unions in Canada by Andras	150
Labor Movement in United States by Jack Barabash	150
Trade Unions in a Free Society by Gerard Dion	200
Code of Ethical Practices	100

Our students are doing very well and I am now convinced that it is only a matter of time until they are ready to repossess their own union.

Sincerely yours,

A. J. Boudreau
Director of Extension

AJB/JS

National president Nels Thibault (left) administers the oath of office to the new Local 598 executive, March 1959. Don Gillis, Don McNabb and Ray Poirier swore allegiance to Mine Mill, but proceeded to work for Steel. Solski Collection

Destabilizing Program Begins: The Report of Allistair Stewart

At its first meeting, the new executive board began the program of destabilizing the union. To discredit the previous administration by way of the sensitive subject of finances, the new officers commissioned Allistair Stewart to audit the local's books. Stewart, a chartered accountant, was a former CCF MP and at the time he did the audit was on the staff of the United Packinghouse Workers, a CLC union. As anticipated, Stewart presented a report that was flagrant in its innuendos, insinuations and deliberate falsehoods. When confronted with threats of libel action, he hastened to recant by stating that there had been no theft of union funds, which he had positively implied in his audit and report to the media.

Stewart spent one month, at a cost of $3,000 and expenses paid by Local 598, supposedly auditing the union's books, knowing all along that the books had been audited by chartered accountants from the union's earliest days and that the union had meticulously followed and carried out all instructions of the auditors.

Among his allegations, Stewart erroneously attacked the building fund for its financial management in building union halls in Garson, Coniston, Creighton and Elliot Lake. He falsely claimed that Local 598 paid higher-per-capita payments to the National Office than other locals did. He issued a distorted picture of officers' salaries and expenses, attacked educational expenditures, and the cost of the children's summer camp, and alleged that the union had lost money on union events such as the opening of the new Sudbury union hall, concerts and the screening and loaning of films such as *Salt of the Earth*.

In response to Stewart's report and the headlines in the media it generated, Canadian president Nels Thibault appointed a fact-finding committee to examine Stewart's charges concerning past financial affairs. The committee was made up of longstanding Mine Mill members, Al King, Mike Kopinak and Clem Thompson, presidents of Trail Local 480, Port Colborne Local 637 and Kimberley Local 651, respectively, as well as William Kennedy, Canadian vice-president.

The committee's report exposed accounting errors and mistakes in every charge made by Stewart. Moreover, it found several improprieties on Stewart's part, including the fact that he had released his report to the press without authorization of the executive and before it had been adopted by the membership, a breach of professional ethics.

The committee found that Stewart did not audit the books at all, but "merely inserted at the end of his report a statement of assets and liabilities as at March 31, 1959, which was prepared by Mr. Favretto with Mr. Favretto's name on the statement."[23] For this dubious service, the report revealed:

> Mr. Stewart received more for one month's time than the regular auditor, Mr. Favretto, received for a complete year's audit plus monthly financial statements.[24]

Regarding Stewart's insinuations that the salaries of the former union officers were out of line, the report stated:

---

[23] *Report of the Fact Finding Committee to Investigate Allistair Stewart's Attack on the Union*, International Union of Mine, Mill and Smelter Workers (Canada), Toronto, 1959, p. 9.

[24] *Ibid*, p. 9, 10.

---

le 25 mars, 1959

Monsieur Claude Jodoin, Président
Congrès Canadien du Travail
100 rue Argyle
Ottawa, Ontario

Cher Monsieur Jodoin,

Je tiens à vous exprimer ma reconnaissance pour la cordialité et la gentillesse de votre réception, lors de notre entrevue à Montréal samedi dernier. L'intérêt évident que vous même et vos officiers portez aux problèmes de Sudbury, nous est un puissant encouragement à poursuivre notre lutte jusqu'au bout.

Depuis mon retour ici, j'ai rencontré à plusieurs reprises tout le nouvel exécutif de Mine-Mill, à l'exception toutefois du nouveau président Gillis, qui a choisi cette période cruciale pour prendre une longue et inopportune vacance--. Ce dernier demeure toujours un point d'interrogation! Nous pouvons toutefois, quoi qu'il arrive, compter sur au moins dix directeurs sur quinze, et ceux-ci sont bien décidés à procéder au grand nettoyage.

Entre temps, les pressions augmentent, tous les vieux trucs sont utilisés, et je suis très heureux de pouvoir compter sur votre puissante organisation en temps opportun.

Sincèrement à vous

A. J. Boudreau
Directeur d'Extension

AJB/PS

April 9, 1959

Mr. Alistair Stewart
459 McAdam Avenue
Winnipeg 4, Manitoba

Dear Mr. Stewart:

This letter will confirm our telephone conversation of to-day. It was a relief to hear you say that you would unertake to completely audit the books of Local 598, Mine Mill & Smelter Workers' Union at Sudbury, and thoroughly investigate their financial transactions over a period of at least five years.

The newly elected executive will expect you on or about April 27th. Mr. Poirier, the new financial secretary will meet you upon arrival, if you will let me know the exact time.

There is no definite time or cost limit imposed upon your investigation, which must be as complete and thorough as possible. The figure of $2500.00 to $3000.00 for the first month was acceptable to the executive.

It is essential that until your arrival here, all contacts be made through my office at the Department of Extension, University of Sudbury, telephone Osborne 4-5248. Mr. Poirier is being so closely tailed, that he is not even sure of the secrecy of his phone calls.

I personally, am looking forward to the pleasure of meeting you.

Sincerely yours,

A. J. Boudreau
Director of Extension

AJB/PS

Mr. Stewart must also have recognized the fact that the wages paid the officers of Local 598 were not high because he himself recommended that the new officers receive wage increases over and above the wages of the former officers immediately.[25]

The committee found it unprofessional of Mr. Stewart not to have clarified questions of facts and figures before writing his report:

It is also a well-known procedure of reputable accountants that in the course of their work they must have the assistance, advice, explanations and co-operation of the individuals who are familiar and responsible for the records being audited. Mr. Favretto always followed this procedure. Stewart deliberately avoided any assistance or explanation from any of the former officers who were at hand and available, or the National Officers who were also available. Certainly, the new officers were not in any position to give explanation or assistance on matters which happened up to seven years prior to their becoming officers.[26]

And, finally, the report pointed out that no charges had been laid against any members as provided for in the constitution of the union: "It is clear to the Committee why no charges have been laid. A complete airing of the case would have exposed the whole lying fabric of the Stewart report."[27]

---

[25]*Ibid*, p. 15.
[26]*Ibid*, p. 29.
[27]*Ibid*, p. 28.

March 25, 1959

Mr. Donald MacDonald
Secretary-Treasurer
Canadian Congress of Labor
100 Argyle Avenue
Ottawa, Ontario

Dear Mr. MacDonald:

It was really wonderful to meet a fellow Cape Bretoner, and especially to have the opportunity to discuss frankly with a man of your wonderful background and experience. In the gigantic struggle now under way in Sudbury, your sympathy and generous offer of cooperation have been an inspiration.

Since my return here I have met the new executive of Mine-Mill several times. They are under terrific pressure, but so far they have been steadfast in their determination to clean up their union. I have mentioned to them your suggestion to retain the services of Alistair Stewart, to conduct a thorough investigation in their financial situation, and they are very much interested. Please let me know of any development along that line. Also, if you have anybody in mind for the position of Educational Director, please let me know.

I shall keep in close touch with you at all times. We certainly need your help.

I am enclosing my expense account for my trip to Montreal. Thank you.

Sincerely yours,

A. J. Boudreau
Director of Extension

AJB/PS

June 5, 1959

Mr. Claude Jodoin, President
Canadian Labour Congress
Ottawa, Ontario

Dear Mr. Jodoin,

The situation here is rapidly reaching a climax. After several months of an intensive, and often bitter struggle for control of the membership, between the "old regime" and the new executive, the fight to a finish is now out in the open.

Our boys are tired of being systematically attacked by their National Office and straight-jacketed by their constitution. They realize now that their hopes of completely cleaning up the whole union from the inside are illusive. Mine, Mill must be destroyed, and disappear from the map of Canada. This can be achieved only by depriving the Commies of their milch-cow, local 598 of Sudbury. A strong group is ready to do the same job in Port Colborne.

So the movement for secession from Mine Mill, by local 598, is afoot. The members will ask for a C.L.C. local charter within the next few weeks. Our well-organized underground has already done a very effective job, and from now on I don't think anything can stop it.

It is obvious that, at this crucial stage, our boys hope for and need the support of the C.L.C. as openly as possible, short of being accused of raiding. Bill England, who is now with us, is doing a magnificent job of coaching from the side-lines. We hope to have Jim Robertson as soon as possible so he can sort of take over the local Mine Mill News which is still completely in the hands of the Commies - (present editor Mel Colby.)

But we would all appreciate it very much if you personally, or if impossible, one of your top officers could make a personal appearance on the scene. The psychological effect would be tremendous. The suggested plan would be as follows: the Extension Department of the University is organizing a special graduation exer...

d their
8:00 p.m.
ations and
y certifi-
n, and
e of Mine
mpire
the press.

e you
. This
timed,
at they
a juris-
was re-
t the time
at, refer-
cepted
t leader-

the gradu-
he three
vill be
ely $40.00

...would have a great psychological effect.

Thank you again, Mr. Jodoin, for your active encouragement in our battle. I would like to assure you that this letter represents the desires and feelings of the new executive of Mine-Mill to a man, except one, Don McNabb, who unfortunately has gone over to the other side for personal reasons.

Sincerely yours,

A.J. Boudreau
Director of Extension

AJB/PS

ALISTAIR STEWART
CHARTERED ACCOUNTANT
WINNIPEG

469 McAdam Avenue,
Winnipeg.

2 July 1959.

Professor A. J. Boudreau,
University of Sudbury,
Sudbury.

Mon cher Alexandre :

I have been away from Sudbury now for a little over a month but that does not mean that I have lost interest in what is happening there. On the contrary it has, if anything, increased. But all I have heard is contained in a letter from Fed Ingham and there was in it just enough to be tantalizing. What were the repercussions to the report? What has been the reaction of the members of Local 598? What is the feeling now in the local? Is the new executive taking over? Do they control Mine Mill News yet? (Obviously they didn't in May. A nice job of sabotage was done in the issue of June 8) What happened at the trials? What is the position with the shop stewards? Have McNabb's wings been clipped yet? The questions are legion and I want to know. After all, I have a $500 investment in Local 598 and I want a return on it. (That $500 is the time I gave to work other than the investigation.)

There has been an interesting development here. Stuart Anderson was the deputy Minister of Finance in the Province. He is quite young yet and I would think quite progressive. He is going to New York as 2 I.C. to the President of Inco. Rumor has it that he will be next in line for the presidency. He takes over his new job in August. I have spent some time with him briefing him on the labor situation in Sudbury and telling him how outrageously stupid where were the tactics of the company. The point I made especially was the necessity of giving at least 12 union members leave of absence from the company with the retention of seniority and pension rights. If I can get him to agree to that then we could run some men against the national board. Or am I out of touch there? Has there been a shift in strategy? Anyway whether there has or not, I have an entry to the highest circles obviously and it is one the Local can use.

The advice I gave Anderson, of course, was not entirely gratuitous as I made abundantly clear. If I have the confidence of the Local then I could act as an intermediary between the union and management - at a suitable fee from Inco. But I also made it quite clear that the services of even St. Peter would be useless unless the union cleaned up the mess and I can only hope that this job is well under way. We must have every steward on our side and then we have to stop hating the boss's guts. Per contra the bosses have to stop hating a decent union and realise that the welfare of all is bound up in co-operation. That will be a tall order with Inco but I have impressed on Anderson that the chance is there and if it isn't taken the company deserves everything which is coming to it.

That is the extent of my news. Now it is up to you.

Toujours à vous,

Alistair Stewart

Sabotaging Cultural Programs

In keeping with Stewart's report, Gillis' next step was to diminish community respect for Local 598's cultural and recreational achievements so that the entire structure could then be dismantled.

As part of the plan designed to destroy Mine Mill, the sabotaging of cultural programs had already been well established. This militant union, which had been so effective in dealing with the metal mining industry and so undaunted in its opposition to post-war reactionary U.S. administrations, had to be stilled.

In the cultural field, the late Paul Robeson, world-renowned actor, singer and civil liberties champion, had found himself a prisoner in his own country when the U.S. authorities confiscated his passport and prohibited him from stepping beyond U.S. borders. The western district of Mine Mill had solved part of this problem by organizing a series of annual concerts at the Peace Arch on the international border at Blaine, Washington. Here, successive concerts saw crowds of up to 30,000 gathered to hear Robeson sing to Canadians despite the U.S. government prohibition.

On the Canadian side, the Royal Winnipeg Ballet had been prevented from performing to a Mine Mill audience. Nation-wide publicity criticizing the ballet for submitting to intimidation and exposing the U.S. administration's unconscionable interference in Canadian cultural matters had been a partial victory for Mine Mill.

In Sudbury, the Gillis executive followed up on Stewart's attack on the local's cultural programs. In April 1959, Weir Reid, Local 598's recreation director since 1952, was unceremoniously dismissed. To head off probable protest against this move, Frank Drea, a reporter for the *Toronto Telegram*, wrote a series of lurid stories about Reid. His Monday, December 21, 1959 article in the *Telegram* was entitled "Ontario Reds Recruit 7-Year-Olds." Reid launched a libel

suit against the *Telegram* which that publication settled out of court with a sizeable payment to Reid. A similar suit against Poirier was also won with a token payment levelled against Poirier. An "Examination for Discovery" (a legal pre-court proceeding) of Ray Poirier, then on the executive of a Steel-infiltrated Mine Mill Local 598, revealed that the stories published in the *Telegram* were planned and concocted by Drea, Poirier and Professor A. J. Boudreau of Sudbury University at several cloistered meeting places in Sudbury.

Church intervention in union affairs reached a new dimension during this incident, when the pupils under the Sudbury Separate School Board were sent home with leaflets calling on their fathers to attend a union meeting in which the Weir Reid issue was on the agenda. The implied appeal to support the Gillis administration was unmistakable.

Pressure on Local 598 Increased

In 1956, the Canadian Congress of Labour (CCL) and the Trades and Labour Congress (TLC) had merged to form the Canadian Labour Congress (CLC), with Claude Jodoin as president. Millard had moved on to the International Confederation of Free Trade Unions (ICFTU). The ascendency of William Mahoney to the office of Canadian Director of the Steelworkers and Larry Sefton to District 6 Director brought increased agitation for Local 598 to leave Mine Mill for ultimate membership in Steel through the CLC as a first stage.

Clandestine meetings between Local 598's new officers and CLC heads, invariably accompanied by Steel's Mahoney and Sefton, were held periodically in hotel rooms around Sudbury and on one recorded occasion in the Ottawa headquarters of the CLC. One such meeting in Ottawa was

Planning the demise of Mine Mill at CLC headquarters in Ottawa. Seated (L-R): William Dodge, CLC vice-president; Donald MacDonald, CLC secretary; Don Gillis, Local 598 president; Stanley Knowles; Ray Poirier, Local 598 secretary. Standing (L-R): James Robertson, CLC member assigned to Local 598; Alex MacDonald, Local 598 recording secretary; Don McNabb, Local 598 vice-president. Solski Collection

revealed by William Stewart, a defector from the Local 598 executive. Present at this meeting were Local 598's Don Gillis, Don McNabb, Edward O'Brien and William Stewart, and for the CLC, Claude Jodoin, Donald MacDonald, Stanley Knowles, William Mahoney, Lawrence Sefton and James Robertson. Robertson had earlier been assigned by the CLC as full-time adviser to the Gillis administration, and to take over the Local 598 *Mine Mill News*.

The program to destabilize the union progressed relentlessly, with well-planned precision. Differences between the National Office and Local 598 were created on any conceivable pretext, aimed at reaching acrimonious heights when drastic action could be taken against Mine Mill.

DEFENDING MINE MILL: LOCAL 598 ELECTION 1959

Acknowledging the threat to the existence of Mine Mill in Canada, Nels Thibault, former long-time president of Local 598, decided to challenge the Gillis administration. He resigned his post as president of the national union and announced his intent to contest the presidency of Local 598 in an election scheduled for November 17, 1959.

In his painstaking and perceptive study of the period, Lang notes:

> The tone of the campaign was set not at a meeting of trade unionists but at a Catholic Social Life Conference held in Sudbury from October 9th to 11th. In his welcoming address to the conference, Sudbury Mayor Joseph Fabbro stated that a possible reason that Sudbury was chosen as the site for this conference "was the feeling here and abroad that we are the hot bed of communism for all the North American continent — a dubious honour indeed." He reflected further:
>
>> If nothing more were gained from this conference we trust our people will realize the grave responsibility they have in respect to the teachings of communism and remain constantly alert to them.
>
> The message was made more clear the next day when the *Sudbury Daily Star* appeared with the headline "Must Prove Sudbury Not Communist Area."[28]

The indefatigable Professor Boudreau, frenzied lest the Thibault supporters regain Local 598 for Mine Mill, was quoted in the *Star* declaring that the election was "a last ditch fight between Christianity and Communism." Boudreau then became a prominent speaker at the various clubs and meetings in the district, with his attacks on Mine Mill widely publicized. In one frantic outburst, he charged that Thibault was operating under an alias and, when faced with Thibault's birth certificate, claimed it was a forgery.

Moreover, exposing himself as the directing force behind the Local 598 executive, Boudreau sent a letter to his students to attend a meeting, at which the executive would be present:

1. to draw up and decide upon a slate of officers and trustees for the forthcoming elections in Local 598
2. to determine and agree upon a platform to be presented to the membership
3. to discuss organizational and campaign problems.

This letter, reprinted in the October 1959 issue of the *Mine Mill Herald*, proved that Local 598 was being run by people outside the union membership.

Meanwhile, steps were taken by outside sources to make Gillis a respected and notable personality. During the Royal Tour of Canada that year, Gillis was presented to the Queen and the developing relationship between Gillis and Prime Minister Diefenbaker was prominently publicized.

The hysterical campaign directed from all sides against the Thibault forces resulted in a record turnout of voters and a victory for the Gillis administration. To compound the loss for Mine Mill in the east, a slate of opposition members in Port Colborne Local 637 ousted the pro-Mine Mill administration which, with several personnel changes through the years, had been in office since the defeat of the CCL raid in 1949. The grand strategy to destroy Mine Mill in Canada was gaining ground.

Whatever steps the National Office took to safeguard the union, the raiders could always depend on the Ontario Labour Relations Board for support. When Falconbridge workers, members of Local 598 in substantial majority loyal to Mine Mill, wished to free themselves from Gillis' control, they sought and received a charter from the National Office for Local 1025, in accordance with the Canadian Mine Mill constitution. On May 4, 1960, their application for certification at Falconbridge was summarily dismissed by the board, with only Gillis himself appearing to oppose the application. Chairman Finkleman reprimanded National President Ken Smith for objecting to Gillis' appearance.

Shortly thereafter, an order for compulsory wearing of safety glasses was seen by Falconbridge workers as a cynical and insincere gesture by management to reduce insurance premiums and not as a safety measure. Scorn flowered into protest, and a general wildcat strike affecting some 70 per cent of the workers occurred on May 16, 1960. The unofficial strike lasted four days. When the men returned to work, penalties were laid against 230 employees, eleven of whom were discharged. Those who were discharged were active Mine Mill supporters, opposed to the Gillis administration. Although the Local 598 executive board resisted taking any action, grievance procedures provided for in the contract with the company were launched to contest the firings, and were carried through to the final stage, binding arbitration. Witnesses provided by the Gillis group testified against the discharged workers and the grievances were lost. The National Office withdrew the charter of Local 1025, and Falconbridge remained in Local 598.

[28]Lang, p. 255.

PER CAPITA TAX WITHHELD

Another stage in the destabilization program was now ready for action. As a local of the International Union of Mine, Mill and Smelter Workers (Canada), Local 598 was obligated to remit a per capita tax payment to the National Office each month. Large and essential expenditures involved in the extensive and costly organizing campaigns throughout the country made the payment from the large Sudbury local indispensable to the operation of the union. To further impede and financially cripple Mine Mill, beginning early in 1960, Local 598's executive deliberately withheld its payments to the National Office.

A further example of the extent to which Gillis was prepared to go to undermine the union was his recommendation to a membership meeting to establish a committee to investigate charges made by the Steelworkers of collusion between Inco and the National Office in the recent contract settlement at the Thompson operations in Manitoba, where Mine Mill Local 1026 had been certified on May 10, 1960.

LOCAL 598 ELECTION: 1961

In the campaign for the Local 598 executive election to be held June 7, 1961, William Stewart openly split with the Gillis administration and ran for vice-president on an opposing slate of loyal Mine Mill supporters led by Al Routliffe.

During the campaign, unabashed by the age-old, hoary stunt of the fraudulent bomb plant, Local 598's secretary Ray Poirier "discovered" a bomb under the hood of his car, while earlier a car belonging to a prominent adherent of the Gillis group was actually dynamited. Abetted by a media thirsting for anti-Mine Mill stories, the Local 598 executive immediately and with much publicity offered a $2,500 reward for the arrest of those responsible — but only if the motivation was shown to be union business.

Some twenty years after these incidents, in a recorded interview on April 23, 1981, in Port Colborne, John Tronko, a former Mine Mill Local 637 officer and later a member of negotiating committees of the Steel Local that displaced Mine Mill, related this version of the bombings.

"During a session in the 1966 negotiations in Sudbury, a few of us were having a few drinks in one of the hotel rooms where we were staying and there was a lot of boasting about cars being blown up in Sudbury during the raids and how Mine-Mill was being accused of all these things. There was an organizer from Sudbury, Albert Desbien, and another chap, half corked and laughing like hell about one of these tricks they pulled off. He said they went ahead and blew up his car and Mine Mill got the blame."

The election was won by the Gillis slate, by a 1,000-vote margin.

Mine Mill's National Executive Board meet in Toronto July 14-21, 1961 in sessions which included a joint one with International officers, to discuss how to combat an anticipated Steel raid in Sudbury. In an obvious move to hurt the National union financially and make it more difficult to combat a raid, the Gillis group had notified the National executive that Local 598 had voted to withhold its per capita payments, not for the first time. In the ten-month period which then elapsed, approximately $200,000 was withheld from Mine Mill. Meeting above are (L-R): Mike Solski (Sudbury), Manfred Hoffman (Bancroft), Jim Patterson (Kimberley, B.C.), Buddy de Vito (staff), Lukin Robinson (staff), Al King (Vancouver), Rod Black (Bralorne, B.C.), Nels Thibault (staff), William Kennedy (Sudbury), Harvey Murphy (Vancouver). Also attending the meeting were Asbury Howard and Al Skinner, International vice-presidents, and Irving Dichter, International secretary-treasurer, as well as Ken Smith, National vice-president, Bill Longridge, National secretary-treasurer, and Gaspare Buscarino, Port Colborne Local 637. Solski Collection

*Mine Mill Local 598
hall on Regent Street
before the siege.*

In August 1961, a new development in the move of the local's administrators towards the Steelworkers was revealed in a *Sudbury Star* story which reported that Steel representatives had been invited to attend a conference of nickel workers called by the Local 598 executive to discuss bargaining proposals. When they became aware of this development, Port Colborne Local 637 and Thompson Local 1026 refused to attend and the conference was cancelled.

It was further revealed that the entire executive board had met with Jodoin, Mahoney and Sefton in a Sturgeon Falls hotel where Local 598 affiliation with Steel was discussed. At a meeting in Sudbury, William Dodge, CLC vice-president, advised the local executive that the only way that the local could affiliate with the CLC was by joining the Steelworkers.

Thomas Taylor resigned from the Local 598 executive board after this meeting was held, and in an affidavit sworn August 25, 1961, detailed these meetings and outlined the collusion of the Gillis administration with the Steelworkers. On the basis of this proof that the Local 598 executive was planning to secede from Mine Mill, President Ken Smith, in accordance with the Mine Mill constitution, appointed William Kennedy administrator of Local 598.

On August 26, 1961, Kennedy obtained an injunction from Judge J. M. Cooper preventing anyone from interfering with his rights as administrator and went directly to the Sudbury union hall and took possession. Sudbury radio stations were alerted and began a day-long frenetic harangue. The incident soon developed into an unprecedented riot scene, as the goons and hoodlums came out. The siege of the union hall added a new page to the history of unionism in Sudbury.

At first, the crowd in front of the building was relatively inactive, with only loud talk and the odd epithet. When Gillis and some of his executive appeared on the scene, the atmosphere changed and became ugly. Led and incited by prominent Gillis supporters, some recognized as among those who attempted to start wildcats prior to the 1958 strike, the violence started. Vicious charges were made at the union building, doors were torn off and rocks shattered windows.

Among the rioters were many non-union members, including several known "town rowdies." Police were present, but stationed somewhat distant from the riot scene. The radio barrage continued incessantly, and the local newspaper and television sound and camera crews were busy throughout the incident. Efforts of those besieged within the building to secure police intervention did not prevail until early Sunday morning, when the riot act was read and the majority of rioters dispersed.

Trapped inside the hall were a handful of men who had dropped in after shift for a social hour in the hall's beverage room. Instead, they found themselves defenders of the union property and at risk of life and limb from the rioters outside.

Albert Routliffe, a Garson miner for 17 years, was one of those who found himself in the union hall when the building was besieged. In an interview some two decades later, he recalled his experience during the siege:

"I was just back from work and quite often I would go over to the hall for a beer, we had a beverage room there. I went to the hall and found out that the district officers had got an injunction authorizing them to take the building back to Mine Mill, and after that it came to quite an exciting evening . . . some of the Gillis executive were in the hall, they were shown the injunction and asked to leave the premises. They all went out except for one. He stayed for a while and then decided to leave. There were probably thirty, forty members in the hall having a quiet beer.

"Sometime about eight or nine o'clock, stones started coming into the hall through the windows and when we looked out there was quite a mob outside . . . most of the windows were busted in the hall . . . several hundred people were outside the building that night . . . how were they mobilized? I would say the executive didn't do it on their own . . . and there were people outside throwing rocks that weren't union members . . . there were hoodlum types outside.

"There were about thirty of us inside the hall and when they started busting the windows and the doors we decided we had to defend ourselves. I know there were phone calls to the police but none of them came out to try to stop the riot . . . I understand there was a cruiser with some police in it parked about a block away watching the proceedings but they didn't seem to be too interested . . . it's a little hard to imagine a similar situation elsewhere and the police doing nothing. There had to be someone behind the scenes somewhere giving instructions.

"We kind of split up in groups at the time . . . a number of fellows were protecting the back door . . . the rioters had put a chain on the back door and pulled it off so the fellows inside put a bunch of chairs in the way. I remember Sproule was patrolling the main floor and some were trying to go up through the windows into the main hall and he was on that most of the night and no one got into the hall that way. Nobody said go here or go there, we just ended up in one place or the other . . . I ended up on the main door, we had a fire hose and I was on it all night until daylight when the police came along and the riot act was read.

"I think it was quite obvious when the people outside couldn't get in that the police got the order that they'd better try and get in to settle things down. When they came to the door I told our chaps to put down the hose and we would talk to the police. There was a lot of tension that night, it was a real riot . . . the fire hose had been on from about eleven at night until the morning . . . it was a nervous situation.

"When the policemen came in they offered to escort us without us getting hurt if we would give up the hall. I didn't see any reason why we should give up the hall . . . we had held it all night against all they could do, and we decided we were going to stay in, we had a court injunction and I didn't see why the police couldn't have acted through the night, and we were going to stay inside come hell or high water and we didn't need police protection to escort us outside . . . and that left the police no alternative but to call the sheriff and read the riot act. I had the satisfaction of standing beside Sheriff Lamoureux when he read the riot act and I felt kind of good about it.

"It would be very interesting to know why no one was arrested or the rioting stopped. I'm sure that if the same sort of thing took place at any other building, church or *Sudbury Star*, it would have been stopped by the police."

Three years later, after Steel had ousted Mine Mill from the Inco operations, he quit his job: "One of the reasons I quit I couldn't accept working underground 17 years as a miner and then be called a steelworker. You just don't change overnight."

The *Globe and Mail*'s Wilfred List, in his August 28, 1961 article on the riot, reported that

> Deputy Chief Guillet said he did not interfere with the gathering at that point [early in the demonstration] because he said they were awaiting Mr. Gillis' return from Port Colborne to hold a meeting. . . . One pro Gillis member . . . tore down the injunction notices and tried to open a door to the hall. The booing, shouting and stone throwing reached its most violent point after Mr. Gillis arrived.

Other observers described the scene as in the "grip of a lynch mob."

After Tom Taylor provided proof that the Gillis executive was planning a move to Steel, National president Ken Smith appointed District 2 secretary William Kennedy as administrator of Local 598. Armed with a court injunction, Kennedy took possession of the hall at 11 a.m., Saturday, August 26, 1961.

Inside the hall: Ken Smith (right) and William Kennedy watch developments outside the hall.

The pace of the attack accelerated Saturday evening after Gillis arrived on the scene from Port Colborne.

Don Gillis (left) and Ray Poirier address crowd from roof of hall: they were not there to promote law and order.

Photos in this series all from the Solski Collection

There was no shortage of booze, an encouragement for rowdyism.

Deputy police chief Bert Guillet blocks the street, making it easier for a mob to gather outside the hall.

Once a crowd assembled, police took no steps to disperse it. Blow-by-blow bulletins by local radio stations ensured the crowd grew during the day.

Jack McDonald, a known local tough guy, having ripped the court order from the door, proceeds to break down the door.

Despite calls to police by those inside, the siege of the hall, destruction of property and threatening of lives continue all night long without police action.

Inside the hall, a handful of loyal Mine Mill members barricaded doors and windows to defend themselves.

Men keep the fire hose trained on the main door all night long. (L-R): Ray Forestall (with hose), Jim Stark, Tony Andrews.

Deputy police chief Guillet warns the crowd outside, many of whom were not union members, against rough-house tactics, but does nothing to disperse them.

Sheriff Lamoureux, with detective-sergeant Tremblay at his side, reads the riot act at 5.30 a.m. Sunday, after a night of violence and destruction of union property.

The results of the all-night attack on the Mine Mill hall: nearly every window and door was smashed under the eyes of the authorities.

William Kennedy, again almost two decades later, recalled the events: "I believe it was a Saturday that I went to the hall with a couple of people to advise whoever might be there that it was a Mine Mill hall and that the union was taking it back from the people who to all intents and purposes had seceded from the union. By nightfall the crowd outside the building had become a mob of rioters and the authorities were forced to read the riot act. What I remember most vividly was the courage of the people inside with me . . . they knew that if this howling mob was ever able to break into the hall it was questionable if they would have been left alive."

Kennedy also questioned the action of the police in not interfering with a mob intent on destroying the building and threatening the lives of those inside: "I can recall when in 1942 goons smashed our union office and the police were conveniently absent although the destruction was in the centre of the city."

Court hearings which followed overruled the union's constitution which provided for administration of any local seceding from the international — a court action not normally found in the records of trade unions in Canada. The power of a trade union to impose an administration over its affiliates has been often exercised before and since this instance.

The courts restored control of Local 598 to the Gillis group and, in addition, granted an injunction restraining National President Ken Smith from interfering with the administration of Local 598.

Don Gillis addresses crowd, many of whom had no union affiliation whatsoever, at Queen's Athletic Field Sunday night, August 27, 1961. Despite the fact that these were the same people to whom the riot act had been read twelve hours earlier, authorities granted them use of public grounds, complete with public address system, to continue their harangue as a prelude to the Steel raid.

Jim Robertson, CLC and Steel staffer (left) who had been brought to Sudbury at the request of Professor Boudreau, joins Gillis at Queen's Athletic Field Sunday night.

The meeting to hear CLC and Steel representatives at the Sudbury Arena on September 10, 1961 was advertised for all members of Mine Mill, but 4,000 of those members were denied entrance. They are waving their membership cards. Photos in this series from the Solski Collection unless otherwise credited.

The Sudbury Arena Meeting

Indications that an open Steelworkers raid on Local 598 was imminent came with the announcement by the Gillis group of a meeting in the Sudbury Arena for September 10, 1961. The main speakers were to be Jodoin, Mahoney and Sefton.

Although the meeting was advertised for all members of Mine Mill, when 4,000 unionists loyal to Mine Mill, including President Ken Smith, Mike Solski and William Kennedy, sought to enter the arena, they were refused admission. When they insisted on their right to attend, a fracas resulted, with the police using tear gas to break up the demonstration.

Inside the arena, hundreds of loyal Mine Mill supporters were determined to raise their voices in opposition to the exhortations of the Steelworkers, CLC officials and Gillis henchmen. Disturbances reached the point at which the police ordered the meeting ended. The next day, Smith, Solski, Kennedy, Thibault and six Mine Mill supporters were arrested for unlawful assembly and later fined $100 each. One of them commented: "Poirier defied the riot act during the union hall siege — a very serious offence — was arrested and fined ten dollars."

Mine Mill officers who were denied entrance to the meeting show their membership cards (L-R): Ken Smith, National president; Jim Keuhl, staff; Nels Thibault, legislative director; Mike Solski, District 2 president; Al Skinner, International vice-president.

Nothing like a little help from police to keep union men from attending their own meeting. Photo courtesy Robert J. Keir

Ed O'Brien of the pro-Steel executive screens members with the help of a policeman who keeps his gas mask handy. Big Turk White looks on.

Inside the arena. The Gillis executive invited CLC president Claude Jodoin and Steelworkers representatives William Mahoney and Larry Sefton to speak; officials of Mine Mill were excluded from the meeting. Photo courtesy Michael Dudowich, Sudbury, Ont.

Instead of union wardens, Sudbury police guarded the doors to the arena. Here, police get caught in their own tear gas along with Pete Pirozik, a loyal Mine Mill member who had gained entrance.

A bandaged head and torn shirt, evidence of how determined the pro-Steel forces were to keep loyal Mine Mill members out of the meeting. Facing the camera are Jim Loftus (right) and Wilfred Gerard, union stewards.

Don Gillis looks on in dismay as Claude Jodoin tries to make himself heard over loyal Mine Mill members, who booed and chanted, "We Want Smith." Jodoin never did speak. Police ordered the meeting to be called off.

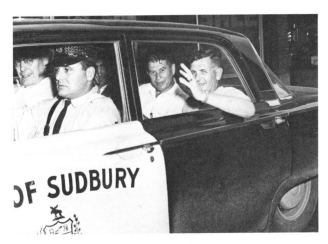

The next day, the victims and not the goons were arrested and charged with unlawful assembly, an example of Sudbury justice of the day. In the front of the cruiser is William Kennedy; in the back are Nels Thibault, legislative director, and Ken Smith, National president. Wilfred Gerard and Jim Loftus, the union stewards who were attacked, were also charged, along with Mike Solski, District 2 president.

Open Steel Raid Starts: 1961

On September 15, 1961, at a meeting in the Sudbury Mine Mill hall, Mahoney and Sefton announced their intention to start a sign-up campaign and urged Mine Mill members to join the Steelworkers. When Mine Mill President Ken Smith attempted to try Gillis under provisions of the union's constitution, Gillis again applied to the civil courts and received an injunction preventing this action.

It was at the September 15th meeting that Mahoney broke the news of Steel's grand coup — Robert Carlin had defected to the Steelworkers. Whether or not Carlin was of any assistance to the Steelworkers is problematical, as he had long since squandered whatever good reputation he had built up in the earlier days of the union.

Because of his early prominence in the Canadian section of Mine Mill, Carlin needs careful consideration. Towards the end of the Kirkland Lake strike early in 1942, Carlin, an executive board member of Local 240, had been sent to Sudbury as an international representative to aid in the organization of Mine Mill in that district.

Carlin had arrived in the right place at the right time. For many decades, back to the early 1900s, there had been union organization in that area. On three separate occasions, local unions of Mine Mill had previously been established, the most recent in the late 1930s when Scotty Anderson was the resident organizer. When Carlin arrived in Sudbury, the area was fully aware of the union, and with nickel-copper mining an essential war industry, its workers were protected by law in their jobs. The combination of these circumstances, added to the dire need for a union, made organization inevitable. Within one year, more than 6,000 workers had become members of Mine Mill Local 598. This extraordinary growth was the result entirely of the efforts of hundreds of rank-and-file workers led by a group of dedicated and tireless men who later became the real leaders of the union.

No sooner had he arrived in Sudbury than Carlin was elected to the provincial legislature. During his five years in the legislature, he spent relatively little time on union affairs. After his political defeat, personal problems too often overwhelmed him and his efficiency in the union deteriorated to the point where he was persuaded to withdraw entirely. The most fitting epitaph to his career in Mine Mill are his own words in an article in the *Mine Mill Herald*, April 1957. Describing the pattern of Steel raids up to that time, he said that "without exception, a potential traitor was invariably, if not before, put on the payroll of Steel. . . . [They] may have found a financial reason for their action, but they will never find a moral one."

The Steel sign-up campaign was now in full swing, with Local 598 stewards, appointed by Gillis to replace Mine Mill adherents, now Steel's major agents on the job. The Local 598 executive, openly seceding, still presumed to carry on as a Mine Mill body, but a growing section of the membership, now fully apprised of the intent to defect to Steel, began to attend meetings. Gillis found it increasingly difficult to command majorities at membership meetings. Motions condemning the Steel raid were consistently rejected from the chair by Gillis, and members demanding recognition from the floor were ignored. Before long, police called in by Gillis became regular features at membership meetings. Finally, the executive board cancelled all further membership meetings. Meanwhile, Inco was not sitting by idly: when contract negotiations approached, on November 15, 1961, the company refused to bargain because of the unsettled status of the union.

The National officers of Mine Mill had attempted to prevent the assets of Local 598 being used to assist the Steel raiders. A petition signed by over 6,000 members had supported taking action, but Gillis had immediately applied for and received an injunction blocking any such action. In turn, President Ken Smith tried to get an injunction preventing Local 598 officers from assisting the Steel raiders. Chief Justice Morand dismissed Smith's motion. In addition, he ruled that all suits involving these issues be put off until the spring of 1962 — in other words, until the Steel raids had been completed. In fact, the matters in question were not brought to trial until January 1963.

Commenting on this series of events, John Lang, in his 1970 thesis, states:

> In granting the injunctions requested by Gillis the courts had put themselves in the position not of an impartial arbitrator but of an accomplice to the Gillis-Steel strategy . . . the courts made possible a situation in which Gillis and five members of his Executive Board

National officers hold a meeting to fight against the Steel application for certification at Inco, Sunday, December 3, 1961. Front row (L-R): *Lena Petroff, Peggy Bertrand, Ted and Sally Grabish. Solski Collection*

Pro Mine Mill meeting at the Sudbury arena, Sunday, January 21, 1962. Appearing on behalf of Mine Mill are (L-R): Al Skinner, International vice-president; Madeleine Parent, Canadian Textile Council representative; John Clark, International president; Mike Kopinak, Port Colborne; Nels Thibault; Ken Smith, National president (speaking); Jack Whelahan (the same Local 598 organizer who had been beaten up by company goons on February 24, 1942); Bill Walsh, United Electrical Workers representative. Solski Collection

were being paid salaries by the entire Local 598 membership, to work for the Steelworkers in the raid against Mine Mill. In addition, all the physical resources of Local 598 and a substantial amount of its financial resources were put at the disposal of the Steelworkers. Not one dollar of Local 598's assets nor any of its office space or equipment was provided for those members who did not wish to join Steel. Once Gillis had suspended membership meetings, this section of the Local was powerless to have its grievances heard.[29]

With the courts blocking all attempts of the elected national officers to apply the provisions of the union's constitution dealing with secession, the raid grew in intensity. The raiders expended vast amounts on media propaganda and payments to accomplices. Mine Mill supporters fought back vigorously, but could not hope to match Steel's treasury made available for newspaper, television and radio propaganda. Nowhere in trade union records can a situation be found such as the one which prevailed in the Sudbury district throughout these developments.

On November 28, 1961, the United Steelworkers of America made formal application for bargaining rights at the Inco operations in Sudbury, presenting the Ontario Labour Relations Board with the required number of cards allegedly conforming with all of the board's regulations.

At Port Colborne, the Steel raid started officially with Local 637 president James Babirad defecting to Steel. A vote conducted by the OLRB resulted in defeat for Mine Mill by 1,033 to 763. On December 7, 1961 the OLRB certified the Steelworkers as bargaining agent for the employees of the Inco Port Colborne refinery.

CERTIFICATION VOTE ORDERED

On February 1, 1962 the OLRB complied with the Steelworkers' request that there not be a hearing on their application before a certification vote. Such a hearing normally is ordered to examine the membership cards presented by the applying union and to verify whether the applicant has complied with all regulations. Instead, the certification vote was set for February 27th to March 2nd.

The vote in Sudbury did not take place in a vacuum: at the time of the Steel raid on Mine Mill, it was clear that the full mechanism of the state was also doing its part. Beginning with a speech delivered by Deputy Commissioner of the RCMP, George McClelland in Halifax referring to Mine Mill as Communist-controlled and urging support for the Gillis faction, attacks on Mine Mill escalated. Justice Minister Davie Fulton endorsed McClelland's remarks in the media the next day. In Sudbury, prominent coverage was given to statements by U.S. Secretary of Labour Goldberg attacking Mine Mill and U.S. Attorney-General Robert Kennedy recommending that Mine Mill be declared a Communist-infiltrated organization. In a similar vein, Canada's Prime Minister Diefenbaker embraced Gillis, appointing him labour representative to a NATO conference in Paris, which Gillis attended in the middle of the Steel raid, in January 1962. The provincial authorities appointed Gillis labour representative on the Ontario Economic Council.[30] All these developments were prominently publicized by the Sudbury media.

---

[29]Lang, p. 304.

[30]Lang, pp. 310-312.

The vote took place as ordered, but without counting of the results as the OLRB considered Mine Mill's objections to various aspects of Steel's application of November 1961 and violations of regulations prior to the vote. On June 4, 1962 the OLRB dismissed Mine Mill's objections and ordered that the votes be counted.

FALCONBRIDGE FORGERIES

At the time that Steel's application for the Inco certification was before the OLRB, Steel had also applied for certification at Falconbridge, a separate application. In the Falconbridge application, an examination of the Steel membership cards presented to the board disclosed an inordinate number of forgeries; twenty-eight of these had been witnessed by James Robertson and fourteen by a salaried Steel organizer. So scandalous was Steel's position that William Mahoney withdrew the application for Falconbridge.

The same people exposed in the Falconbridge forgeries had also been involved in the Steel sign-up campaign at Inco. It could then be readily assumed that a close examination of the cards purportedly signed by Inco workers would disclose a proportionately large number of forgeries. The OLRB, however, which had refused a hearing on the Steel application prior to the vote, also refused to reconsider the application.

STEEL'S MAJORITY FIFTEEN VOTES

The results were finally announced on June 12, 1962, some three months after the vote. Of the 14,333 eligible voters, 7,182 had voted for Steel, only fifteen more than the number required for a majority.

After the vote, the board rejected Mine Mill's protests against violations of the statutory 72 hours of silence preceding the vote. It also rejected Mine Mill's contesting of 71 ballots that were not stamped by the returning officers, as well as others which indicated support for Mine Mill but which were claimed by these officers to be spoiled ballots.

EVALUATION OF THE CONFLICT

So flagrant were the violations by Steel that sentiment throughout the Sudbury district expressed itself in widespread demands for another vote. Even the *Northern Miner,*

never before a champion of Mine Mill, in its August 2, 1962 issue, editorialized as follows:

> For over a year the workers in the nickel industry at Sudbury have been deeply disturbed by the attempts of the Steelworkers to dislodge the long-time holders of power there, Mine Mill. While these may not have affected operations, they certainly kept the people at the area in an uproar. A vote as to which union should receive certification for bargaining rights at International Nickel was "won" by such small margin, 15 out of 14,133 votes cast, in favour of Steelworkers, that many persons refuse to believe it expressed workers' desires. The other union has made allegations of improper or careless actions, including one embracing a block of 71 ballots. This matter is now before the courts. The indecisiveness leads many to say the best thing the Ontario Labour Relations Board could do would be order a brand new vote. But it will be necessary to await the findings. The confession of Steelworkers that forgery was committed at Falconbridge helps make it impossible for large numbers of people in the camp to have confidence in the voting at International Nickel.

But the board majority was not to be deterred from its intent to award the spoils to the Steelworkers. The votes of Chairman Finkleman and the CLC labour representative for the Steelworkers were not unexpected. The dissent to the board's majority report came from R. W. Teagle, industry's representative. His minority report declared: "I dissent. I would have directed a new vote in this case." In giving his reason for his dissent, Mr. Teagle presented only one issue, that the board's no-propaganda rule had been violated by the applicant.

The U.S. publication, *Business Week*, in a December 5, 1959 issue, underestimating the power of the forces arrayed against Mine Mill, paid a reluctant tribute to the union:

> There are a number of more clearly discernible reasons why Mine Mill has been able to stand off challengers:
> • One is a matter of history. Mine Mill is the lineal continuation of the old Western Federation of Miners, which battled for the rights of miners in the old tough days. Oldtimers respect Mine Mill because of memories of the federation; younger workers like its long history of militance for miners
> • Another is social: In many remote areas Mine Mill halls are about the only centre of community activities; in some, there is no place else to go that is not company property.
> • Perhaps more important, rank-and-filers have heard their leaders described as Communists for so many years — back into the old Western Federation days — that the charges are shrugged off now; they have completely lost meaning. Members believe what they are told, that the charges are a corporation conspiracy to take away the militancy of "their" Mine Mill and turn it into a loose organization of company unions.
> Few really look for — or, in some instances, hope for — changes in Mine Mill, like Ishmael grown lean and tough in the desert, perhaps the leanest and toughest of all unions.

Don Gillis, Progressive Conservative candidate in the federal election, is hit on the head at the Chelmsford union hall during political rally featuring Prime Minister Diefenbaker, June 3, 1962. Mine Mill members protesting Gillis' use of the hall he had closed down in November 1961 were further angered when stewards at the door refused to admit Mine Mill supporters. Michael Dudowich won an award for his photograph of the event. Photo courtesy M. Dudowich, Sudbury, Ont.

DEFEAT OF GILLIS AS TORY CANDIDATE

Although the result of the Sudbury balloting had been announced on June 12th, the OLRB did not officially award the Inco certification to Steel until October 15th, 1962. In the interim, the Gillis executive term of office had ended on June 30th. Between these two dates, a federal election took place, with Gillis, as a much-touted favourite of Diefenbaker, the official Tory candidate in the Nickel Belt riding. To display his support for Gillis, the Prime Minister made a special campaign visit to the riding.

When Gillis, responsible for closing down all the area union halls since November 1961, chose to hold his political rally at the Chelmsford union hall, his unpopularity was manifested in the demonstration that ensued. Gillis was hit on the head by a placard and the car in which he and Diefenbaker had arrived was almost overturned. The election was an overwhelming defeat for Gillis with the Liberal candidate O. J. Godin doubling his vote.

His term of office in Local 598 ended and the official status of Local 598 still undecided, Gillis once again called in the civil authorities to intervene in union affairs. He delivered the keys of the union offices, properties and all other assets to the sheriff.

Reflecting on that situation, Tom Taylor, in an interview for the Laurentian University archives in November 1980, said that "when Gillis turned over the keys to the sheriff that was a terrible thing to do because then the representation of the union was lost to the men on the job . . . everything was cut off, especially the welfare plan which was very important to people off sick, and all the other services were taken away from us, and that was a great loss."

Prime Minister John Diefenbaker is surrounded by guards and protesters' jeers as he appears at the Chelmsford union hall to support Gillis. The election resulted in an overwhelming defeat for Gillis. UBC Collection

A New Mine Mill Leadership

The National officers called a membership meeting where a *pro tem* executive board for the local was elected, with Tom Taylor as president. In keeping with the practice established by the Gillis executive, a group within the local sought an injunction to prevent the new executive from assuming control of the union's assets. On July 25, 1962, Mr. Justice M. C. Fraser drew up a court order governing the administration of Local 598 until a permanent executive was elected. The Taylor executive was to administer the local, together with a three-man committee including two former Gillis executives, Poirier and Hickey. The court also ordered an election to be held, supervised by the OLRB; but the election was not ordered until after October 15th, when the OLRB awarded certification at Inco to the Steelworkers.

In the election on October 24, 1962, 12,500 Local 598 members voted decisively to defeat the entire Gillis slate and elected the slate headed by Taylor. Cost of the election, paid for by Local 598 members and conducted by the Ontario Department of Labour as ordered by Mr. Justice Fraser, was $23,124.14.

Concerned about depleted Local 598 funds, one of the first actions taken by the Taylor executive was to commission the union's chartered accountant to audit the local's books for the period when the local's assets were in Gillis' control.

Itemized expenditures on projects that were not justifiable union matters added up to almost $200,000 for the short period the Gillis group was in power. Examples as presented by the auditor's report included:

$55,192.90 spent in 1961 and 1962 and listed in a "defend the union" account.

$15,145.80 spent on lawyer's fees for the legal defence of Poirier in the personal libel suit brought against him by Weir Reid.

$2,273.70 to send Gillis and two others to a CLC convention without membership approval.

$45,000.00 to Robins and Robins* in legal fees.

A total of $199,454.48 was spent on matters not legitimately of trade union concern and resulting entirely from the Gillis administration's role in the overall conspiracy to destroy Mine Mill. Moreover, during the ten-month period when union membership meetings were cancelled, all expenditures were without membership approval, contrary to constitutional requirement.

In February and March of 1963, Mine Mill applied to the OLRB to have the Steel certification at Inco revoked due to irregularities. The report of Malcolm Robb, Q.C., published by Mine Mill under the title *A Study in Sham Abuse*

---

*This amount included a $400 legal fee to David Lewis, counsel for the United Steelworkers, for his opinion on the legality of cancelling the per capita. Since the Gillis executive did not want to put this amount before the membership, it was arranged that the account be paid and shown on the account of Robins and Robins as a consultation fee in connection with the Falconbridge walkout. (Information from *A Study in Sham Abuse and Fraud: Application for reconsideration and to revoke and set aside a certificate as bargaining agent* by Malcolm Robb, Q.C., IUMMSW, Sudbury, 1963, pp. 21, 22.)

Mine Mill campaign for an honest vote at Inco, Queen's Park, November 19, 1962. (L-R): Mike Petroff, Ernie Taylor, ———, Floyd Gates, Larry Legault, ———, Laurence Murray, William Longridge. Solski Collection

Mine Mill delegation attends Ontario Labour Relations Board hearings in the second campaign to regain Inco certification, Toronto, July 1965. (L-R): Tom Taylor, Manfred Hoffman, National vice-president Harvey Murphy, board member William Kennedy, Robin McArthur, Ed Levert, John Nelligan, Local 598 president Nels Thibault, National president Ken Smith, Darwin "Beaver" Benson, Mike Farrell. Solski Collection

and Fraud (IUMMSW, August 30, 1963) provided a concise history of the dubious methods used by the Steel union leadership and former Mine Mill officers to destroy Mine Mill. However, the labour board's decision, handed down July 4, 1963, denied the application and refused either to revoke its decision of October 15, 1962 or to hold a new vote.

CAMPAIGN TO REGAIN INCO: 1965

The disclosure of Steel's violations of OLRB rules governing certification, plus the disputed ballots in support of Mine Mill and the forgeries exposed in Steel's application for Falconbridge, convinced many Sudbury workers that awarding the Inco certification to the Steelworkers had been a miscarriage of justice. Encouraged by manifestations of support, a substantial core of determined Mine Mill workers began preparations to launch a campaign to regain the Inco certification.

To overcome the devastating financial handicap incurred by the loss of the Inco check-off, voluntary dues payments were made to Local 598. Hundreds of Inco workers imposed double dues upon themselves, one a compulsory payment to the Steelworkers and the other a voluntary payment to Local 598.

It was destined to be a long struggle, most of the way uphill. The Mine Mill campaigners were faced with a mixed bag of obstacles. After laying off 2,200 employees, Inco took full advantage of a disrupted and divided work force. It refused to negotiate from where Mine Mill contracts had left off and was insisting on bargaining from scratch with the Steelworkers. The Steelworkers had appealed for unified support. Understandably, the uncommitted wished for an end to inter-union conflict and were apathetic now that the OLRB had awarded the certification for Inco to the Steelworkers. Afterwards came the practical problems of signing up thousands of workers and collecting the legal initiation fees from men who were already operating under a bargaining agency and having their dues checked off monthly.

Undaunted, dedicated Mine Mill activists persisted. After some two years of tenacious pursuit, Mine Mill was able to apply to the Ontario Labour Relations Board on May 11, 1965 with 7,369 membership cards, 49.2 per cent, later increased to 50.1 per cent, well above the 45 per cent of eligible voters required for a vote to be ordered.

The Steelworkers, however, launched a determined effort to prevent a vote by introducing a series of objections, and it was not until seven months later that Steel was forced to agree to a vote ordered for December 7, 8 and 9, 1965. Meanwhile, a Steel raid at Falconbridge was again defeated and an application to the OLRB dismissed when Steel could not produce the required number of cards.

STEEL WINS AGAIN

On December 10, 1965, when the board announced the results of the vote, Mine Mill had failed to regain the Inco certification. The surprising element was that the vote, with close to 100 per cent turnout, was 8,207 for Steel and 6,174 for Mine Mill — 1,195 less than the number of those who had signed Mine Mill membership cards and paid the initiation fee required under OLRB rules.

The reason for this anomaly was generally conceived to be the concern of those who had signed Mine Mill cards but later voted for Steel that the conflict would not be ended if Mine Mill were to win. The Steel campaign in this latest contest was even more vicious, disrupting and acrimonious than in the 1962 encounter. The wavering workers were convinced that if the vote were lost, Steel would not go away. Continued strife and disruption was a future that did not appeal to them. Thus, results of the vote seemed to reflect the decision that peace was more likely if Steel remained the bargaining agent for the Inco workers.

Forced to accept this last vote as an indication that Inco was lost to Mine Mill, perhaps forever, the union in eastern Canada concentrated on servicing the remaining Sudbury district membership at the Falconbridge operations, the Local 598 contracts and the few small locals elsewhere that survived the Steel raids.

Mine Mill ranks in western Canada had withstood the Steel attacks and the union continued to function successfully on behalf of the membership there. However, Mine Mill was no longer the predominant union in Canada's non-ferrous metals industry, and the same situation prevailed in the United States. There were now two unions competing for the allegiance of the industry's workers in North America. Before long, Steel union officers in the United States and in Canada were making overtures to Mine Mill to consider the possibilities of a merger of the two unions.

Labour day picnic celebrations during the second campaign to regain Inco certification. (L-R): Emile Prudhomme, Pearl Moir, Joe Astgen, Bob Peterson, Local 598 president Nels Thibault, National president Ken Smith (speaking), veteran organizer Tom McGuire, board member William Kennedy.
Solski Collection

Al Skinner, International president of Mine Mill, addresses joint meeting of Mine Mill and Steelworkers staff held at the Royal York Hotel, Toronto, April 29, 1967, outlining terms of the merger agreement about to be signed by officers of the two unions. The agreement was subject to approval at the forthcoming annual convention and to ratification by a secret ballot vote of all Mine Mill members in Canada. (L-R): Al Skinner; Harvey Murphy, Mine Mill National vice-president; Larry Sefton, Steelworkers District 6 director; Joseph Moloney, Steelworkers International vice-president; William Mahoney, Steelworkers Canadian director; Ken Smith, Mine Mill National president; William Longridge, Mine Mill National secretary. UBC Collection

Merger Proposals: 1967

This new and hitherto remote possibility brought to the fore the necessity for Mine Mill officers to consider anew aspects of the relationship between the two unions, aside from the previous two decades of slanderous and destructive assault on Mine Mill as a whole and on individual leaders within the union. Objective conditions had undergone qualitative changes: world tensions had eased, with Cold War rhetoric no longer as shrill and pressure on dissidents softened; McCarthy was dead and McCarthyism discredited. With the U.S. involvement in Vietnam threatening an uncertain future, the need for the broadest possible unity of workers was essential. An additional positive factor was the emergence of a new international leadership in the United Steelworkers of America with the departure of David McDonald and the installation of William Abel as International President. Most important was the recognition that a work force united in one union could exert greater pressure on the industry and achieve greater gains for the workers than a work force divided amongst itself.

Mine Mill leaders in both countries decided to meet with Steel in their respective regions and investigate the details and mechanics of a merger that would be acceptable to both organizations. After lengthy negotiations, an agreement was reached and Mine Mill leaders brought the results to the membership.

In Canada, a convention was called for June 23, 1967 in Winnipeg for delegates from all Mine Mill locals to hear and discuss the recommendation that a merger of the two unions be accepted and that a referendum vote on the matter take place. Convention delegates voted in favour of the merger, but the Sudbury Local 598 delegates representing the Falconbridge workers (except for Robin McArthur, the local's president) voted against it.

When the referendum held on August 3rd overwhelmingly approved the merger, Mine Mill in Canada virtually ceased to exist, with only the Falconbridge workers preserving the Mine Mill Local 598 identity. Court actions launched by the Falconbridge workers ended with the merger declared illegal, and the Sudbury district properties and assets of the Mine Mill union were awarded to the Falconbridge workers' Local 598.

Since the church anti-union activists placed their main emphasis on the red-menace, communist-conspiracy fraud and vilified Mine Mill's officers, one wonders what the reaction of church stalwarts was when the merger of Mine Mill and Steel was consummated and Steel provided staff positions for these self-same Mine Mill officers. Bouvier and Boudreau have disappeared from Sudbury and they did not disclose their opinion on that development.

Falconbridge's Local 598

There remains today a single Mine Mill local, Sudbury Local 598. Over 2,000 members belong to the functioning union of the hourly-rated employees of the Falconbridge Nickel Company that identifies itself as the inheritor of the name and traditions of the Western Federation of Miners and the International Union of Mine, Mill and Smelter Workers. Without organizational ties with Canadian or American labour federations, cheek-by-jowl with the large Steelworkers Local 6500 representing the Inco employees, Local 598 has carried on for more than fifteen years, negotiating contracts, fighting grievances and conducting strikes against the company.

The special convention that approved the merger of Mine Mill and Steel was held in Winnipeg on June 23, 1967. A referendum vote held August 3rd ratified the merger, and Mine Mill virtually ceased to exist. Photo courtesy Mike Farrell

The future of this isolated organization is a matter of speculation. Can it carry on indefinitely in its present form? Will it ultimately become an integral part of the organized Canadian labour movement? Will it disappear altogether from the scene, or is it possibly the rebirth of a new Mine Mill trade union? Today, there are still some who think that, since history records successive ebbs and tides in the life of the Western Federation of Miners and Mine Mill, the union will rise again out of its ashes, in youthful freshness and vigour, and once more be the legendary union of hard rock miners everywhere.

For over ten turbulent years, staunch old-timers held out against blandishments, threats and betrayals, and stuck with Mine Mill despite sabotage from within and pressures from outside forces. Men and women who had lived and worked in years when there was no union or protection from brutal bosses, and who had witnessed race discrimination and wage levels barely above subsistence recognized what was at stake. But through years of continuous growth of the industry, the ranks were diluted by new employees who knew little of the history of the union and were newcomers to unionism. They took for granted the wages and working conditions won for them by the union, rarely appeared at membership meetings, and did not participate in union activities. Those who did not understand or adequately judge the purpose of the smears against their union were easier victims of the raiders.

The real story of the last days of the Mine Mill union in Sudbury is not that the Steelworkers succeeded in the raid. The real story is that the staunch adherents of Mine Mill refused to lie down and die, but fought back valiantly against the forces marshalled against them. They carried with them into their new union the traditions and militancy of the International Union of Mine, Mill and Smelter Workers.

Sudbury Local 598 delegates representing Falconbridge and Port Colborne delegates who refused to go along with the merger. Falconbridge succeeded in preserving the Local 598 identity: it is the sole remaining local of the legendary Mine Mill union. First row (L-R): Jim Tester, Royal D'Amour, Norm Stephen, Don Montgomery, Ron Green, Bill Laporte. Second row (L-R): Mike McCormick, Ed Nitchie, Emile Prudhomme. Third row (L-R): Laurie St. Jean, Jim Gallagher, Ron Levert, Roy Scranton, ———, ———, ———. Fourth row (L-R): Bill Martin, Joe Astgen, ———, Lorne Stevenson. Photo courtesy Jim Tester

Conclusion

While much has been achieved through the continuing effort of the trade union movement to improve conditions for working people, there remains unresolved one issue which undoubtedly is in the minds of many Canadians, that is, the creation of a genuine Canadian trade union establishment. In natural resources and manufacturing, we have long since been aware of the need to be masters in our own house. Equally important is the need to have our own trade union movement, completely autonomous and altogether free of foreign domination. This does not imply isolation from labour organizations elsewhere: co-operation with labour bodies everywhere is of obvious benefit to all. Freedom of action for Canadian trade unions is clearly essential for many reasons.

The trade union is an instrument through which workers bargain with employers for wages and working conditions. As such, all trade unions are similar in structure and intent; however, there are variations between trade unions as to tactics and strategy, objectives and philosophies concerning the role of unions in the socio-industrial world in which they function. Currents in the Canadian labour movement are determined by the actions of the diverse trade union organizations. These currents may be characterized as of the right, centre and left. On the right are those unions which proclaim themselves to be "pure" and "business" unions. They avoid all activity beyond the bread-and-butter issues and deal only with the employer. In the centre are groups which declare themselves to be politically oriented towards social democracy within the prevailing industrial system. As a rule, they uphold the bread-and-butter position in dealing with the employer, but they participate in political election campaigns outside the confines of a narrow definition of trade union functions. On the left are the few unions which attempt to blend the bread-and-butter issues with political, industrial and social realities. Such a union was Mine Mill: it participated in all aspects of its members' lives outside the narrow confines of the trade union; it attempted to look after the health and welfare of its members and their families from the cradle to the grave. Unions such as Mine Mill developed new trade union concepts, fought precedent-setting legal battles with industry, and led Canadian workers in establishing improved wage and working conditions as well as improved quality of life. They were instrumental in convincing federal and provincial governments to introduce legislation favouring trade union organization and laws governing working conditions. Mine Mill was notable for its early establishment of an autonomous Canadian organization.

Today, there is growing fear that history may very well repeat itself. Currently, extensive unemployment and unprecedented levels of inflation, coupled with reports of unconscionable profits in key industries and financial institutions, have resulted in the increasing insistence of working people generally and trade unions specifically that more attention be paid to the needs of the many rather than the benefits for the few. After a decade of detente, Cold War clouds are gathering on the horizon, threatening once again to overwhelm us. Tactics of Cold War architects may differ, but the strategy is unswerving: the first move, as in the past, is to silence all opposition. This is already evident in the variety of legislative measures instituted by the U.S. Reagan administration. In the past, such moves against militant or socially-oriented trade unions originated in the United States and were soon adopted by elements in our country. In the 1950s, it was clear to those of us in the heat of the battle that the orders to destroy Mine Mill came from below the 49th parallel. We hope, through this brief study, to succeed in alerting working people, who are always the true victims of repression, to the strength of the forces that may be brought to bear against them and the necessity of maintaining their own principles and their own organizations.

In the period under review, Mine Mill was admittedly the most militant and therefore the labour organization most fiercely assaulted. Labour today is presenting a militant posture on the many issues threatening the welfare of working people, issues that encompass threats of a cataclysmic world war, as well as attempts to thrust the full burden of economic regression on the wage earner. To carry on a viable battle against these threats, Canadian trade unionists must maintain the traditions of independence, education and organization pioneered by unions like Mine Mill.